NATIONAL LAMPOON®

ROAD TRIP USA

ALL THE PLACES YOUR DAD NEVER STOPPED AT

Published by National Lampoon Press

National Lampoon, Inc. • 8228 Sunset Boulevard • Los Angeles • CA 90046 • USA • AMEX:NLN

NATIONAL LAMPOON, NATIONAL LAMPOON PRESS and colophon are trademarks of National Lampoon

Road Trip USA: by Harmon Leon
Photos by Brad Kuehnemuth and Harmon Leon
Cockfighting Cartoon by Michael Cappozzola

p. cm.

ISBN-10: 0978832302
ISBN-13: 978-0978832308
$15.95 U.S. - $19.95 Canada

Book Design and Production by
JK NAUGHTON

Cover by
MoDMaN and Sam McCay

PRINTED IN THE UNITED STATES OF AMERICA

1 3 5 7 9 10 8 6 4 2

MAY 2007

WWW.NATIONALLAMPOON.COM

NATIONAL
LAMPOON®
PRESS

by Harmon Leon

Photos by Brad Kuehnemuth and Harmon Leon

Road Trip Into The Diseased Underbelly Of America

Aaah, the great American road trip – what surprises does it hold? Numerous questions need to be answered. Do hobbits live in our nation's wilderness, lying in wait, ready to steal your shoes at truck stops? Are hitchhikers really misunderstood adventurers, like Lewis and Clark, and not scary people who will steal your shoes at truck stops? Is it legal to kill a hobo in some States? Is it illegal to steal people's shoes?! Yes, questions need to be answered – and I shall do that question-answering!

Humdrum guidebooks, written by THE MAN, stress that road trips are truly American adventures that every citizen should enjoy (USA! USA! USA!). They use words like, *the love of the open road, wanderlust,* or even a *keen sense of adventure* to describe the experience, stressing you never know what lies around the next bend. Every road trip has a beginning and an end, but they say it's really the journey that matters *(except if the ending is really kick-ass such as Mount Rushmore or the birthplace of Jonas Salk).* Between Point A and B is the true meat of a road trip. That's when you're on the asphalt glide in Zen harmony with the road, realizing that you're supposed to be wherever it is that you currently are *(flaw in logic: what if you're supposed to be at Disney World, and instead find yourself in an Alabama jail cell?!).*

The moment you take that sharp curve, into the realm of the unknown, is an awestruck instant like no other. Bullcrap! Sometimes it's really flippin' terrifying! Why? America is scary!

Seriously. Leave the confines of your comfort zone and you can encounter some frightening stuff out there in the hinterlands of the USA's open roads. Safety-wise, I'll take the Tenderloin District of San Francisco any day, with its *Night of the Living Dead* crack-heads, over, say, being stuck in an isolated Mississippi town where suddenly you're the outsider playing by their rules! Yes, America is really scary – especially if you search for it!

From virtually any starting point in the country, drive a few hundred miles in whichever direction and you'll experience the vast diversity of the diseased underbelly of America in terms of culture, inhabitants, and landscape. My goal is to set out off the beaten path, and find this true *diseased underbelly of America.* With a sense of adventure, and complete abandonment of common sense, I will venture on the endless American highway to places against my better judgment. Yes, I will embark on a cross-country road trip in search of the *true* America filled with *true* Americans, but most importantly I will search for myself! *(Don't think of putting the previous on a postcard because I already have the copyrights.)*

"That's very deep and you sound just like Jack Kerouac... but without all the speed and alcoholism," you must be now be saying, "or *Thelma and Louise...* but without Thelma or Louise."

My road trip sojourn will be an epic expedition of grand scale, reminiscent of The Knights of the Round Table *(only without all those pesky British),* as I set out like a brave knight on a crusade for the true meaning of America, bringing you, my little Sir Galahad, along for the ride. *(okay?!)* The trip will be like *Easy Rider,* except I'll be Dennis Hopper and you – the readers – will be thousands of Peter Fondas. *(I just hope we don't get blown away by thousands of rednecks in the end.)* This is not going to be your father's road trip. No. It won't even be your uncle's road trip *(your father's brother).* Nor will it be your friend's *(your friend)* father's road trip. We wont be stopping at the World's Largest Ball of String, or a jack-a-lope display. I want to go to the worst towns in America, meet bad people, eat horrible food, and sleep in really awful accommodations – basically encounter American culture at its vilest, oddest, most bizarre, and frightening.

Goals Of Our (But Mostly My) Diseased Underbelly Road Trip Of America:

1. To See the *True* America!
2. To Avoid Being Ritualistically Murdered!
3. To Avoid Being Ritualistically Sodomized!
4. To Avoid Being Ritualistically Murdered Then Sodomized While The Town Elders Watch!
5. To Find the Worst Place In America To Go On A Honeymoon!
6. To Find My Wally World – My Diseased Underbelly Amusement Park of Americana!

Live vicariously through my four-wheelin' exploits, as I devise one of the most hell-bent American road trips of all time, *(with the exception of fugitive Charles Starkweather whose road trip left 11 people dead in his wake),*

I'll provide insights on interacting with shady regional superstars such as Louisiana cockfighters, Mormon polygamists, circus carnies, racists, and wild boar hunters – all who live outside our comfort zone. I'll try and play by *their* rules, in such illustrious places as Branson Missouri, Celebration Florida, and the hometown of the KKK. Dodging being pegged as a fish-out-of-water, I'll bring along elaborate-and-cunning disguises to pose as a member of the local subculture in order see the *true* America from the inside out.

Also, I'll show how to take normal, stupid tourist locales – filled with the obese adorned in fanny packs – and turn them into a place for exciting activities that the mere sane would never think of *(such as counting nude people, etc...).*

Yes, my American diseased underbelly expedition shall provide road trip insights and logistical secrets, but most importantly the inspiration for you to plot and take your very own screwed-up road trip *(without legal obligations to us)* into the low points of America and its underbelly *(which happens to be diseased).*

Let's go!

Road Trip Checklist

Before the odometer reaches 1 and your car smells like a cross between spoilt meat and feet, there are a few preparations needed for a successful road trip into the diseased underbelly of America:

1. **Bring a car (very important)**
   My first choice is a hot-red Cadillac convertible like Hunter S. Thompson's Great Red Shark. Not having the necessary budget for this, I instead rent a green Geo Metro *(at least it has air-bags).* Be sure to get full insurance so you can practice various stunt driving maneuvers. A comfortable car is important for road trips, being it not only acts as your transportation, but sometimes your sleeping quarters, kitchen, and in lucky cases the place where you have sex.

2. **Road tripping without "tripping out."**
   Meticulously plan every aspect of your trip and leave no room, what-so-ever, for spontaneity. Put yourself on a strict time schedule where severe punishment will be inflicted if broken *(such as having to run laps around your car, eating your weight in cheese, or taking a Time Out in the back seat while parked in a Denny's parking lot).*

3. **Create the proper ambience inside your car**
   Do not bring along CDs or any form of outside music other than what is provided on your AM and FM car radio. This will enable you to get a true taste of where our country's headed

as you descend into the underbelly of America. From classic rock stations and country music, to Jesus preaching and the vast array of right-wing talk radio, you will descend into pure loathing within hours on the road! Again, do not bring along CDs or any form of outside music.

4. **Don't crap in the car!**
   This should go without saying, but in some cases it doesn't.

5. **Bring along a babe in a short skirt**
   (When available)

6. **Road snacks DO's and DON'Ts**
   Ha-ha. Isn't it funny that you're on the road and you're eating Beef Jerky, which you normally don't eat and bought at a kitschy truck stop. Ha-ha-ha, indeed! Forget beef jerky, as well as snacks like Cheetos *(they will make your fingers orange and your steering wheel orange as well)*. Instead, invest in a whole pie—yes, a whole, entire pie right by your side. Think of it, as you drive, you can frequently dip your entire hand in a pie of your choice, just like a mighty bear trying to scoop up freshwater salmon from a mountain stream with his bear *(except in your case, human)* claw *(hand)*. Or something like that. Mmmm, pie!

7. **Remove dead hooker from trunk of car**
   This can only present problems later down the road. Thus before leaving town purchase a wood-chipper and do what you need to do.

8. **Drink red bull instead of water!**
   Yes, large amounts of energy drinks will not only keep you from falling asleep at the wheel, but it will also give you that crazy wired kind of energy of a crack head who strangles kittens with his bare hands.

SAN FRANCISCO, CALIFORNIA

Nudespotting

POPULATION 739,426

TOWN MOTTO I Left My Heart In San Francisco.

***MY* TOWN MOTTO** Don't You Dare Call It Frisco!

SAN FRANCISCO FUN TIP Never call San Francisco "Frisco," unless you want to sound like that kid in school who wore the hockey helmet and didn't play hockey. Same holds true to calling it "San Fran," or SFO. If you happen to call it "San Francis-key," you will have to be removed immediately from city limits.

WAYS TO GET YOUR ASS KICKED By calling it "Frisco!" Haven't you been paying attention?!

WEIRD LOCAL SMELL Obese tourists who call San Francisco "Frisco."

EXTREMELY USELESS INFORMATION People think Mark Twain once said, "The coldest winter I ever spent was a summer in San Francisco." This isn't entirely true. His actual quote was, "The coldest winter I ever spent was in Alaska because it's pretty fucking cold up there. Canada would rank second for the same reason."

CULTURAL HIGHLIGHT Rice-a-roni, those Victorian homes seen in the opening credits of the Bob Saget sitcom "Full House," over-priced clam chowder served in a sour dough bread bowl.

AN IDYLLIC LOCALE FOR People who don't call the city "Frisco!"

LEVEL OF CREEPINESS 1-10, depending on the type of nudity encountered.

Why not start the road trip off in the very damn city in which I live?! When in San Francisco forget the usual tourist hoo-ha of such over-rated attractions as Fisherman's Wharf *(boring)*, The Golden Gate Bridge *(over-rated)*, Chinatown *(how many dead hanging ducks in windows can you see in one day?!)*, Haight-Ashbury *(there's a Gap store dead center in the locale of the Summer of Love)*, Alcatraz *(it's an old prison where people our grandparents' age were gang-raped in the showers)*, or riding a picturesque cable car *(boring and over-rated)*.

Do you want to get in line with the flock of tourist sheep with their fanny-packs and big smiles, holding their identical copies of Fodor's pocket guidebooks of San Francisco, while wearing their T-shirts that say *"I Got Crabs at Fisherman's Wharf!"* Hell, no.

Why not meet the *true* citizens of San Francisco, not clothed like most tourists would be, but *nude*. Beneath our clothes, we are all nude. Each San Francisco citizen encountered is a potential nude person deep down. I'm not kidding! Bearing that in mind, there's a lot of opportunity to encounter naked people while on a road trip, especially in San Francisco – being this is the town that created the Summer of Love.

Like spotting Bigfoot or the Loch Ness Monster, to prove my point and let you follow in my road-trip-foot steps, I'm going to pose the noblest challenge of modern time, rivaling that of Madame Curie and her exploration in radiation: I will tally how many naked people I can see in one day (my goal is 1,000). Hell, if you're on a road trip, why not have it entail seeing 1,000 nude people in one day?! Let me pave the way – I know it's a tough job, but someone's got to do it.

STUFF NEEDED FOR NUDE QUEST:
A CATCHPHRASE: "Nudetastic!"
A NUDE COUNTING DEVICE: A small abacus
A DEVICE TO ENLARGE THE NUDITY: A magnifying glass
MY GOAL: To see over 1,000 nude people in one day
The clock is running. Let's go! Bring on the nudity!

NUDE SIGHTING #1: BAKER BEACH IN DECEMBER

CLOCK: 10:00-10:45

Morning. I awake with a smile; my naked-day lies before me. My nudespotting holds no discretion *(though females would be much nicer).* I start with a sojourn to Baker Beach – a nude beach roughly a ½-mile long on the outskirts of San Francisco, just south of the Golden Gate Bridge. Normally, this would be a major place bustling with nude activity. One problem; it's a cold-ass day in winter. Everyone at the beach is fully clothed. Some wear ski jackets.

I'm about to write this off as a nude-loss, when spotted off in the sandy distance are a few scattered pink objects. You guessed it, naked people! Abacus in hand, I skip like a merry schoolgirl towards freezing cold nude sunbathers. Looking like beached whales, these are the survivors from the season, the true diehards. They won't let the fact that it's REALLY FUCKING COLD, or common sense, stop their naked pursuit of basking pale bodies in the winter sun. Bless them. I salute you nude brethren!

Climbing on rocks, I get a better perspective. Some wear shirts, but no pants. All are middle-aged men and older. All lie naked on their own. Maybe nude-extremists are branded as loners, due to their bold/brash nudity, which chased others from their lives. Can't nude people make friends? They could pair off and share in some good, nude conversation:

EXAMPLE:

"I'm really fucking cold."

"Yes, me too."

Some get nude for a few minutes, and then desert the idea. A big-bellied man puts on pants. Like a clever monkey he uses a stick as a hammer to build a makeshift shelter out of driftwood and towels. Once constructed, he again gets nude, posing as if to say: "I'm king of my newly found naked domain!" I feel like knocking over his naked-protective fort.

A new-age, longhaired, nudist does naked yoga. He does a naked headstand, parting his legs in a nude spread-eagle. Surprisingly, he too is on his own.

LIVE NUDE TALLY:

Six overweight men, one with a proclivity for naked handstands.

If You Must Go

Baker Beach
Lincoln Blvd and Bowley St.
San Francisco, CA 94129

NUDE SIGHTING #2: URBAN OUTFITTERS CLOTHING STORE-80 POWELL STREET, SAN FRANCISCO

CLOCK: 11:15-1:35

If there's a department store, there's a dressing room. That means clothes coming off, which equates to... nakedness! Beneath a door, pants drop to the floor. I haphazardly, grab clothes and get closer to the nudity for a proper nude-count.

"Can I try this on?" I ask the tiny salesclerk with the large attitude.

"You need a dressing room to try on a hat?" she inquires.

"I don't like to try hats on in public, okay?"

Quickly, I grab other items so I'm not branded as a pervert wanting to glimpse naked people; rather, one who is on an almost sacred mission. Through a door, I see a bra-strap. This is a very good start.

Below, a pair of shoeless feet step out of a skirt. Like MacGyver I pull out my cell phone. Using its concave reflective surface, I try to get the image of the nude person in the next changing-stall. There's something resembling a bottom. Or an elbow. Or a bottom. Maybe a knee. Can I count this as a nudespotting victory?!

Due to the ambiguity, I use the dressing room opportunity to explore my own personal nudity. Standing in the small cubical, in front of the mirror, I flaunt my nakedness whilst making several muscle poses.

"Nudetastic!"

Yes, I'm very nude. One of the items I grabbed, a bowtie, is utilized to accessorize my Samuel Jackson, making it more formal;

one that could attend fancy occasions like events involving the Queen of England.

There's a series of knocks on the dressing room door.

"Are you doing okay in there?"

I glance deeply into the mirror noting my formal nakedness. "Yes. Yes. I'm doing very good, indeed!"

LIVE NUDE TALLY:

Two, if you count both myself and a concave image of what might have actually been an elbow. Or bottom. Or maybe a knee. Onward.

If You Must Go

Urban Outfitters
80 Powell St.
San Francisco, CA 94102
(415) 989-1515
(But keep in mind that what I did could be, well, illegal. Duplicate the feat and you may be seeing more nude men than you'd like, behind bars.)

NUDE SIGHTING #3: GIRLFRIEND'S HOUSE

CLOCK: 2:07-2:30

What a better spot to see someone naked, then at the home of your girlfriend.

"I need to see you naked," I state without explanation.

"Well, maybe later." She passes the comment off like "some sort of joke."

I look her in the eye with brutal seriousness. "I need to see you naked now. It's very important to me. I'll explain later."

My girlfriend, always the exhibitionist, begins stripping. She's Canadian, her people are very congenial and understanding that way.

"Nudetastic!"

Two hours and twenty minutes later, I realize I must move on after a slight "segue" of events. Sure, during that time span I saw continuous nudity from all sorts of angles, but it only involved a person who I see naked all the time anyway. Also, I'm not sure it's in the rules to probe those who are to be observed and counted. The German judges might not allow this, but I'm going to petition and enforce that this nudespotting escapade be allowed to stay in the books. Victory is mine!

LIVE NUDE TALLY:

One naked girlfriend.

> ***If You Must Go***
>
> Get real – Like I'd give you my girlfriend's address?

NUDE SIGHTING #4: INTERNET CAFÉ

CLOCK: 3:10-6:10

The nude future is here – now! This is an amazing era. One simply needs to go to an Internet café to see nudity. Venturing to Java City, I buy some Internet time and then surf to the sleazy section of the Internet. Under "webcams," I'm fascinated by the hundreds of choices for live nude video conferencing.

- Click Here To Chat With Me And My 18 Year Old Pussy!
- Live Sex 24/7. With 3 Camera Angles You Never Miss A Move!
- I Shove Anything That Will Fit In My Ass... Live!

These seem intriguing, if not slightly physically impossible and grammatically incorrect. I go to the cunningly-named "Live Tit Talk!" for some in-depth conversation with a live naked minx, about politics and the Marxist theory of economics.

"Chat with a girl live! It's like one fantastic chat orgy," the screen beckons.

Putting the $3.95 free trial on my credit card, I'm stopped by this message:

"Forbidden!"

I click a few more links.

"A Security Violation Has Occurred!"

I click to another place. I'm told to download viewing software. Something almost happens, then doesn't. I find myself back to the payment page.

Momentarily, I get a video image of a young vixen, resting on a pillow in a poorly decorated room, sowing her own oats. But, how do I know this woman is "live" at this very moment, and not a nude woman filmed earlier who is now wearing clothes elsewhere?

I finally access Tit Talk. There is no video image; just people typing to the model.

"Make your fingers wet and play with your melons"

"Wow, you are so beautiful!"

"Where the hell is the live nude woman." I type. I'm beginning to think the organizers are solely after my hard-earned money!

"Signup is FREE! Only nude and private chats require a purchase."

What? Huh? I need to fork over more cash for breast chatter?! Once again, I pull out the credit card to pay $3.95 per minute. I get the image of a tired looking woman sitting in a lawn chair. She is live. By no means is she nude. My time clicks away.

"When will you get naked so I can count you?!" I type.

She answers back, "I don't know, maybe in one year." Great, that will cost me several hundreds of thousands of dollars. Ads flash in the text area offering private chats for $14.95. This is a godddamn live-sex-internet pyramid scheme. There's probably fine print stating my credit cards have been charged $10,000. Most importantly, I've wasted three hours of valuable nude-spotting time. Technology has slowed down my live, nude viewing. And even worse, I'm asked to leave Java City and also asked never ever to come back (under any circumstances).

LIVE NUDE TALLY:

One. Maybe, but I can't be sure if she was live. The Internet is actually the most annoying, expensive, time-consuming place to see live, naked people, and Internet cafes are most likely not the best locale to try and do such.

If You Must Go

Java City Bakery Cafe.
1475 Market St.
San Francisco, CA 94103
(415) 552-4449

NUDE SIGHTING #5: 24 HOUR FITNESS LOCKER ROOM

CLOCK: 6:38-7:27

It's time for the lightning round; the locker room of 24 Hour Fitness. If I can't find a naked person here, then I'm a nude-spotting disgrace. It's shouldn't be a question of seeing a nude person – it's more like how many.

Fully dressed, I camp out in the locker room. The one problem; locker rooms provide the nudity of only one sex. In this case – male. I'm not gay. Really.

The baseball game is on TV. I try to act absorbed.

"Go Niners!" I shout, which translates to "Go Nudity!"

Sitting down on a bench, ready to count, I've brought a book to help pass the time. The thing I don't like about locker rooms is there's always some creepy guy watching and leering as you undress. Whoops, wait a minute, I'm now that creepy guy. But I'm doing this for science. Or something like that.

So far exercise enthusiasts are modest about showing the Full Monty. Getting restless, I scour the shower room every five minutes.

"No! No! No!" I mutter after each disappointed excursion. The co-ed sauna holds the same disappointment. I can't believe this shit. There's actually guys taking showers in swimsuits.

Suddenly the clouds part, the nude floodgates open. It's raining fat, old naked men. Hurrah! My plight wasn't in vain. I count them off with my abacus quicker than an auctioneer selling hams. Yes, fat, old guys, with flabby asses and bulbous bellies that practically cover their gray pubic-hair region.

"Nudetastic!"

This is a glorious sight from one whose mission is to track nudity. Again, I'm not gay.

LIVE NUDE TALLY:

Twelve elderly naked bodies.

If You Must Go

24 Hour Fitness
1200 Van Ness Ave
San Francisco, CA
(415) 776-2200

NUDE SIGHTING #6: LUSTY LADY STRIP CLUB

CLOCK: 7:45-7:50

"Private Booths. Naked Naughty Nasty. Live Nude Shows."

For a mere 25 cents, all this nudity inside the luxury of my own private, comfortable stall. This will be the cheapest nude-spotting of the day.

Outside, in the foyer, a line of solemn men wait for the booth light to change from "In Use" to "Vacant."

Inside the small cubicle, the floor is covered with wet tissues and some sort of stiff liquid. And a smell. Eeeeew. *(Mental Note to Self: Don't touch surface areas or walls.)* That's the price I pay for budget nudity.

I place one quarter into the slot. The screen goes up. Inside an enclosed mirror area, three nudies shake it for the locals. The reflections of the other solemn-faced spectators are caught in the mirror. That, along with the smell, make this jaunt as erotic as a trip to the dentist.

Music by The Bangles is piped in as the three nudies dance joylessly in front of each glass window. One gives me an internal medical examination where I think I see her internal organs. Another puts her bottom against the glass. Within the confined space, the naked strippers remind me of three turtles put inside a small, crowded fish aquarium. The screen goes down. That was the wisest quarter I've ever spent.

NUDE TALLY:

Three bored looking strippers. I saw nudity, and for cheap. But I felt like compulsively washing my hands afterwards. And the bottoms of my shoes.

If You Must Go

Lusty Lady Theatre
1033 Kearny St.
San Francisco, CA 94133
(415) 391-3991

NUDE SIGHTING #7: PRETENTIOUS SAN FRANCISCO UNDERGROUND ART PARTY

CLOCK: 10:40-12:17

At almost every San Francisco art party, there's always a stupid, drunken hippie dancing around naked. It's guaranteed, like bad toupees on aging magicians.

The warehouse is filled with dancing urban hipsters. Some crap performance art brouhaha commences, so complex that my simple mind can't comprehend. There are more bindis than funny hats at a Pope convention. Some wear sinful fetish gear. Others dress as superheroes. The zany choice for wardrobe has to do with their... CREATIVITY!

My intuition paid off. Amongst the brood is a goateed man with a large leaf over his cobblers. He holds a drink. I wonder where he keeps his wallet? Hitting nude-pay dirt, I approach.

"You are naked, aren't you?"

"Do you think I'm naked?" he retorts, turning the tables.

"Yes, I DO think you're naked," I confirm, explaining the leaf is merely a nude accessory.

"No one really cares. Anyway, it's passé to be naked."

No one cares?! No one cares indeed! I'll be the judge of that. What's this pretentious naked man trying to say, that nudity is sooooo 1990's?!

LIVE NUDE TALLY:

One who wore a leaf to hide what I presume was a very small penis.

If You Must Go

Cafe Cocomo
650 Indiana St.
San Francisco, CA 94107
(415) 824-6910

NUDE SIGHTING #8: RANDOM HOMELESS MAN PEEING AGAINST MY CAR

CLOCK: 12:18-12:19

Coming out of the pretentious art party, I make my way to my car. A figure with a baseball cap and shopping cart hunches by the passenger side, emitting a huge liquid stream that travels down the gradual incline. Hurrah, it's a random homeless guy peeing on my car!

I'm first angered by his actions. Then I couldn't be more delighted; I witness his partial nudity. This is unexpected nudity indeed, for I see his sloppy John Henry as he continues to relieve himself on my vehicle. His tool sharply catches in the moonlight, perfectly silhouetted against a brick wall.

"Nudetastic!"

"It's cool man. It's cool man," he says fumbling to put away his monster, noting my advancement to unlock the door.

"Thank you," I inform him with honesty. This is great, for I needed to earn some nudespotting points, being that time is running out. As I drive my urine-soaked vehicle, I know just the place to go to top off my day.

LIVE NUDE TALLY:

One random homeless man's disgusting Johnson.

If You Must Go

Mariposa and 19th St.

Although I can't promise that particular homeless man will pee on your car, there are a usually a range of urinaters to choose from.

NUDE SIGHTING #10: POWER EXCHANGE SEX CLUB

CLOCK: 12:30-1:49

At San Francisco's only straight sex club, people go to have sex – most often nude! For scientific purposes, I've brought along my trusty girlfriend/assistant (See Nude Sighting #2).

"$15 to get in if you check your clothes and wear a towel. It's $75 to get in otherwise," says the weighty bouncer. We pay the $15 and are told where to check in our clothes, which we so clearly don't do. The poorly-lit atmosphere is like a haunted house. I expect the wolf man to pop out with a boner. There's various theme rooms; a prison cell, a wedding chapel, a medieval banquet room, a Frankenstein dungeon. For some reason, they're playing the music of Yes.

One thing about straight sex clubs, they're inhabited almost entirely by men who somberly lurk from room to room clad in towels. That, and Thai transvestites. The few women present are built like meaty truck drivers. How weird; no one you'd actually want to have sex with ever frequents a sex club.

Attempting humor, my trusty girlfriend/assistant climbs into some table/dungeon device. Immediately 6 men in towels descend on the scene.

"Move on, there's nothing to see here!" I state.

The walls are sticky. I avoid accidentally bumping into anyone wearing a towel. A guy wearing chain mail has an open wank. I must stay far beyond shooting distance from this cowboy. Two naked women are tied together on a post and are being caned, while the largest woman I've ever seen, in the midst of grand role-playing, gets whipped. These sex club-goers are dealing with issues.

Hoards of vultures descend, watching a fat woman suck a man's meat-sausage, with a content look. She's still at it twenty minutes later.

Like Mad Max's Thunderdome, primitive men in loin cloths cheer on the action of a girl in a Bo-Peep outfit spanking the bare bottom of another woman while being fanned with a peacock feather. Some reach under their towels, taking the action into their own hands. Eeeeew! The crowd disperses when someone in a towel gets sick on the floor.

After passing a large topless female bouncer, a man in glasses wearing an ill-fitting wig and granny dress approaches my girlfriend.

"Do you want to play pool?" he asks. Sure, most people come to sex clubs for the fine pool playing opportunities. When she says "no," the man in the granny dress sputters, "Well, how about oral sex?" He thrusts out his tongue, adding, "I have the mouth of a lesbian!"

Like Robert De Niro in *Raging Bull,* I give the man in a granny dress a look that says, "Are you trying to fuck my wife!"

The last image I'm left with at Power Exchange is a man sitting on his own, watching a porno, spanking the monkey. Ewwww.

LIVE NUDE TALLY:

Four naked women, six naked men. Except I'm not only turned off by the nudity; I'm turned off by the whole human race.

If You Must Go

Power Exchange
86 Otis St.
San Francisco, CA 94103
(415) 487-9944

NUDECLUSIONS:

Well, I failed at seeing 1,000 naked people. Instead, I only saw 37. Perhaps you on your attempt to nudespot will fare much better. But I'm sure you'll find out like I did that, other than leggy supermodels, the human body is disgusting. We should all be ashamed!

Diseased Underbelly Salute To...

Small Towns That Make A Big Deal Out Of Their One Claim To Fame

1. Corn Cob Pipe Capital of the World: Washington, Missouri

Don't get too excited, but the Missouri Meerschaum Company, is still the world's oldest and largest manufacturer of corncob pipes, which has put Washington, Missouri on the map. Again, settle down!

If You Must Go

Corn Cob Pipe Museum
400 West Front Street
Washington, MO 63090
(636) 239-2109

2. Town without a Toothache: Hereford, Texas

The city's reputation as the "town without a toothache" evidently began in 1948, when Dr. F.M. Butler attributed local lack of cavities to natural fluoride in the area's water. Butler's discoveries were later verified by the Texas Department of Health.

If You Must Go

Hereford is located in the Texas Panhandle where U.S. Highway 60 and U.S. Highway 385 intersect, about 21 miles north of Dimmit, 30 miles south of Vega and 46 miles southwest of Amarillo, and positioned 34.82 degrees north of the equator, 102.39 degrees west of the prime meridian. Which sounds like a long trip for a glass of water that might prevent tooth-decay – brush your teeth, you lazy bastard.

3. **Turf Grass Capital of the World: Savannah, Georgia**

Tifton, Georgia also claims this title. I think the two cities should fight it out using conventional weapons, which will costs thousands of lives, to determine the true title-winner.

If You Must Go

Savannah is positioned 32° degrees north of the equator and 81° degrees west of the prime meridian.
Tifton is located at 31°27′24″N, 83°30′23″W
Set your missile sights, turf fans.

4. **Cherry Pit Spitting Capital of the World: Eau Claire, Michigan**

Eau Claire was originally the "Spitting Capital of the World," but somewhere along the line they decided to add cherry pits to the equation. The city holds an annual competition, in which they claim "Pit-Spitting is for any age!" Much more entertaining is their "Cherry Pit Spitting Special Olympics."

If You Must Spit

Especially during harvest time...
www.treemendus-fruit.com/int.htm

5. **Jackrabbit Capital of Texas: Odessa, Texas**

Goddamn they have a lot of jackrabbits here! Goddamn!

If You Must Go

Odessa is a city in Ector County.
(The community straddles Ector and Midland counties)

BERKELEY, CALIFORNIA

Getting Kicked Out Of A Religious Cult

POPULATION 102,743

TOWN MOTTO Some people call Berkeley "Beserkely." Laughter then ensues.

BERKELEY FUN FACT The '60's were invented in Berkeley. In case you forgot this fact, some aging hippie will make sure to remind you. Take a walk down Telegraph Avenue and you'll see some of the original cast members.

CULTURAL HIGHLIGHTS Pretending the '60's never ended. For a while there was a naked guy who roamed around Berkeley. People referred to him as "The Naked Guy."

EXTREMELY USELESS INFORMATION William "She Bangs" Hung was a civil engineering student at UC Berkeley. In case you don't remember who William Hung is, clearly that means his 15 minutes of fame are up!

AN IDEAL LOCALE FOR Hippies, tree-huggers, hairy-legged girls, the overly politically correct, burnt-out drug casualties, trust fund gutter punks asking for spare change, those who like to go to parties where hummus is served.

LEVEL OF CREEPINESS 10 if you voted for Bush.

A Mecca for liberal moonbats, Berkeley is a city known as home to numerous kooky religious cults. So when visiting this little town in the East Bay, why not check out a few? Think of it... a support group of like-minded people with similar mind-controlling interests, proving once and for all they are the only people on the whole entire planet who actually care!

Transcendental Meditation, which almost sucked in the Beatles, can be found here in Berkeley. Same with CARP, which is the student arm of the Unification Church, headed by the Rev. Sun Myung Moon, (known playfully by many as *Moonies).* Of course, the worst cult of all is here: the cult of those still alive who followed the Grateful Dead; whose members seldom bathed and worshipped the god Jerry by eating lots of acid and playing hacky-sack in a drum circle.

Better yet, instead of spending your *Diseased Underbelly Road Trip* time checking out a cult, why not turn the tables and try to get *kicked out* of a cult. These organizations want you to stay a member forever and ever, often times soaking you out of lots of money. That's why it takes real skill to be so annoying that a cult will, instead, ask you to leave and *never come back.*

Yes, it's time to "Get your shit together!" and join a religious cult in order to get kicked out!

The criteria for the cults we choose will include:

1. Creative, Interpretive Dancing
2. Kickboxing
3. Sci-fi

Our *(but mostly my)* first attempt at joining a religious cult *(in order to get kicked out)* is a large, major "Science-based" organization that is notorious for suing publications who print yarns about their large, organized cult affairs. To give you a clue of its identity, the founder's name rhymes with L. Ron *Blubbard* and he wrote the sci-fi book *Battlefield Earth.*

It's highly important to set some standards and get something out of the entire experience. That's why the cult you decide to join must have one or more of the following:

1. Free food
2. Lots of cult-babes
3. Kickboxing

For my cult indoctrination, I'm wearing the "funny" T-shirt that says *"Alcatraz Psycho Ward Outpatient."* The headquarters looks not unlike a well-kept gift shop. I attend the large Science-based cult's weekly Sunday service and group evaluation.

Inside, are four people, two of whom work at the headquarters, a man who is sleeping and myself. A large bust of the man who wrote *Battlefield Earth* is perched in front, while on the pulpit a guy in a white shirt and tie conducts a religious ritual of tomorrow, beyond my earthly comprehension.

"With your two hands, measure your head," he requests. "Now, measure your mouth. Now measure your feet."

This goes on and on. Then he starts spouting something, not to far from being a nursery rhyme.

> "Imagine you own your body. *(pause)*
> Now, imagine someone else owns your body. *(pause)*
> Now, imagine a demon owns your body. *(pause)*
> Now, imagine you own your body. *(pause)*
> Now, imagine someone else owns your body."

This also goes on for a good half-hour.

I'm still not yet sold on calling the man who wrote *Battlefield Earth* Mein Führer, god, lord and savior. So I take their free 200-question personality test that will determine exactly how much of the Science-based cult I am actually needing.

SAMPLE QUESTIONS

Q. Are you a slow eater?
Q. Do people enjoy your company?
Q. Are you in favor of color bar and class distinction?
Q. Would you use corporal punishment on a child aged ten, if it refused to obey you?

This is tricky, but since I want to be kicked out, I answer all with "yes" with the exception of the one about people enjoying my company. Then I check off the rest of the 200 questions in a record three minutes.

When I finish a man with an accent, shirt and tie *(the standard costume for the Science-based religion worker)* scientifically feeds my 200-question personality test into a computer *(for scientific, computer-like results).*

The man with the accent *(shirt and tie as well)* herds me into an office with a large poster, displaying the ministry hierarchy of the Science-based religion. At the very top is a large cruise ship of the *Love Boat* variety.

"What's the boat all about," I ask the man with the accent. I'm told it's their highest form of ministry, only for those who are advanced in the Science-based cult religion *(they get to be religious on a cruise boat in the Caribbean!).*

"Does the boat have a really good food spread?" I ask.

"The buffet is incredible!" he adds with delight.

BINGO! An incredible buffet spread! I'm beginning to like this cult already.

"Are there a lot of hot babes involved in (Science-based cult)?" I ask.

The man with the accent thinks for a moment, smiles, then answers, "That shouldn't be the reason for joining."

"So, there are a lot of hot babes!" I press further.

The man with the accent looks uneasy. "There's some attractive women, but it isn't appropriate for me to say so."

BINGO!^{2} A cult with hot babes! I'm almost ready to sign up.

Our moment of religious, Science-based cult cruise ship fantasizing is short-lived. The man with the accent presents my 200-question personality test. I see a flat line across the very bottom of the Unacceptable State region.

"The test shows that you've had a major trauma in your life. Why don't you tell me what it was?" he pries.

"I was once abducted into a cult," I explain.

According to their scientific graph, my personality is withdrawn, depressed, but on the flip side, I'm very aggressive. Hurrah, I am very aggressive about being withdrawn!

"Can you tell me why you are withdrawn and introspective?" asks the man with the accent.

"I like to read a lot."

"Do you use drugs?" he pries further.

"Only caffeine, nicotine and… heroin," I mumble.

"Do you smoke pot?" he asks, perhaps not hearing about my mumbled love for heroin.

"Oh *yeah!"* I exclaim. "Are you holding any?"

He is not.

"Smoking pot is why the graph registers so low. With *(Science-based cult)* you'll learn to enjoy things without drugs."

"What about Pink Floyd and Ben and Jerry's ice cream? When I'm high, both of those are lots, lots better!"

The man with the accent has trouble explaining why those two things would be better with Science-based cult. He goes on to tell me I need to sign up for Science-based cult's many courses to improve my life. He also tries to sell me a copy of the Science-based cult's seminal book, which, without giving away the title, rhymes with "Diabetics."

I pull out my checkbook, put it back, then pull it out again. Before signing a check to Science-based cult, I tell the man with the accent a story I heard about their founder *(who wrote* Battlefield Earth*)* and how he used to take teenaged girls out on his sailboat and mentally torment them. I elaborate with an imaginary scenario where he forced them to rub down his hairy back with oil.

Also, I tell him how the founder of the Science-based cult once told a fellow sci-fi writer, "If you really want to make money, start your own religion!" The man with the accent says I'm no longer invited to join their Science-based cult. Bah!

If You Must Go

Really? No, I mean really? Oh, well, can't say you haven't been warned. 63 Shattuck Square Berkeley, CA, 94704, and that's all we're saying.

Sunday is when the Hare Krishnas have their big weekly hoedown in Berkeley. To some the label of "Hare Krishnas" conjures up the image of guys in sheets, dancing around bus stations with shaved heads and a lack of material belongings. I see them as a group of cult religious enthusiasts who would potentially like the sport of kickboxing.

I arrive there ridiculously early. Inside is a distinct odor that smells not unlike pee *(I am hoping this has nothing to do with the initiation ceremony).* I'm wearing the "funny" T-shirt that says "*Not Enough Sex Makes You Go Blind,*" but the lettering is really blurry *(thus the humor).*

I'm asked to remove my shoes *(I hope I get them back!).* Out of the five people currently inside the Krishna temple is a Hare Krishna handyman, in the process of fixing a door. The rest of the Krishnas are in the kitchen whipping up some Krishna goulash.

"You are only required to shave your head if you live in the temple," the Krishna handyman explains as I note his long hair in a ponytail.

"Oh, then you can be a *'hairy'* Hare Krishna," I add with a chortle. *(I'm so very witty!)*

The Krishna handyman remains stone-faced.

"Actually it's pronounced *'Hare'* Krishna and not 'hairy', he explains.

"It's a joke," I explain. "I'm doing a play on words."

He still fails to laugh, providing valuable insight into what a Hare Krishna handyman finds funny.

The Hare Krishna handyman gives me a full tour of the temple, including portraits of everything from baby Krishna fighting a large snake to a pig battling some guy with a mean face.

"Will a lot of hot babes show up later?" I ask.

The Krishna handyman looks stern for a moment. "It's not appropriate for me to say so."

"So, there *are* a lot of hot babes!" I press further.

"Well..."

BINGO! Another cult with hot babes! I'm almost ready to sign up.

"If I'm really into kicking can I still become a Hare Krishna?" I ask, striking several poses. The Hare Krishna handyman momentarily gets excited.

"I used to be into Kendo *(Japanese sword fighting),"* he spouts, then segues into tales of his days in the Marines.

"If I join, could I possibly teach kickboxing classes here at the temple?" I inquire, striking more poses. Before he can answer, I add "Would it be all right to live here in the temple? My roommate is *such* a dick!"

The Hare Krishna handyman starts fiddling with his tools. He says that the decision is up to a member who is in the kitchen preparing the Krishna goulash.

BINGO! Free Krishna goulash! Forget the Science-based cult started by the man who wrote *Battlefield Earth.* Krishnas might be my new cult home.

With time to kill before the Krishna hoedown begins, I contemplate my future in the Hare Krishnas over a few pints of Guinness, for it might be my last being the Krishnas don't condone drinking, illicit behavior, and consider sex only to be used for procreation *(huh?!).*

When I return, it's a full-blown Krishna jamboree. The place is packed with Krishnas dancing around, playing drums, tambourines, cymbals and various other instruments. There's still that familiar pee smell. People are lying face down on the floor with their arms stretched out. The more important Hare Krishnas are gathered around a microphone leading the monotonous chanting.

"Hare Lama. Hare Krishna. Hare Lama. Hare Krishna."

The Krishna dancing leaves plenty of room for interpretative dance moves. I do the old mime trapped in a box schtick followed up by dancing "the robot," with various "beeps" and "boops." This is accepted. Then I test the Krishna's love of kickboxing. I throw in a few kickboxing maneuvers complete with loud sound effects. The music and dancing build, and so does my kickboxing as I throw in some high roundhouse kicks. I accidentally knock over a drum. Dancing Krishnas clear a path for me as I pretend I'm Jean Claude Van Krishna Damme.

I notice only a very few Krishnas are taking advantage of chanting into the microphone.

"Hare Lama. Hare Krishna. Hare Lama. Hare Krishna."

Thus I pretend it's the Rock and Roll Hall of Fame All-Star Jam. I perch myself between two robed Krishnas and start going at it into the mic, with the same fervor I had for my kickboxing maneuvers.

"HARE LAMA! HARE KRISHNA! HARE LAMA! HARE KRISHNA!"

For flavor, I add some scatting.

"Do-ba-dee, Do-ba-dee, doooooo!"

There's nothing like the sensation of having a Hare Krishna frown at you and take away your access to a microphone. Afterwards, I take the opportune moment to ask the recommended robed Hare Krishna if I could immediately move into their clubhouse. I'm flatly denied.

There's nothing lonelier, no greater feeling of being "lost," than being rejected by a religious cult! And damn, they both had free food and hot cult-babes, and a mild interest in kickboxing.

So my quest continues. I won't rest until I find a cult with free food, hot babes, and members with kickboxing proclivities. Until that day, the open road lies ahead. Onward!

If You Must Go...

Berkeley (New Jagannatha Puri Dham) Temple
2334 Stuart St.
Berkeley, CA 94703
(510) 540-9215

PEA SOUP ANDERSEN'S
BUELLTON, CALIFORNIA

I Love Goddamn Pea Soup!

I come across a giant billboard that reads, "Pea Soup Anderson's 110 Miles." This is very informative and gives me time to think about me and my pea soup consumption.

Where else but the middle of freakin' nowhere could a specialty restaurant like this survive. Pea soup as a main selling point for a restaurant's appeal could only prevail in the hinterlands of the open road.

"Pea Soup Anderson's 110 miles."

"Hell yes!" I cry, "Save a bowl at the table for me!" My dreamy thoughts are tapped by visions of entire swimming pools filled with steamy pea soup as revelers hold enormous piping bowls and participate in ornate limbo contests, where perhaps a menu consists of over 150 pea soup varieties – everything from Spicy Jalepeno to Chunky Monkey.

"Pea Soup! Pea Soup!" I chant for the next hour and twenty minutes. Now you might think I'm too cynical for the enjoyment of simplistic pea soup at a pea-soup-themed restaurant. This cannot be farther from the truth. In fact, during high school I used to be one of the most animated pea soup supporters. I was president of our school's "Pea Soup Appreciation Society," a collective group who gathered weekly to discuss, share facts, photos and thoughts about bowls of green pea soup. The club consisted of myself, Jingox – the flamboyant exchange student – and the shy girl with glasses who always got hit in the face during dodgeball.

I pull off at the Buellton exit and proceed down the "Avenue of Flags" *(my guess is they named it such due to all the damn flags lining the street).*

Parking my rental car, I depart from the vehicle, skipping like a schoolgirl in a pink frilly dress at a Sunday picnic; my pea soup awaits. I stop in my tracks.

I'm deceived. Pea Soup Anderson's is *not* a restaurant that exclusively sells only pea soup; it merely *showcases* pea soup as their specialty item. What a bunch of bullshit. By no means is there Pea Soup Pie or Pea Soup-sicles. That's deception in advertising. Pea Soup Anderson's is a pimp-slapped whore!

Grabbing a booth, it's very disappointing the staff isn't dressed in giant flamboyant pea outfits whilst talking in deep, silly voices. The waiter, dressed merely as a waiter, asks for my order.

"Pea Soup! Pea Soup, you stupid bastard! Pea Soup!"

Though there're food items on the menu other than blessed pea soup, the deal with Pea Soup Anderson's is, when ordered you get *a bottomless bowl of pea soup*; yes, all the pea soup you can eat. America *is* the beautiful. It's like somehow in 1946, Mr. Anderson bought a gigantic tanker full of surplus pea soup for a ridiculously low price from some shady, underworld soup-baron. Since that day, this has been Mr. Anderson's life mission – to deplete his colossal pea soup supply, sacrificing all worldly and conventional dignity.

The paintings on the wall would lead you to believe otherwise. According to their lore, a hoard of elves are in constant production of pea soup, chipping away at individual peas. Yes, poor elves ripped from their homes, put on freight cars and shipped off to the camps in order to fulfill Pea Soup Anderson's *über alles* dream of mass pea soup production. In particular, a giant, jolly elf named

"Happea" has a large mallet perched over his head, ready to hammer-down on "Pea-Wee," a sad looking elf who shakily holds a chisel to a singular pea. To me, this symbolizes giant corporate America, raising its mighty hammer, ready to strike down on, well, tiny unhappy elves. Or something like that.

This has all the trappings of a classic urban legend in the same genre of the crispy rat discovered in a bucket of Kentucky Fried Chicken. But instead, found in a bowl of pea soup would be an unfortunate severed elf's head, green as a ghastly consequence of poor labor conditions.

Reading the back of the menu, I learn more.

As history has it, Anton Andersen purchased the current restaurant spot in 1924 and built his soup empire. The original owner died in 1905 and was buried *exactly* where the parking lot now stands. It sounds like something out of Poltergeist with demonic peas terrifying tired and hungry travelers, or "pea-soupers" as they brazenly refer to their loyal pea-soup enthusiast army. With the demand for his split pea soup steadily increasing, poor Anton was faced with the uncanny problem of what to do with one ton of peas. He solved it by putting them in the window. Now, the thriving pea-soup restaurant purchases *50 tons of peas each year*, enough for three-quarters of a million bowls annually, and most likely three million cups of yearly pea soup. If you stacked up those bowls they would reach all the way from here to Bun Boy restaurant *(home of the World's Largest Thermometer)* in Baker California. Goddamn, that's a lot of pea soup!

My pea soup arrives. It's green.

"Is everything all right?" asks the jovial waiter, pestering me every five minutes. "Would you like to have more pea soup?" *(They really keep pushing the pea soup.)* Yes, through Pea Soup Anderson's "All the pea soup you can eat," I discover my pea soup limitations – one bowl. With the last spoonful consumed, it's back in the my new rental *(Grand Am)* and onward to the fabled Hoover Dam.

On the way out, I take a quick peek upstairs at the Pea Soup Andersen's Art Gallery. I expect various giant portraits by various established artist of the day, or perhaps a ceramic Jeff Koon's bowl of split-pea. What I do find is several pictures of John Wayne adorned in a cowboy hat. What are they trying to say – pea soup is as American as John Wayne, or John Wayne is as delicious as a bowl of pea soup?!

If You Must Go

Andersen's Pea Soup
376 Avenue of the Flags
Buellton, CA 93427
(805) 688-5581
www.peasoupandersens.net

Road Trip Quick Tip...

SLEEPING IN YOUR CAR

Why pay for a motel, when your car can double as a mini-motel? Much like Capsule Hotels in Japan where you are provided an area just large enough to fit your body, overnight car-sleeping is more comfortable than you think-if you make the proper preparations:

1. Buy some very small soaps and place them in your ashtray. Then hang a few hand-towels from your rearview mirror to create that comfortable motel feeling.
2. Put a bible in your glove compartment.
3. Have a recording of a loud couple making love and place it in your back seat. Periodically, pound on your seat and scream, "Can you keep it down, I'm trying to sleep! Do you want me to call the manager?!"
4. Place a mint on your headrest with a card that says, "With Our Compliments!"
5. Buy a magazine. Rip out a picture of someone's head, and then cut out the eye-portion of their face. Tape the eyes over your own eyes so if someone approaches your car, they will think you are simply awake, sitting up, ready to kick-some-ass!
6. The best location to park your car overnight is the parking lot of a State Prison or County Jail. No need to worry about being robbed-all the criminals are locked up inside.
7. A fully inflated air-bag makes for a very comfortable pillow.
8. For added protection have a huge man named Ajax sit in your passenger seat with a baseball bat ready to knee-cap any intruders who might try to interrupt your blissful sleep.

Pleasant dreams O road trip warrior, pleasant dreams!

29 PALMS, CALIFORNIA

Tour Of Duty In Fake Iraq

POPULATION 11.001

TOWN MOTTO "The Largest Marine Corp Base In the World!"

MY TOWN MOTTO "Better than Magic Mountain!"

FUN FACT In 1991, the town of 29 Palms was the setting for the vicious murder of two local teenage girls by a troubled marine!

WEIRD LOCAL SMELL Fake explosions and flop sweat.

EXTREMELY USELESS INFORMATION 7,200 meals are served in dining facilities daily.

WAY TO GET YOUR ASS-KICKED Scream, "No Blood for Oil!"

CULTURAL HIGHLIGHT It's better than a Renaissance Fair and has more thrills and spills than the Batman Returns Stunt Show!

AN IDYLLIC LOCALE FOR Marines and those portraying fake Iraqi villagers.

LEVEL OF CREEPINESS 8. This place is nearly as creepy as the real Iraq under US occupation, if not somewhat safer.

Down a dusty desert road, past the barbed wire, a sign reads in both English and Arabic, *"Slow Down Prepare to Stop. Military Traffic Point."* Two Marines search a car with its doors opened. An interpreter wearing a keiffiyah translates military orders through a bullhorn, while another marine with a mirror on a pole checks for explosives.

"One of the most dangerous things that could happen at a checkpoint is you could be subjected to a coordinated effort by the terrorists to injure you or to blow up some of your vehicles," informs the large battalion leader, who talks slightly out of the side of his mouth.

While we walk side-by-side with tanks whizzing by, suddenly, two Arabic men in a blue car speed towards the checkpoint. One dramatically leaps from the vehicle – a direct fire shooter with an AK47 – and starts sprinting madly towards the troops, dropping to the desert floor, taking the checkpoint under fire.

The Marines, returning the fire, suppress the gunman. But the ploy was a diversion. A white pickup truck *rigged with explosives,* comes barreling through the other side of the checkpoint. Not losing their 360° security, the Marines open fire and take out the truck before it can get close enough to detonate the car bomb.

Highly entertained, I practically applaud! This rocks as hard as the B*atman Returns Stunt Show* at Six Flags Magic Mountain. Wait. This is *much* cooler than the *Batman Returns Stunt Show.* Why? This is Fake Iraq!

Like many of you, I've always wanted to road trip to Iraq, but it seemed waaaaaaay too dangerous. *(All that darn killin' might be the reason.)* Here's the next best thing: Fake Iraq. It's a mere 60 miles from Palm Springs; just a simple insurgent stone-throw away from the town of 29 Palms *(is 29 Palms Fake Iran?),* with its strip malls, McDonald's, and Red Barn Realty.

Fake Iraq is set up by the US Government in the Mojave Desert to conduct a simulated military exercise to replicate real-life battlefield training missions. Forget Universal Studios with its long lines and annoying tourists. Fake Iraq is like Disneyland's version of *It's a Small Iraqi World,* but with a war twist, where the sound of gunfire permeates the cold desert morning air. And much like Disneyland, you can get a first-hand feel of what it must be like for Marines in Iraq, without all those pesky car bombs.

It gets better – just like at a Renaissance Fair, they actually hire actors to play Iraqi villagers. I kid you not! And where do they recruit fake Iraqi villagers? Craigslist!

Under a listing for *ACTORS WANTED* an ad trumpets auditions for the parts of Iraqi citizens on live sets built to resemble an actual village in Iraq. The listing said, improv skills are helpful, you know, like the kind you learn at Second City. *(Do fake Iraqi villagers play word-ball to warm up?)* I picture something out of *Team America,* with out-of-work Hollywood actors talking an improvised gibberish fish-language while swinging their arms wildly in the air. Those cast in the role of a lifetime must stay the entire duration of the operation, and are forewarned they might spend days on end without showering during the 24/7 military training scenario. *(Sounds like potential for some weird Abu Ghraib simulation)* They are paid $150 per day.

Setting my road trip sights on this idyllic hellhole destination, I phone the number listed in the Craigslist ad, and get a casting office in Hollywood. Not only do they cast fake Iraqi villagers *(for fake Iraq),* but also extras for such Tom Cruise *(fake heterosexual man)* movies as *Collateral! (Extras are paid less than Iraqi villagers.)* The thrill for me, I always wanted to be a war correspondent in Iraq. But I'm way too chicken, that's why I decide to be a war correspondent in *fake* Iraq.

POSSIBLE HORROR MOVIE SCENARIO

The Marines actually find fake WMD's amongst the fake Iraqi villagers, thus justifying invading fake Iraq, after which time they construct the largest naked fake Iraqi pyramid known to humanity. A fake civil war breaks out amongst the fake Iraqi villagers who start role-playing slaughtering each other.

Fake Iraq is located on the Marine Corp Air and Ground Center in 29 Palms; the largest Marine Corps base in the world, spanning 932 square miles of desert, three-quarters the size of the state of Rhode Island *(our smallest state).* This is the last stop for Marines right before they get shipped off to Iraq.

"Is it okay to park here?" I ask the Marine, who looks about 13 years old, working at the Visitor's Center.

"Sure," he replies. "We'll use your car for target practice!"

Ah, military humor gets me every time.

Well, I'm late to meet Gunnery Sgt. Cox – my personal tour guide for fake Iraq – at the gate of the Marine base at 0700 hours *(I hope I'm not court-martialed or forced to run laps.)*

As we get into his jeep, he explains about cultural differences in Iraq. "It's rude to talk with your sunglasses on." And then, "It's just a rude thing to do in general!" *(I quickly remove my sunglasses before he makes me drop and do push-ups.)*

Driving a few miles on a desert road towards the fake Iraq city limits *(affectionately nicknamed Waudi-Al-Sahara),* rounding a desert bluff and things take a turn for the surreal. A fake Iraqi police car blazoned with Arabic writing speeds by us, as we encounter a tin shanty town, where women in burkas and men in traditional headdresses walk to-and-fro on the sparse desert streets while the freezing desert air blows right down to the bone *(the weather in fake Iraq is either sweltering hot in the summer, or like today, record low temperatures).*

A tattered Iraqi flag *(not a fake Iraqi flag, but a real one)* waves high over an Iraqi Army base *(a fake Iraqi army base).* Burnt out shells of cars with fake Iraqi license plates dot the landscape, where stop signs read in both English and Arabic.

"Is that a real garbage truck or a role-playing garbage truck?" I ask our guide, as an Iraqi garbage truck collecting trash goes by.

""Everything is in play," he replies.

A total of 375 buildings comprise the glory that is fake Iraq. Unlike the local mobile home park in nearby 29 Palms *(where residents live in rectangle boxes),* fake Iraq offers homes *(made from yellow, rectangle metal shipping containers),* strategically stacked on top of each other to provide the fake Iraqi villagers the finest in simulated-city accommodations *(the irony here, these are the same type of containers used in "real" Iraq for waterboard interrogation).*

"How does it compare to real Iraq?" I ask the large Marine battalion leader who's taken over tour guide duties, while we come into the proximity of a fake Iraqi hospital adorned with a red crescent moon.

"Sometimes near dusk, when the lighting is right, I will have a moment when I actually think I'm back there." *(Pause.)* "There are times when it really freaks me out."

I nod my head, noting the armed Marines on every corner while a house search is already being conducted... putting on a production that makes Disneyland's Pirates of the Caribbean look like an elementary school talent show. A role-playing scenario is already in progress, where the actors portraying Iraqi villagers show off their "art."

IT'S SHOWTIME!

One actor wearing a traditional robe and cap comes to the door of his metal shipping container house. Using his "improv skills," he acts surprised to see a long line of fully armed Marines outside with their guns poised *(apparently searching for something in the fake Iraq villager's possession).* The head of the household, a man adorned in a robe and keiffiyah, is summoned. Also utilizing "improv skills," he greets the Marines with a startled look and big smile, shaking the squadron leaders hand. The first actor acts as a translator *(though I heard the other guy speak English minutes earlier when I was waiting for the Port-o-Potty).*

"Ask him what's in this blue bag out here," one marine shouts with concern. The two actors come outside to show there are no fake WMDs in the blue bag.

The commotion causes yet another actor to "improvise" and come to the door. It's a tense fake situation here in the desert, as the Marine squadron leader goes inside and the three fake Iraqi villagers are patted down from head-to-toe, searched for role-playing weapons. When the rest of the Marines enter the house, one actor becomes very combative, raising his voice in Arabic (but not too combative; he's paid $150 per day) – putting on a performance worthy of a Fake Iraq Golden Globe.

AND... *SCENE!*

I give a light golf clap; appreciative of the show the Marines just put on for us *(guessing their presence here is to liberate these actors and spread democracy throughout fake Iraq).* The actors portraying the Iraqi villagers are kind of like that basketball team that always plays the Harlem Globetrotters; no matter how many times the groups face off, they are never going to win.

The large battalion leader remarks after the curtain drops that the majority of fake Iraq villagers are actually *real* Iraqis recruited from heavily Arab-populated Dearborn, Michigan. "It's great because they are really Iraqis. It's not like we got some American guy pretending to be an Iraqi."

"Did you ever have Americans trying to portray Iraqis?" I ask, while a group of Marines begin practicing knocking down doors of houses with a battering ram.

"That was what we began with," he says. "We'd have Marines who would be the opposing force. But it's impossible for them to portray the same sort of thing."

Knowing about the casting office in L.A., I add like a big Mr. Smarty Pants. "Would you get Hollywood wannabes?" I thought the place would be filled with starving actors leaning against a tank and talking about their latest Burger King commercial audition.

(Smiles) "There were a good numbers of those."

"How did that go?"

"We have a good number of Marines coming back who have been to Iraq before, and they know what to expect from someone playing a part and to be convincing."

"What about really good actors," I inquire. "Like Joey Lawrence?"

After their performance, the four middle-aged fake Iraq role-players, now out of character, sit outside the metal shipping container house smoking and drinking tea by a campfire *(a real campfire, not a role-playing campfire).* Taking on the role of James Lipton, I conduct a little *Inside the Fake Iraq Actor's Studio.* A round table discussion about their craft commences as two veiled women look on from around the corner.

"This is like a typical Iraqi town, you are a typical Iraqi person living in your house living a regular life," one of the actors *(who I dub the Sean Penn of fake Iraq)* explains, as I'm taken inside. No expense has been spared on the elaborate interior décor of the fake Iraqi house *(essentially two tattered couches set against unpainted wooden board walls).*

"We got the mayor here," interjects another actor in a green army jacket gesturing towards the man in the keffiyah, explaining the casting office assigned certain roles from a list. "Tomorrow, we're going to have a town meeting and you're going to see the Mayor and you're going to think, 'Oh my God, what's going on here? It looks like we're in Iraq.'" *(Cool. Sounds like the Hall of Presidents with animatronic Abe Lincoln, only instead it'll be real humans.)*

"When he's got the Marines there, he's a different man," he says, boasting about an acting ability Juilliard students would envy. He, in turn, gives a morose look. "That's why we put those kind of people in those roles." *(His role in this mock-town is Iraqi army major.)*

I look over at the Mayor of Fake Iraq *(or Real Mayor of Metal Shipping Container Town).* He is the Marlon Brando of the group, playing not just one, but *two* different characters here in fake Iraq. "The first role I do here is family leader," he says in a monotone voice. "They come to my house. They search my house. They ask how many weapons I have. Then the other role I do is the mayor and I have town meeting with all my sheiks."

"We do scenarios," says another robed actor, explaining their purpose is to expose the troops to Iraqi culture. The protocol: "A team of Marines walks by. You greet them. Sometimes they search your house. They ask questions. You answer questions. It's not very hard at all."

"Actually, do you want to know how real this is?" pipes in the actor who plays the Mayor's advisor. "Often when troops go to Iraq they often remark, 'Wow, this is just like the Mojave Desert.' Or those who've had a tour of duty, come back and exclaim, "It just gave me a flashback like I were in Iraq or something." *(Then come the screaming nightmares.)*

Right now there's 90 actors in fake Iraq. On the last few days before the Marines are deployed there will be 400.

"The last four days we stay here 24 hours a day. So whenever the Marines come by, you have to get up and be ready and do anything they ask you to." *(My mind wanders to thoughts of Private-Lyndee-England-shenanigans.)*

Under the watchful eye of our marine tour guide, all the fake Iraqi actors *(but actual* real *Iraqis)* stress several times how much they love America. As the Marines continue to look on, I make sure to agree as well.

IT'S TIME FOR THE *HAUNTED MANSION* RIDE!

We follow at the heels of three large Marines, the fake Mayor *(or real Mayor of fake Iraq)* and the man who portrays his advisor. We're going to the Mayor's house! I clearly know this because the word's *Mayor's Office* is painted on the door.

"Welcome to our house," the fake Mayor's advisor says with pride.

"Yeah," says the Mayor.

"The Mayor's house!" the advisor says once again.

Unlike other buildings in fake Iraq, the Mayor's house is three stories tall *(three shipping containers stacked on top of each other),* with a large yellow sign in Arabic. The décor is also more elaborate being they mounted a few posters on the bare, plywood walls.

"This is the main room where we have the meetings," says the advisor, gesturing towards a row of chairs against each side of the shipping container complex. "As you can see, the Marines sit on one side, and us and the Sheiks sit on the other side."

The Mayor pulls a large, grainy photo off the wall, ripping off the plastic cover to give me a better look. "This was the last unit. The last one we had. This is the battalion commander with all the Sheiks, the Marines, advisors and everybody."

"That's him," the advisor says, pointing to the Mayor, playing dress-up, wearing a suit. "We are the two famous people in this town."

"It's not a perfect office, you know, but we do the perfect job."

"Should we go upstairs?" asks the Mayor.

"No," the advisor abruptly interrupts. "Nobody goes upstairs but me and the Mayor."

(I wonder if upstairs is like the part of Disneyland where Mickey Mouse is smoking a cigarette with his mouse head off, and seeing it would ruin the illusion.)

"We control the town, all of it. I'm the advisor and he's the Mayor," he boasts with pride.

As we're about to leave the fake Mayor's house, I notice – for some reason, hidden away in a wall cranny – a large portrait of a handsome blond man.

"Is this a picture of Kevin Costner?" I question, raising an eyebrow, wondering if it's connected to *not being allowed upstairs.*

"No, that is not Kevin Costner," the advisor quickly snaps, changing the subject. "Like I said I'm the advisor and he's the Mayor."

HURRAH! IT'S THE *INDIANA JONES STUNT SPECTACULAR!*

It's showtime once again!

In this scene, an actor seems to be portraying a man who stands in the middle of the street, talking loudly in Arabic, looking confused while Marines scream at him for walking away from his car at a roadblock. A tank is positioned at the other end of the road with soldier's assault weapons directly positioned on him. The man, keeping in character, still screams loudly while waving his arms wildly.

"Emshee!" a Marine yells *(translation: "Get moving!")*

His acting in the role of confused-man-screaming-in-the-middle-of-the-street is very convincing. I could easily see him making the transition to serious stage actor once the war is over. *(Okay, so it will be a while.)*

I catch up with him after his performance as confused-man-screaming-in-the-middle-of-the-street, complimenting him on his role. Going by the name Fassi, prior to coming to fake Iraq, he was a struggling actor in L.A. for 10 years.

"I used to do background acting a lot in movies and commercials," says Fassi. "I've done a lot of movies like *The Mummy, Scorpion King, Three Kings.* I did, ah, *Siege.* All kinds."

"Do you still want to be an actor?" I ask.

"I tried but there is too many people struggling," he replies with a tinge of bitterness. "I give up." Fassi has a confession. "Actually I like this job much better. Because you're not on stage and you're not on camera. This is natural work; you feel it," he says.

"You live in a regular town and you act like in real life. Being here really makes you feel happy a lot." Fassi smiles, as I watch a group of Marines conduct another house search of fake Iraqi villagers. The problem Fassi has with Hollywood is the typecasting of Middle Eastern people.

"They want bad characters. I don't want to do bad characters. I want to do a good character. *(I assume that confused-man-screaming-in-the-middle-of-the-street is a "good character?!")*

Fassi's overall opinion on being a thespian in fake Iraq: "I like it here more than in L.A., because in L.A. I don't have that much work."

And plenty of work there is. He gets to play several roles ALL DAY LONG!

He elaborates. "Sometimes I'm interpreter. Sometimes I play like a trick man. I stay at the house, and they go inside and I have like a little walkie talkie. I play stupid." *(Moves hands.)* "Sometimes I play crazy. Sometimes I play insane. I play different characters."

"Insane?" I ask.

"Sometimes I play insane," he again clarifies. "I did it like twice. They let it happen twice. Then they said they didn't want it. So I stop doing it."

I ask Fassi if he could give me a little taste of "insane."

"I just went 'Eeeeeu!'" *(He sticks out his tongue and moves hands. Then he does it again.)* "Eeeeeeu!"

"Did you add that to the role?" I inquire.

"Sometimes I add it. But they don't like Hollywood stuff. So I stopped doing that."

The large battalion leader also has a critique of the performance; not of Fassi's but of the Marines.

"The superior will talk to them later and say, 'Why did you tell him *Emshee*? Why didn't you ask him a couple of questions, or *Shisma*; what's your name. It's more friendly that way.'"

There's suddenly a loud explosion. This is followed by another loud explosion

"What are we hearing back here?" I question with concern, *(wondering if we're being attacked by fake insurgents who will mock behead the nearest fake journalist over a role-playing Internet?!)*. Gunfire starts erupting from all parts of fake Iraq.

"Almost every lane has to react to an IED. It's a totally harmless simulator but certainly makes a signature, so the Marines are aware that something is going off there." He clarifies it enhances the realism.

Neat. It's like the same way 3D effects enhance the realism of the *Terminator 2: Battle Across Time* attraction at Universal, where the Terminator battles to prevent the extinction of mankind at the hand of the evil cyborgs.

The large battalion leader explains that "realism" once backfired and the pyrotechnics accidentally lit one of fake Iraq's mosques on fire.

Pointing to a burnt out shell of a shipping container with sort of a domed roof, I ask,

"So is that the mosque that you accidentally burnt down?"

He makes clear, "It wasn't a mosque, it was supposed to *represent* a mosque. We didn't burn down a mosque," he quickly illuminates to avoid a holy war if his words are misconstrued.

Meanwhile, members of an armed marine platoon are now trying to secure a bridge under a certain time limit, while taking fire from fake Iraqi villagers in the metal shipping container houses. Marines take position in the ditches. The tanks position themselves, ready to drive through. The sound of gunfire fills the air. There's the same adrenaline thrills of paintball or a giant video game come to life *(you know, like the video games these 18-21 year olds were playing on their mom's couch mere months ago)*.

The wind kicks up and desert sand blows hard.

The battalion leader explains, "They have to move through the town, past the populated area, and there's a sniper they have to react to. When they finally come to this point they take fire from the buildings across the way, and they identify three or four terrorists over there who are firing on them."

Cool. Sounds almost like the synopsis for *Resident Evil 4,* which incorporates fast-paced gunplay, quick controls, and shootouts involving massive crowds of enemies in large open areas, while the fake Iraqi villagers take on the roles of video game villains who fire fake bullets at the real Marines from the windows of the shipping containers.

"They need to deliver the use of force, the ethical use of force, where it's required, when it's required and treat people who are not involved in this thing in an appropriate manner."

Delivering the "ethical use of force" looks fun. I guess the main difference between this and paintball; in only a few weeks, paintball fun will be replaced by *real* actual bullets, *real* IEDs and *real* car bombs that explode carnage every which way but loose. But for now, it's just like paintball. *(And paintball is fun!)*

Once again having to use the fake Iraq Port-o-Potty, momentarily I'm on my own. It's very surreal to walk through the streets of fake Iraq, with groups of armed Marines on every corner. *(This must be what it's like to have to use the Port-o-Potty in real Iraq.)*

FEAR FACTOR LIVE

I'm now watching a plotline unfold, straight out of an episode of TV's *24.*

A fake villager in a black robe gets out of his car and starts arguing with three armed Marines. There's a little bit of Oscar buzz about this actor who is fake Iraq's version of a Middle-Eastern Liam Neeson, delivering a tour-de-force performance. Looking pissed, he smokes a cigarette and gestures wildly, showing a multifaceted side to his character portrayal. He is made to lift up his robe to prove he's not carrying any weapons.

The battalion leader describes the scenario. "The Marines stop the car at the initial barbed-wire checkpoint and the husband says,

'My wife is pregnant. I have to go to the hospital right now.' Normally, you'd get everyone out of the car. But of course this woman is in labor.

"Her husband says, 'She is not getting out of the car, we need to go right now!'"

A cameo appearance is made by one of the few female actors on set today, who brings to mind Meryl Streep circa *The French Lieutenant's Woman,* adding her own unique stamp to the role of pregnant-woman-in-car.

"Is she a real pregnant woman?" I ask, wondering if that's why she was hired for the role for $150 per day or if she's role-playing pregnant *(and making $150 per day).*

"No!" the battalion leader snaps, strongly clarifying like one would if they wanted to avoid a lawsuit *(that's how good of an actor she is!).*

AND... *SCENE!*

Afterwards, the large battalion commander gets a little sentimental about fake Iraq.

"Waudi-Ha-Sara is not a real Iraqi town," he says with a bit of chagrin. He mentions a desire for a larger palm grove and mud-brick to be used for construction authenticity of the metal shipping container houses. "This place will never be finished!" He then gets positive about the ongoing growth of fake Iraq, which will continue to grow and grow as long as there's a war going on. "If I ever come to work one day and say, 'Wow this is exactly like Iraq,' I have to quit. Because I'll know something is wrong with me. Because this will always be a work in progress."

I nod my head as another group of Marines takes a turn knocking down doors with battering rams.

"This is why it's such a fun and fantastic place to work," he summarizes, giving credit to the great American/Iraqis that work here to *make this fun.* I ponder the use of the word "fun" as he takes a moment to reflect. Then, like a little kid, he breaks into a big smile. "Ah, it's a fun place to work!" Like we're off the record, he turns to me with privileged information, "Like I told you, if I want chai I can get chai." He leans in closer. "I've even had the opportunity to have some good barbeque down here from time to time."

Before leaving fake Iraq, and venturing back to the regular world where there is only real Iraq, I stroll through the fake Iraq marketplace. It's a full-on production to the level of Andrew Lloyd Webber's *Cats.* Dozens of actors role-play selling what looks like a random assortment of crap bought at a thrift store (tires, a refrigerator, sewing machines, shoes, a child's bike, etc.), where Marines can actually barter for stuff using fake Iraqi funny money. This is my favorite part of town in fake Iraq.

"Yellah! Yellah! Yellah!" one actor screams, holding up a Cosby sweater.

Another shouts, "Special price for you my friend." *(On what? A set of tires?!)* "Special price for you!"

"Yellah! Yellah! Yellah!"

I almost buy a child's bike *(that's how convincing the actor is)* as I wonder why there's a Barbie doll for sale? Is this for the Marines?! Role-players emerge from around every corner like orphan extras in the musical *Annie*. The screaming builds, becoming intense and louder. Passing a sloppily spray-painted sign that reads *Café Lewis* with someone pretending to sell buckets turned upside down on a table, I remember the words of the actor who portrays the town's Iraqi army major. "This is not a playground. I mean we don't have robots here. We have human beings and we have to train them. I mean they're not going to Disneyland. This is a war!"

Leaving this cog in the machinery of war, I think maybe we're all better off going to Disneyland!

If You Must Go

Marine Corps Air Ground Combat Centers (MCAGCC)
29 Palms, CA 92278
www.29palms.usmc.mil

SAN LUIS OBISPO, CA

Pretty Inn Pink: The Madonna Inn

My drive south on Highway 101 is scattered with bland, identical strip malls, which indicates I'm passing a town. Most look like places where people in the Witness Protection Program would live. After driving four hours, a shockingly large neon sign appears on the horizon. Pulling into the parking lot, I almost hit a horse-drawn carriage. This must be the place. This must be my Holy Grail!

The Madonna Inn is a Taj Mahal; a brilliant pink brushstroke on the canvas of central California. It's a cross between Vegas and a gingerbread house. If Willie Wonka were emperor, all hotels would be like this 109 room wonderland, nestled on twenty-two-hundred acres in San Luis Obispo. Elvis would love this Graceland, doing kung-fu kicks in the middle of the lobby. The Madonna Inn is an ideal place for an eight-year-old girl in a frilly dress to visit with her grandmother.

Completed on December 24th, 1958, each room is uniquely decorated. The most popular is the Rock Room, which is like staying in a comfortable cave, complete with rock waterfall showers. A spiral staircase takes me to my French Victorian room. The best way to describe the furnishings is "pink... very pink!" Pink carpet, pink walls, pink curtains, pink bathroom! I'm getting a cavity just looking at this place. I'm not in a hotel room, but a space in the game Candyland. There should be a giant Neapolitan ice-cream bar to slide down, rather than a staircase. I expect the shower to spray grape soda and the sink to gush chocolate syrup. This would be a great location to shoot a porn movie!

Inside, the main dining room is a Liberace wet-dream. All booths are pink leather, with pink table cloths. Gold cupids, winged angels, chandelier lamps and pink flowers dangle from the ceiling. A big Victorian dolly in a white dress is mounted on top of a moving swing. I'm having an acid trip without the acid. Santa would love to come here on his off-season. On the level of kitsch, this makes "Circus Circus" look like a Romanian sweat shop. Subtlety is not king here.

I perch myself at the pink bar. There's a large ballroom with more pink tables and gold-framed mirrors.

On stage a guy on saxophone plays "Tequila" accompanied by a guy on piano. The bald guy on saxophone has glasses and looks like a social studies teacher, and his partner on piano is the science teacher. About a half-dozen people samba on the wooden dance floor. This is Nazi Germany on a Friday night. The average age is about 100. The bartender comes over for my order.

"Do you have any house specialties?" I request. I'm given a menu with pictures. The first specialty is called "Pick and Shovel." It's simply a beer with a shot of liquor. Bizarre choice for a specialty in a place with dangling cupids. Instead I order the "Pink Cloud," comprised of strawberry schnapps, white creme de cocoa, grenadine and cream, topped with whipped cream and sprinkled with pink sugar. I hope it's served by an Oompa-Loompa!

The band starts playing "Billie Jean." A younger man dances with what I hope is his grandmother. I want to request "The Safety Dance."

In a perfect world, this would be my ideal place to conduct a fist-fight. Not a mere shoving match, but a full-on, throwing-across-pink-tables, breaking gold cupids, fist-fight! These people would go into sugar-shock.

After my second Pink Cloud I visit the bathroom. The restroom has *the best urinal ever!*

"This is the coolest thing I've ever seen!" I spontaneously exclaim.

It's like peeing into a cave. A light sensor activates a sprinkling waterfall from above. The sink is like washing your hands in a giant oyster shell. It's so-o-o-o cool that both men and women come to marvel.

"I just had to see it," says a blue-haired woman.

Returning, I ask the waitress if any celebrities come here.

"Yes, Ernest Borgnine." I bet he has.

"His wife Tova sells her products in the gift shop," she adds. *(I don't ask what those products are.)*

The band plays their last song, which is "Staying Alive."

"You'll have to fight over who gets the last dance," says a very old man to two old woman. It's 11:00 and they're giving last call! Not even enough time to have another Pink Cloud. Damn, 11:00! What now?! Am I supposed to go back and sit in my very pink room?! How can I sleep with all this sugar pumping in my veins? It's time for us to go back to our individually-designed theme rooms, get in our jammies and tinker off to nigh-nigh land.

After a good nights sleep, dreaming of sugar plum fairies and gumdrops, I go to the coffee shop for breakfast. The waitresses are clad in German Heidi dresses. Big pink cakes and lollipops are on sale by the register. At the next table, the conversation goes like this:

"We petted horses!"

"Were they nice horses?"

I put pink sugar in my coffee. The Heidi-waitress comes over.

"Can you sum-up working at the Madonna Inn in one sentence?" I ask.

"There's plenty of nice people," she says about her eight-year experience here.

"Have you met any celebrities?"

"Yes."

"Have you met Ernest Borgnine?"

"Yeah," she says, astonished by my knowledge.

Before leaving this fairytale land, I check out the gift shop. Not only can I purchase my very own gold Cupid, but also extravagant lamps, life-size children dolls and many things made of porcelain. There's also plexi-glass toilet seats for $375, containing a choice of barbed wire or dollar bills. Maybe I should do my Christmas shopping early?

The Madonna Inn is America at it's best. A pure sugary spoonful of Americana. A place where all the good little boys and girls go! A place that is sooooo good for all the wrong reasons. My teeth still hurt from the experience.

Viva La Madonna Inn!

If You Must Go

The Madonna Inn
100 Madonna Road
San Luis Obispo, CA 93405
(800) 543-9666, (805) 543-3000
Rooms from $168 per night.
www.madonnainn.com

MADONNA INN
VACANCY
COCKTAILS
COPPER CAFE
Pastries
STEAK House

LOS ANGELES, CALIFORNIA

City Of Broken Dreams And Bad Reality Television

POPULATION 12.9 million

TOWN MOTTO The City of Angels

***MY* TOWN MOTTO** You Need Knee-Pads To Make It In This Town!

HOLLYWOOD FUN FACT The Hollywood Sign used to read Hollywoodland. On September 18, 1932 out-of-work actress, Peg Entwistle, committed suicide off the sign's "H."
Hurray for Hollywood!

WEIRD LOCAL SMELLS Desperation, plastic surgery, freeway engine fumes.

EXTREMELY USELESS INFORMATION The TV show *Alf* was filmed in L.A.

HOLLYWOOD CULTURAL HIGHLIGHT There's more fake breasts than funny hats at a Pope convention.

HOLLYWOOD IS AN IDYLLIC LOCALE FOR Actor wannabees, sharky agents, Scientologists, those who are pretty on the outside and ugly on the inside, and Mel Gibson.

LEVEL OF CREEPINESS 10

Hollywood is the land of crap reality TV shows. If you're going to roadtrip to L.A. why not do so by being on a TV show, and have them pay for your lodging and expenses? It's much, much easier than you think.

Reality TV shows are constantly looking for something "real" to mock and humiliate. So why not turn the tables and on your trip to Hollywood, humiliating instead reality television, all while making a little cash?

Let's set our target on daytime courtroom TV shows. We've seen these TV shows where the judge doesn't take crap from anyone.

Take your pick: *The People's Court, Judge Judy, Divorce Court, Judge Joe Brown, Judge Lopez.* There's a fake court show for almost everyone. And they've all got things in common: black robes, yelling and fake *(yet solemn)* wood grain paneling.

"Submit your case," beckons each TV judge's website, providing contact info for those with small claims brouhaha and the need to resolve them on television. All you need is a sensational story that's waaaaaay over-the-top, not to mention risqué enough to make a Midwestern housewife momentarily stop her afternoon vacuuming.

Follow my lead; the case I submit:

> It was my roommate's bachelor party in Vegas. I gave my friend Mike $700 to hire some strippers for the party. When it came time for the strippers to take it all off, they weren't chicks, THEY WERE DUDES!!!!!

Within hours I get an email from the *Judge Joe Brown Show* ("Defender of womanhood, promoter of manhood"); a syndicated TV judge who hasn't taken crap in his TV courtroom for eight years. I call the associate producer.

He's ecstatic to hear from me.

"I can tell you this, I've seen a lot of stuff, but I don't think I've ever seen anything like this come across my desk before," he excitedly professes, confirming I've jumped the first hurdle and soon will be partying it up in L.A.

"Basically my friend ruined my good friend's bachelor party in Vegas," I confirm.

"No, I read your story and I think its completely crazy," he confides with enthusiasm, sharing, "Sometimes we read stories like this and sometimes they embellish for fun like they write these stories and they're just full of smoke. But if you're serious, I'll totally see if we can help you out with this."

Confirming seriousness, we roll up our sleeves and get into the details of the case.

"From his point of view he thinks it was a funny joke. Like a 'ha-ha-ha I was just messing around'. But meanwhile you get no strippers."

"Well we got strippers," I reply. "But they weren't chicks."

(Shocked.) "So you were all slapping dollar bills and getting lap dances and at the end it was *wabam?!*"

"Yeah."

"You're joking me. Like really?!" he exclaims. "Like, I'm in serious disbelief right now. I've been doing this show a lot and I've never heard anything like this. Like it's just ridiculous to me," he blurts. "So they never took off their bottoms and were giving everyone lapdances, and then at the end of the night did they just said 'Surprise'?"

"It certainly was a surprise all right! You could hear a pin drop," I snarl. "Some people just freaked out. Then everyone started yelling at each other."

"Basically, they're all thinking, 'Oh my god am I gay now because I just got a lapdance from this guy?!'"

I bitterly confirm this information.

(Impassioned anger.) "Mike *(who hired the strippers)* was like, 'Screw you. This was funny! You're being a big bunch of babies. You can't take a joke,'" I spew, adding groom Hal's wedding has since been postponed due to the hidden secret that **dare not speaketh its name.**

"What a creep. Holy mackerel!"

"It really pissed people off and I feel responsible. That's why

I think your show would be the best way to resolve this," I reason *(wondering why the hell he'd think anyone would want to go on national TV and profess accidental-lady-boy-lapdancing).*

The TV court legal system is then explained.

"On our show if a plaintiff wins their claim, whatever they win, we pay. So therefore the defendant gets off without having to pay you back. *(Huh?!)* Yes it sucks. The defendant gets off scott-free. It's kinda a bunch of bull."

The benefit of avoiding *real* actual court, he explains, is that even if I won I'd still have to hound down the defendant for the money. The best solution recommended is to settle legal matters as TV entertainment!

"On our show if you win you don't have to worry about that process. You get a check from us within 30 days for the amount that you win!"

There's more enticement to avoid the real legal system in favor of television.

"We're located in Hollywood, California. It's a free trip, hotel and all that fun stuff," he allures. "We'll give you some spending money. Maybe go to the strip clubs...."

"Yeah, but not the lady-boy strip club!" I angrily clarify.

But there's another hurdle before I get my trip to La-la-land: I need to provide evidence the bachelor party actually took place.

"Like I said, it's not that I don't believe you but my bosses are going to say, 'Show me proof that they're not just making this up for a quick buck. And a quick free trip to L.A. because they think it's funny.' Because we do get those," he shares. "And we have to protect ourselves from those!"

He request my Circus Circus receipt as well as photos from the infamous bachelor party, including myself with one of the strippers.

"I mean clearly, you got to understand that this story at first glance almost seems far fetched. I'm not calling you a liar but from an audience perspective I've got to protect the sanctity of our show."

“Sure.” I say *(Photoshop work lies ahead for me).*

“I take every case seriously until I see something that makes me think otherwise,” he states.

Then the ugly side of courtroom TV shows has reared its hideous head.

“At this point you have to understand you are now verbally committed to doing our show,” he stresses. “So if any other shows contact you, you have to say sorry, ‘I’m already working with the show, I can’t talk to you.’ Ignore them!”

“Ignore them,” I repeat.

“The problem with some shows are,” he bemoans. “Even though they do it illegally they will contact the defendant before they contact you and try to book them first and say ‘I have the defendant on board,’ which technically they are not allowed to do.”

“Really?!”

“Yeah, it’s kind of sketchy. But I’m not going to mention shows because I can get in trouble for it.”

TIME TO PLAY HARDBALL

The Judge Joe associate producer was right. TV’s finest legal-resolvers are very concerned with trying to resolve my lady boy stripper problem. *(Damn. I only need one trip to L.A.)*

The People’s Court comes knocking. After hearing Judge Joe wants a piece of my courtroom pie. The producer pleads, “Please don’t sign anything with the Judge Joe Brown Show!” I tell her I’m flattered but I’m still fielding other offers.

Then, the *Judge Maria Lopez Show* wants to work fast, being I now have TV courtroom heat. The producer hurriedly e-mails, trying her damnedest to land the big Thai-lady-boy-bachelor-party-stripper case: “I’d like to strike a deal with you today considering that other shows are calling you. We work very quickly in television... and I want to bring you to New York City the first week in August... I promise, I’ll make it worth your while.”

Well butter me sideways! I’m hot crap in the TV courtroom world. With cockiness, I phone her, ready to play court TV hardball.

"So are you guys willing to wheel-and-deal?"

"Listeeeeeen," she says with a nasal voice. "That's what we do. *(Ha-ha)* It's so funny," she says, "I definitely know some of the producers of that show. *(Ha-ha-ha)*"

She sweetens the deal offered by the Judge Joe Brown people, enticing me with more cash.

"So, do you want to come to New York or do you want to go on that other show?"

I make her work harder and arrogantly state my loyalty to the Judge Joe producer. Besides, New York isn't in my road trip plans.

"Who is the other guy?" she asks, raising her voice. She throws out a name. When I confirm it, she shrieks, "No waaaaaaaaay. Don't tell him," she murmurs, being he once worked for her. "He used to be in love with me!" She then does a crude impersonation of him. "He's kind of 'Uhhh!' 'Uhhh!'"

"He told me not to talk to any other shows," I inform her.

Her ethics are unfazed. "I mean yeah, whatever. Don't worry about him." She pits the shows against each other. "Judge Joe Brown doesn't have the same sense of humor and understanding that our judge will," she explains like a used car salesman. Then my ego is fed: "We get a lot of small claims that I think are just boring. *(Snickers)*"

"I'll let you know by Friday?" I snip.

"The producer abruptly whines, "Why do you want to go to Judge Joe Brooooown?! Come on! I mean I don't want to pressure you, but at the same time I want to pressure you. Ha-ha-ha-ha *(Long cackle)* You get it. You know."

(Almost bored) "I'll think about it."

"Don't go to him. Come on, stay with me. *(Pause.)* I can't believe the only person I know over there, that he and I would be going for the same case. It's hilarious!" she proclaims. "I love that I know him. *(Pause)* Oh god, he sat in my office and just like drooled over me," she brags *(embarrassing statement if ever printed)*. "I'd also love to take his case."

(Long cackle).

LOS ANGELES, CA

IT GETS ANNOYING

It's time for the Judge Maria Lopez producer to dance the tango. The next day I send her an e-mail saying the Judge Joe Brown folks would double your appearance fee and give me an extra night in L.A.

Mere moments later she responds saying they'll match that. I choose to ignore her. She responds hours later with:

I'm willing to give you 300 bucks and an extra night in NY...

Then comes a parade of Instant Messages. I finally e-mail back making really unreasonable demands that includes a case of Yoohoos and a gold crown, as my loyalty remains with Judge Joe. In fact, I've already assembled a cast of misfits to play the appropriate bachelor party roles. With two improv-acting friends recruited to portray defendant Mike and disgraced groomsman Hal, I make extensive notes and send each a bullet-point sheet of the entire back-story. Booking a room at Circus Circus on hotels.com provides the appropriate needed receipt *(after Photoshop).*

What about pictures of lady-boy strippers? I live in San Francisco, how hard can that be?! In fact, we've got a restaurant called Asia SF. The entire staff is comprised of Asian trannies. Venturing there, photos are snapped with my arms around one of the staff-trannies. When a musical number is performed on top of the bar, photos are shot at a really low angle to make it look like they might be stripping in a hotel room. When complete, I send the photos to the associate producer.

The next day I get an email saying, "Those are great!"

I'll soon have my road trip to L.A. paid for *and* be put up at the Hyatt on the Sunset strip *(defendant Mike gets a crappy hotel across town).* It's stressed that I shouldn't wear hats or sports stuff being it would make it seem like I didn't care about the case.

MY DAY IN TV COURT

It's 8:00 a.m. and a audience members are lined up outside the Judge Joe Brown soundstage. I got the free trip to L.A., but now I have to work for it. I'm in character already, wearing a suit and a mean "I could eat babies" grimace. Jilted groomsman Hal walks by my side.

Scrutinized at a security checkpoint, our picture phones are confiscated and set next to someone's seized bottle of vodka. Gesturing to the bottle, the guard says, "It happens more often than you think!" We're then herded into the green room with the other plaintiffs who are eating complimentary donuts.

"It's not your fault that the dog was running in the street. It's the owner's fault and he needs to take responsibility," one of the many producers coaches a girthy woman, regarding her TV court case. She's catty-cornered from the girl whose boyfriend refuses to pay for wrecking her car, and a jittery exotic dancer from Virginia.

"I'm so nervous my heart is racing," she blurts. "I'm scared that I'm going to faint. I'm serious." *(Could it have been her confiscated vodka?!)*

"I just hope I don't get too angry out there," I snap, ready to fly off the handle.

"That's my concern too," she says. "I'm sensitive. I'll cry," she declares.

The show's bubbly head producer butts in on our heart-to-heart in order to coach us on how to make good TV. "It's an arbitration but it's also television, so you can be animated. It's okay to interrupt the other person. Feel free to have a little back-and-forth with the defendant," she says, moving her hands to illustrate this. "Make your words really clear with some passion."

I nod my head with a permanent scowl on my face. My defendant's plan is to also act as nervous as possible. Tucked away in his green room, every time someone knocks on his door, he sits on the couch in a rocking motion, hugging his backpack. "Is he going to be mean to me?" defendant Mike asked the producer, as though he's afraid of Judge Joe.

"Work with the judge, okay?" the producer continues. "Give him something to go on. Give him something to keep talking about it.

She hands me a copy of my TV court statement for my approval. "Do I have to use the words 'male genitalia?'" I ask, pointing to the words 'male genitalia.'

"Use any way you want to frame it," pipes in the associate producer from the phone, whose lanky build towers over us. "You can say *penis.*" He confirms this with the bubbly producer. "Is penis okay?" Then he spells it out. "But you can't use the word c-o-c-k or d-i-c-k."

(Pause) "How about s-c-h-l-o-n-g?"

"Here's the thing with this case, it's a light case. In the sense that no one got killed *(do murder trials come to the* Judge Joe Brown Show*?!)* No one got beaten up. No one destroyed anyone's property. No one busted up someone's face."

"My soul's broken," mumbles faux jilted groomsman Hal, too ashamed to even make eye contact.

"Have fun with it. Let your personality come out. This is a funny story. You can say, 'in hindsight it's a little bit funny, but on the day it happened it wasn't funny.'"

Rubbing my clenched fist, my blood begins to boil. "It wasn't funny then and it's not funny now!" I clarify with hate burning in my eyes. "You think this was a joke?! It's not funny; it's a matter of principle!"

"You see, I was testing you," the lanky guy, slightly taken back, explains. "I wanted to see where you were at with this whole thing. The defendant was saying that it was a big joke. He thinks it's funny. That's his whole thing. 'Ha-ha big deal.'"

"This was supposed to be a good memory," the bubbly producer adds her two-bubbly-cents, along with the cliché, "Because, hey, what happened in Vegas didn't stay in Vegas," she recites with a smile. "I'm sure it's a hard story to tell people now."

"That's why I'm kind of nervous going on TV and admitting this actually happened," Hal mumbles, looking at his shoes. "This was supposed to be my first and only stag party!"

"I understand," she says with a consoling look.

With the weight of this dark secret resting on his shoulders, he adds, "My fiancée brings it up all the time now."

"Oh, she does! You should definitely express that!"

Wow! Maybe they really do care and truly want to resolve matter rather than just exploit our story.

IT'S TV COURTROOM SHOWTIME!

Led through a maze of hallways to a bustling set, passing the courtroom audience (paid roughly $60 to sit here all day), my goal is to see how many times I can get them to go "Oooooooh!" in unison. Kind-of-hot TV bailiff, Miss Sonia, calls our case to the stand. I almost lose it when defendant Mike appears, dressed like he rides the special bus to school. With somber expressions we walk with serious determination through waist-high swinging doors, both taking our respective stands.

Judge Joe, with posture so casual he might rest his feet up on his judge stand, sets up the scenario by launching into a long rambling diatribe, "Every now and then there's some levity that comes into the courtroom!"

I think the lanky producer duped us. Some people are already chuckling. We've been set up as the TV courtroom comic relief, between heavy cases like the freeloading roommate who borrowed something he didn't return. I scowl harder. Weren't we assured this wasn't a joke and we weren't going to be exploited for laughs?!

As I start describing the bachelor party scenario, "...so I gave the defendant $700 to hire two strippers...." Defendant Mike, utilizing body posture so rigid he looks like he's in the military, loudly pipes in with, "WRONG! WRONG! WRONG!"

I wave my Photoshoped Circus Circus hotel receipt, but Judge Joe interrupts. "And what was so different about these strippers?" he asks, knowingly setting me up for the big courtroom zinger.

Pausing for dramatic effect I lean forward. "They weren't chicks... They were DUDES!!!!"

"Ooooooooh!" erupts the courtroom in unison. They totally lose it.

"Can you even imagine?!" someone remarks from behind me.

The supposedly impartial, fake TV courtroom suddenly becomes a free for all. It becomes more like Judge Joe talking and us trying to interrupt him. Trying to get a word in, Judge Joe won't let us finish or even tell us to shut up; he just keeps talking and doesn't get mad.

For no reason, Mike starts repeating "I object!" a lot, speaking directly into the microphones on the stands *(even though we were told they are props)*. "You said get some strippers. That's all you said, "'Get some strippers!'" he barks. "That's all you said!"

"I asked for strippers. I didn't ask for *The Crying Game!"* I retort, to more courtroom clamoring and another moan of, "Ohhhhhhhh!"

Defendant Mike starts objecting again. "LIAR! LIAR! LIAR!" he keeps yelling. "Like you asked I went and got some strippers; hot, Asian strippers!"

"I didn't say that," I sneer. Throwing a little subtle racist undertone to the whole story, I add, "You know how I feel about *them."*

"You were the one that went into the bathroom with one of the lady-boys," defendant Mike turns the tables.

"Ooooooooh," spouts the audience *(who-gets-roughly-$60-for-the-day)*.

With classic Jerry Springer talk-to-the-hand timing I come back with, "I only went into the bathroom because I wanted to throw up!"

Gesturing to the jilted groomsman, I hint that his bathroom rendezvous is the reason why his wedding is now postponed. He, in turn, looks like a petrified deer, unable to form words, harboring the dark secret of that fateful Vegas night.

"How come you kept getting the lapdances from them, and you were the only one who knew they were trannies?" I throw at defendant Mike.

"Ooooooooh!"

This ignites Mike to go off on another round of ranting "LIAR!" and "I OBJECT!" and then, "It was funny. It was a funny joke. Everyone thought it was funny!"

"Can I see the photographs you brought," Judge Joe finally commands.

I hand sort-of-hot TV bailiff Miss Sonia copies of my photos depicting Vegas lady-boy strippers *(Asia SF staff members).* Immediately they're projected on the large courtroom screen.

The authenticity of the Asia SF staff members – posed with me and my huge smile – instigates another rumble throughout the fake TV courtroom. "Ooooooooh!"

Judge Joe takes time for another long, rambling, analogy. "Do you do any hunting?" he asks.

"What?!"

Posing the question again, he elaborates, "It's like when you set a duck decoy out and you try to get these other ducks...."

I'm sure his long, southern-type analogy has something to do with the case, but goes on for so long that when finished there's an awkward pause. Mike chimes in with, "But this case has nothing to do with ducks!"

It seems the producers predetermined that they really wanted a bad guy. And lady-boy-purchasing Mike has been set up as the bad guy as the judge throws wisecracks at him. I slam-dunk my closing arguments, delivering the classic line, "It's like I told him to go buy oranges... and he came back with *a banana!*" The courtroom loses it. More scowling. I throw out another correlation, "Or, it's like I told him to buy pillows... and he came back with *A BANANA!*"

Before the judgment is handed down, the Judge Joe twist is

the audience gets to vote on who they think should win *(much like they do in real courtrooms).*

"If you thought they were getting what they expected," advises Judge Joe, "vote yes."

Defendant Mike interrupts the proceedings. "Is this going to be tabulated by a Diebold machine?" There're literally three or four loud groans inside the fake TV courtroom.

"I'd have another name for you if this wasn't being broadcast," replies the testy judge. "If they had a *Judge Joe After Dark* it would be a different story. We're on broadcast TV so there are certain things I can't say."

The tabulated votes appear on a large screen, 86% to 14% in my favor.

"If you hired these people then obviously you might like what they have to offer," bellows Judge Joe, trying to make defendant Mike admit he's gay *(weird)*. "If there was a time for you to come out of the closet, this is the time for you to do it, you got a good audience." With a slam of the gavel, "I award the judgment to the plaintiff!"

I give a cocky Tom-Cruise-with-a-head-full-of-Scientology, "Yes!"

Defendant Mike pretends to wipe away a tear, as he's led from the courtroom. I swagger out uttering, "Lady Liberty must be smiling!"

Backstage, as our remote mics are being removed, the lanky producer comes over, looking jubilant at the TV spectacle. He says with a smirk, "It's good it's a hurdle. It puts closure on things. Maybe you can all be friends now?"

"No way," I snap, still in character. "If I see that asshole in the parking lot afterwards, he better watch out!"

"Hey, hey, you don't want to do that," he responds, concerned I'm going to go after him. "He basically got called gay on national television."

True, and that does make for some good TV, not to mention a hell of a road trip stop!

If You Must Go

The Judge Joe Brown Show
CTLA Studios
5842 Sunset Blvd,
Hollywood, CA
Tickets are available at: 323-860-0200
www.judgejoebrown.com

Road Trip Quick Tip...

Changing A Flat Tire

Step One: Realize you have a flat tire.

Step Two: Stop your car.

Step Three: Get out of car and look at said flat tire.

Step Four: Swear. Say things like "Son of a bitch!" or "Goddamnit!"

Step Five: Pull out cell phone to call local service station to come and fix flat tire.

Step Six: Pay person from local service station money. *(See Step Four on swearing to be used when you're overcharged.)*

Step Seven: When tire-fixing is complete, treat yourself to a hot fudge sundae for a job well down!

Step Eight: Get back in car and continue on journey.

CONGRATULATIONS!
YOU'VE FIXED A FLAT TIRE!

Nevada Quick Tip...

DISCOVER THE BEAUTY OF STATE LINE CASINOS!

Some of the *shadiest of the shady* are the casinos in Jean, Nevada, right off of I-15, on the Nevada/California State Line. That's why they're so flippin' great. Perched directly over the border, these establishments are for hardened gamblers who just can't wait, and don't have the patience, to drive that extra 20 miles to Las Vegas. They need to gamble NOW! ("If I don't gamble right away, goddamn it, I'm going to fucking hurt somebody!")

The State Line casinos allow you that magical opportunity to gamble alongside drifters, people harboring terrible secrets, and the plain confused *(who might actually think they are in Vegas).*

It gets better. The Nevada Landings Casino is located next to a prison! That's right, an official Nevada State Prison. Hurrah! Yes, while you're gleefully putting coins into the nickel slots, right down the road is a prison with its high stone walls, elevated watch towers, and barbed wire – housing hardened, incarcerated criminals – some of whom have even murdered people! To me, nothing screams "vacation fun" louder than that. The greatly confused might actually mistake the correctional facility for a prison-themed casino.

I think this casino/prison hybrid locale originated for two reasons. First, it sends a firm message for those who might consider ripping off the casino in any WAY, SHAPE or FORM *(such as stealing an extra helping of 99 cent shrimp cocktail while casino employees aren't looking)*. Secondly, much like Alcatraz, which hosts a spectacular view of bustling San Francisco, this Nevada State Prison establishes the cruelest and most sadistic form of punishment for those locked away on gambling-related charges. From behind their cell doors most likely they can hear the clanging of slot machine coins, while the aroma of $6.99 prime rib dinners wafts towards them in the warm desert air. Yes, a cruel, sadistic punishment indeed! And the best part is, prisoners who manage to escape could fit in with the shifty crowd at the Nevada Landings Casino – a perfect getaway destination *(something to consider when sharing a blackjack table with some new buddies)*.

If You Must Go

Nevada Landing Hotel & Casino
2 Goodsprings Rd
Jean, NV 89019
(702) 874-1767

LAS VEGAS, NEVADA

Vegas, Mon Amour!

Vegas is the Paris of Central Nevada. It has so much to offer: fabulous smorgasbords, senior citizens gambling away their kidney dialysis money, a false sense of reality, and much, much more.

There are many hidden treasures which can be found and explored in this city of subtlety. It's a mere 45 minutes from my beloved Hoover Dam. Vegas is a great road trip destination, being that experience was immortalized in Hunter S. Thompson's classic book, *Fear and Loathing In Las Vegas.* Reaching Barstow on the edge of the desert, you can vividly imagine picking up a hitchhiker in the midst of an ether binge, silently admiring the shape of his skull as huge bats and manta rays swoop and screech around the car. The only thing missing from that book is more references to the Hoover Dam.

I pull the green Pontiac Grand Am into town for some pre-dam fun. Although Las Vegas is considered a gambling Mecca, there are many more fun alternative activities to a-bettin' and a-whorin' that won't deplete your hard-earned kidney dialysis cash.

1. LARRY KING IN WAX

Yes, everyone enjoys the wry insights of informative talk show host Larry King, and some would argue that he's already fairly wax-like. So the only thing better than his astute anecdotes would be, of course, seeing his actual likeness carved completely in wax! Settle down. I know this sounds too exciting to be true, but it actually does exist at Madame Tussaud's Wax Museum. Once again, settle down!

Fun activity: count Paraffin Larry's age spots!

If You Must Go

Madame Tussaud's
3377 Las Vegas Blvd. South
Las Vegas, NV 89109
(702) 862 7800
www.mtvegas.com

2. GROWN PEOPLE CRYING

I always find it a treat to see a man my father's age crying in Las Vegas. Not everyone is a winner and, in fact, Las Vegas is crammed with losers, both metaphoric and literal. So what might be a rare event elsewhere is common here. Take time off from wolfing down 99-cent shrimp cocktails to witness the glorious marvel of adult men weeping in the public areas of the "America's Playground."

Where:

Every casino. Most pawn shops.

3. GET MARRIED TO YOURSELF

The Viva Las Vegas Wedding Chapel boasts: Immediate Arrangements, Free Reservations and No Deposit Required. Hot damn! If you're lucky, you might be asked to be a witness to one of these sacred, if hurried, events, or become an insta-spouse yourself!

I enter the small chapel, where a helpful woman sports an orange face.

"I'd like to find out about getting married immediately. What do I need to do?"

“You’ll need to go to the courthouse and get a marriage license,” says the woman with the tangerine complexion.

“Is there a three-day waiting period like for buying a gun?”

“No.” *(Pause)* “You can get a license this afternoon. How many people will be attending your wedding?”

“Just myself! I’d like to get married to myself!”

But the Ronald McDonald face-paint lady insists that, unlike sex, you have to drag at least one other person into the situation to make a marriage happen. Deeply disappointed, I make my excuses and leave.

If You Must Go

1205 Las Vegas Boulevard So.
Las Vegas, NV
(800) 574-4450

4. THE GAMBLER’S POSSESSIONS MUSEUM

Located at any Las Vegas pawnshop. My museum stop is at Sahara Pawn. Inside is a shrine of items exchanged for cash for one more lucky spin of the wheel. A fun activity is seeing how many wedding rings can be found.

“Can I help you find anything?” asks the suspicious sales clerk.

“Yes, I’m interested in immediately buying a gun, a chainsaw, and a large bag!”

I’m told there’s a waiting period on the gun. I shrug my shoulders, make my excuses and leave.

If You Must Go

Sahara Pawn
2400 S Jones Blvd. # 15
Las Vegas, NV 89146
(702) 253-7296

WHERE TO STAY: HOOTERS HOTEL AND CASINO

Vegas is all about subtlety. A great example is the huge billboard for Tao Tao Chinese Restaurant. Plastered along the strip, it shows the crack of a woman's ass and reads, *"Tao Restaurant–Always a Happy Ending!"* But I think this overtly sexual innuendo may be *too* subtle for the mind of the average Vegas-patron.

If You Must Go

Tao Tao Chinese Restaurant
3740 E Flamingo
Las Vegas, NV
(702) 458-2920

Speaking of subtle, when staying in Vegas, there's only one choice for accommodations: Hooters Casino!!!! *(Note all the exclamation points.)* For me, I stay at Hooter's Casino with the same smug ironic detachment like one would if they wore an old-school *Dukes of Hazzard* T-shirt. *(Get it? I know it sucks that's I'm staying here and it's funny).* This newly constructed casino has that soon-to-be-bankrupt glow written all over it. The place is filled entirely with guys. Yes, packs of middle-aged men pounding back Budweiser, leering at the tackily dressed Hooters Girls, who might be considered hot if you were at a suburban shopping mall in the Midwest. Yes, the casino is filled with men, and women who look like they were dragged here by men.

Hooters is all about the "funny" double-entendre *(it's a double-entendre lover's paradise!).* If you're a big fan of '70s *Three's Company* humor, then much laughing will be had on your part. Get ready to laugh, cuz here's a few examples. The Do Not Disturb signs read, **No Knockers!** *(I'm laughing already)* You see, this phrase could be applied to both big breasts and the pounding on one's door by the hotel's housekeeping staff. Road signs are placed in the casino that say **Curves Ahead!** *(More laughing on my part.)* Again, this could refer to both a sign denoting a standard deviation in the road, or large milk-sacks of women who work at this establishment. Another sign features a big breasted waitress

holding a plate of food reads, **Look at 'Em.** *(Oh Pleeeeeeeease!)* Once again, your mind is not sure whether to look at the food or the woman's huge meat-pillows? *(Do yourself a favor and look at both.)* Regardless, you're convulsing with laughter.

Besides the ridiculously-clad Hooters girls, the casino also has an eatery called The Dam Restaurant. *(Double-entendres are their main course!)* Their waitresses are mostly frumpy looking women in very concealing '50s diner outfits. Those who apply to work at Hooters and get assigned to the Dam Restaurant must be an inside joke amongst the casino employees:

(Looking over application). "Well...we don't have any openings for Hooters girls, but we got this damn diner...."

If You Must Go

Hooters Casino Hotel Las Vegas
115 East Tropicana Avenue
Las Vegas, NV 89109
(866) LV-HOOTS (584-6687)
Rooms, from $50 per night.

LIBERACE MUSEUM:

WHAT YOU SHALL SOON LEARN ABOUT LIBERACE:

1. Liberace was not gay.
2. When tired, Liberace had trouble making it to his home two blocks away.
3. Old people really like Liberace.
4. Liberace liked to cook "Liberace Lasagna."
5. Liberace Museum employees don't like French accordion players.

Vegas is the American Dream. Where else could a freak like Liberace not only call home, but even have his own museum? It's time to pay it a visit and see what secrets there are to be found.

But first a little needed preparation.

PREPARATION

When visiting this shrine, you should be appropriately presentable at the museum dedicated to the life of Liberace. You don't want to be taken for an average Liberace enthusiast, but, like myself, a Liberace fan of the hugest magnitude in order to get the full Liberace VIP treatment.

ATTIRE

Liberace was famous for his elaborate and flamboyant gowns. You should attempt to imitate the attire of the man some called "Li" and devise your own interpretative version. This might entail a trip to the Salvation Army, after which you will be able to create a makeshift gown which will look simultaneously haphazard and meticulously designed. Maybe wear many drugstore rings or perhaps a big furry, silly hat.

ADOPT A FLAMBOYANT PERSONA

Again, this will help with Liberace Museum VIP treatment. Follow my lead as I adopt the persona of François LaRoch – famous French accordionist from the band Les Petites Accordions *(Translation: The Little Accordions).*

UTILIZE A BACKSTORY

François is a self-proclaimed Liberace protégé. His excitement at visiting the Liberace Museum is the equivalent of a King Tut fan visiting King Tut's tomb.

ONWARD TO THE LIBERACE MUSEUM!

The Vegas city bus drops me off at a strip mall. Surely this can't be the Liberace Museum. I'm in the suburbs of Las Vegas!

Somehow I imagined it as an annex next to Caesar's Palace, complete with secret doors and Odd Job from the Bond movie *Goldfinger* as the doorman. Instead it's near a 7-11, where an Aikido Center used to be. Where are the iron gates to hold back the throngs of weeping fans like at Graceland, screaming "Liberace! Liberace! Liberace!"

The museum is divided into three buildings, the largest is near the 7-11; the two others are at the far end of the parking lot by the old Aikido Center. Yes, I have arrived!

> *It always seemed to me that when you have*
> *something beautiful, it's a shame not to share it.*
> – Liberace

The first building houses Liberace's pink rhinestone cars and pianos. There are very few people inside. No one is under the age of 70. I enter, falling on my knees in ecstasy. If I knew how to make myself openly weep on command, I would be doing so at this very moment.

"I em so veery hep-py!" I say in broken English.

A soft-spoken gentlemen with fuzzy hair and pastel jacket stands behind the front desk. His look suggests one who's never seen this reaction at the Liberace Museum. I gather my composure, rising to my feet, and wave a twenty-dollar bill in the air.

"I 'ave come from France for zis mo-ment!"

"Well...enjoy the museum," says Fuzzy-head, handing me a ticket, then commences to nervously straighten Liberace literature.

"Et eez because of Liberace, I now play zee accordion," I remark, clutching my heart.

Fuzzy's eyes go to my gown and black feather boa. "That's nice."

Liberace literature is still being straightened, as I point to a portrait on the wall.

"Et eez him!" I exclaim, letting out a schoolgirl shriek.

"Remember to visit the other two museum buildings," he says, softly, unimpressed by my Liberace idolatry.

Perhaps I was wrong. Maybe he sees the ecstatic fanfare constantly and has now become jaded to these petty rituals. *(Or maybe he just sees through my crappy French accent and makeshift gown.)*

Just then a woman in stretch pants approaches.

"Is that really the world's largest rhinestone?" she asks, pointing to a large, goddamn rhinestone with a plaque that says "World's Largest Rhinestone."

"Why yes it is. Liberace acquired the rhinestone from…"

And so fuzzy-haired man joins stretch-pants woman in an enthusiastic rhinestone discussion. I'm left alone and French.

"Allo! Allo!" I cry, feebly waving my hand.

I get indignant, mumbling some curses in fake French, wondering why does the curator devote all his attention to an ordinary woman in stretch-pants when he could be spending his time with a very famous French accordionist, as I'm left alone to marvel at Liberace's many ornate cars and pianos.

"He sure had a lot of cars," I find myself whispering aloud.

> *One of the many perks of making it in show business is the fantastic people you meet. Legendary performers, royalty, statesmen, religious leaders.*
>
> – Liberace

A wall displays photos of Liberace with very famous people; from Popes to Telly Savalas. There's Liberace with the King of

Sweden and Liberace with Elvis *(the King of Rock and Roll),* along with pictures of Liberace hugging poodles and koala bears *(which makes me go "Aaaaah!"),* not to mention a great deal of photos of Liberace with handsome menservants and boy jockeys *(to a slightly lesser degree, this also makes me go "Aaaah!").*

Above an award from the Boy Scouts of America a video monitor shows Liberace in a huge bubble bath, smiling *(is there a connection?!).* The fuzz-haired man peeks around the corner. Much to his chagrin we make direct eye-contact. I take the opportunity to ask him where the restroom is, first describing it by using mime.

"It's to the right of the pink Rolls Royce," he directs.

"Merci!" I reply, then ask, "Ez et a bathroom once used by the fa-moose Liberace?"

"No!"

I leave in a huff.

Before venturing to the next Liberace building, behind a dumpster I ditch my makeshift gown and hat. Maybe this will help Liberace employees open up to me like a wayward son. I also decide to change my persona to Numan Sherman III – music student interested in the Liberace College Accordion Scholarship *(if one exists).* Perhaps then I'll be able to discover the truth behind the following questions:

Q: Did Liberace, or "Mr. Showman," fake his death so he could get out of showbiz and pursue his dream of being an ultimate fighter?

Q: Did Liberace give 1/3 of his income to the Big Brothers of America program?

Q: Did Liberace secretly meet Lee Harvey Oswald in Dallas and give him a foot massage?

Strangely, all the museum workers become very tight-lipped upon any insinuation that the gayest man *in the history of gay* was actually gay. Maybe I can get them to go into detail about this in a roundabout way. Approaching museum-worker Pauline, who is very knowledgeable about everything from when

Liberace first started playing the piano *(at the age of four)* to what his real first name is *(Walter)*, I explain to her why I want the scholarship.

"I want to be just like Liberace in every capacity," I say in a breathy voice, then wink. "If you know what I mean."

"Oh, that's just wonderful!" she beams.

I pause for a moment. "Was there a Mrs. Liberace?"

Pauline immediately turns a bit nervous. "No, but he was engaged three times."

She directs me to a picture of Liberace circa 1955, standing next to a woman.

"Wasn't he engaged to Bea Arthur at one time?"

"No!"

"Oh! So he was a *life-long bachelor*," I say with a wink.

"He was dedicated to his work."

"Was he very close to his mother?" I inquire.

"Extremely."

Pauline quickly changes the subject, *(the topic is Liberace's elaborate rings)*, while I jump in with, "Wasn't Liberace a guest villain on *Batman?*"

"Yes, in the "Devil's Fingers" episode," she clarifies.

"Didn't he try to make the Dynamic Duo into sheet music?"

"That's correct."

I pose a theory. "Wasn't his appearance on *Batman* marred by Adam West's huge on-set jealousy of Liberace?"

"I'm not sure," she replies, mildly puzzled.

"Wasn't his character, *Chandell* also a life-long bachelor?"

Pauline ignores my comment.

A group discussion breaks out between Pauline, myself, and the few patrons in the building; the kind of group discussion that could only happen at the Liberace Museum! We gather around a pair of gold-cast Liberace hands.

"He was the most charismatic performer I've ever seen." Interjects a very old woman.

"And so handsome," adds a second, not-quite-as-old woman.

“My only regret is I never got a chance to see Liberace and Judy Garland perform live,” confesses a soft-spoken old man in a lavender sweater.

“I heard he went to college on a wrestling scholarship,” is my contribution to the conversation.

The momentum of the discussion comes to a halt, as I get a firm “No!” from two members of our Liberace discussion group *(lavender sweater man racks his brain trying to recall this fact).*

> *I'm the first to admit my stage costumes have become an expensive joke. But I have fun with them and so do my fans.*
>
> – Liberace

Liberace wouldn't be Liberace without his costumes. Pauline told me that the first costume he wore was a white tuxedo with tails, which at the time was very “flamboyant.” After the show a reporter asked, “Liberace, what will you wear next?”

Looking at his sister's gold-lame gown, he proclaimed, “A gold-lame tuxedo.” The rest is Liberace history.

The last building in the Liberace complex is dedicated to Liberace's famous sequined, bejeweled and rhinestone studded costumes.

I use the opportunity to ask bubbly lady at the door questions I've never asked anyone else on the whole entire planet before.

“What was Liberace's shoe size?”

“Size 12,” she answers in a perky fashion.

“What did Liberace do on his days off?”

“He'd dress casual. Sometimes he'd even wear jeans. But on stage it was a different story,” she says gesturing at the costumes with her arms. Then she adds in a soft, serious tone, “He never needed to use laser lights on stage!”

Minutes later, I find myself in front of Liberace's bicentennial suit. This involves a glittery red, white, and blue hot pants with knee-high red boots and a cape. As I study the hot pants suit with grave seriousness a woman next to me decides she wants to share:

"I remember seeing Liberace perform in 1958. He actually winked at me on stage."

I have something to share: "Did you know Liberace had a fierce rivalry with Wayne Newton?"

She let's the comment soak in.

"Well, I don't blame him. I never did like Wayne Newton."

We return to staring at the hot pants outfit in silence.

I stop in the Liberace Gift Shop before leaving. It's a bit disappointing; mostly postcards and ceramic pianos. I was expecting Liberace Casserole Pot Holders and life-sized Liberace dolls-complete with changeable outfits. One great find is the *Cooking with Liberace* cookbook. Figuring this is the last chance to find out the full scoop on Liberace, I tell the two Gift Shop ladies I'm a writer for *Piano World* magazine in order to get some answers.

"How come the museum doesn't have any photos of the great loves of Liberace's life?" I inquire. *"Piano World* magazine wants to know!"

"Why would we do that?" snaps the older of the two Gift Shop ladies.

"I figure his love life would be an important part of his life,' I reason. A fog of tension rolls in. I elaborate. "Wasn't he engaged to Charo before he died?"

"No!"

The two Gift Shop ladies now avoid my glance. An unnecessary task of polishing little miniature pianos commences.

"So there wasn't a Mrs. Liberace?" I press on. *"Piano World* magazine wants to know!"

Judging by their reaction, I believe I've shown disrespect in the sacred shrine. The younger of the two elderly Gift Shop Ladies speaks very frank and clear.

"Liberace was engaged *THREE* times to *THREE* different women! You can find their pictures next door!"

With that she puts an end to the discussion. It seems that the only people in the world who don't know Liberace was gay are the people who work in his own damn museum.

I complete my quest by going next door to the Liberace Restaurant and Bar, where I'll treat myself to a Brandy Alexander in Liberace's honor.

The establishment turns out to be incredible; the bar is shaped like a giant white grand piano. The bartender – a pure product of Las Vegas – takes my order as I relive my highlights of the museum, as he responds with a loud, distinct laugh.

"Liberace opened the restaurant because he enjoyed cooking," he explains.

I tilt my head and picture "Li" in the kitchen, flipping chicken steaks.

"And right there is where Frank Sinatra and the Rat Pack used to sit."

The bartender, seeming like he has juicy stories to share, lowers his voice.

"Liberace used to have his own furnished studio apartment in the back of the restaurant."

"In the back of the restaurant?!" I question.

"Yeah, it was so elaborately decorated that it appeared in *Better Homes and Gardens.*"

This sounds a bit creepy.

"Why did he have a studio apartment in the back of his restaurant?"

"If he was too tired to go home, he could just sleep here in back of the restaurant."

"How far away did Liberace live?"

"About two blocks."

(Pause.) "Oh!"

Apparently Liberace had a big problem getting a limousine or taxi for that long two-block journey. I imagine the most hedonistic acts known to humanity taking place in the studio apartment, involving everything from Siegfried and Roy's white tigers to Frank Sinatra eating scrambled eggs off of underage hookers' stomachs – all overseen by Liberace in his bicentennial hot pants outfit.

The bartender, though, seems cool. Maybe he'll give me the full details and open up about some Liberace gossip.

"How come everyone at the museum clams up when you mention Liberace's love life?"

I was wrong.

"I don't know," he abruptly says. He immediately starts stacking glasses and goes into the next room. I'm left alone with my Brandy Alexander. The mystery of Liberace remains unanswered to this day!

If You Must Go

Liberace Plaza
1775 East Tropicana Avenue (at Spencer)
Las Vegas, NV 89119-6529
(702) 798-5595

LIBERACE MUSEUM

The Hoover Dam Has Sold Out!

The Hoover Dam is a pimp-slapped whore. There's no point in seeing this water-holding-back piece-of-shit.

Why such a hostile reaction to one of America's most beloved road trip destinations?

It's not that I always hated the Hoover Dam. Why in fact, I use to be one of the most animated supporters of the Hoover Dam. In high school I was president of our school's "Hoover Dam Appreciation Society," a collective group of ragtag misfits who gathered weekly to discuss, share facts, photos and thoughts about the Hoover Dam. The club consisted of myself, Mingko-the exchange student, and the shy girl with glasses who always got hit in the face during dodgeball.

But all that changed on my first glimpse ever of my fabled Holy Grail.

I've spilt Mountain Dew on my lap. But it doesn't matter, I'm mere minutes away from my beloved Hoover Dam, cruising past Boulder City, anticipating my first glimpse, ever, of the famous dam I've only seen in photographs. There's a song by Sugar about the Hoover Dam. I think some of the lyrics go like this: "Standing on the edge of the Hoover Dam…" I forget the rest, but still it's a dam-reference. If I had that CD, I surely would be listening to it at this current moment.

One thing I've learned from my road trip experience is American's are really fat. I'm not kidding. Outside of most major cities, you'll find roly-poly, unexercised fat-asses. These thoughts are confirmed as I make final turn through the canyon and encounter Hoover Dam.

- "That's the Hoover Dam all right. Yes sir-ee!"
- "Hoover Dam, yes indeed, there it is. God damn it, yes! The Hoover-God-Damn-Dam!"
- "I'm in Hoover Dam-heaven! Now that I've seen the Hoover Dam I can kill myself because the rest of my life will be entirely anti-climatic!"
- "The bees! The bees! Get the bees off me!" *(To be said only if you have a great fear of bees and you feel that bees are surrounding you.)*

All these hours of driving have amounted to this. And my initial reaction is, the Hoover Dam... sucks donkey dicks! It's swamped by and infested with tourists. Hoover Dam has clearly sold out! What the fuck is this shit. Is this some sort of joke?! This was supposed to be *my* Hoover Dam, now it's caked with busloads of tourists, and tacky gift shops selling Hoover Damwiches. How did this happen? When did the word get out about Hoover Dam. The Hoover Dam is a pimp-slapped whore.

With a bad taste in my mouth about dams in general and presidents of the 1930's who were responsible for building them, I immediately get the hell out of Hoover Dam-ville! To think, I used to be a fan of this nonsense.

If You Must Go

Hoover Dam is located approximately 30 miles southeast of Las Vegas, on the Nevada-Arizona border.
Information: (702) 494-2517
Tours: (866) 730-9097
www.usbr.gov/lc/hooverdam/

Cruising down Interstate 15 at a ridiculously high speed, I pull in to Baker, California, just outside the state line. Where there once was a vacant lot in my heart suddenly sprouted flowers. I see it: The World's Tallest Thermometer. And it's beautiful; gracefully stabbing up to the heavens with a large illuminated reading of 97 at the top, reflecting today's temp.

The World's Tallest Thermometer, standing at 134 feet, was built to that height to commemorate the hottest temperature ever recorded in Death Valley *(in 1913)* and, at that time the hottest on Earth – a record beaten only once and by two degrees in Libya.

Why have I only now discovered this rare pearl of a tourist attraction? All my animosity about the Hoover Dam has transposed into warm allegiance for the World's Largest Thermometer. What an unearthed national treasure, which one could only encounter on a massive road trip into the heart of this great land of ours.

If You Must Go

World's Tallest Thermometer
72155 Baker Blvd
Baker, CA
(760) 733-4660

Diseased Underbelly Salute To...

Hidden Treasures Of Our Ancestors

Little do speeding motorists know, but there are rare treasures to be had at the Ute, Nevada Exit off of I-15 in between Vegas and the Arizona border. To the naked eye, it looks merely like an exit leading to absolutely nowhere, darting off into the desert horizon. A word to the wise; take some time to pull off the road and explore. With a broad smile on your face and a zippity-do-da song in your heart, you'll soon discover one man's discarded garbage is another man's rare treasure. Much like the dinosaur bones found at the La Brea Tar Pits, these artifacts give clues to past civilizations and their habits.

GARBAGE FOUND ON THE SIDE OF THE ROAD AT THE EXIT FOR UTE NEVADA

Beer Bottles
Beer Cans
A Wrapper From A Package Of Bacon
A Dead Baby Corpse In A Plastic Bag (not really)
Sweatpants
One Shoe
A Jack In The Box Cup
A Pair Of Very Large Underwear
An Adult Corpse In A Plastic Bag *(not really)*
A Kentucky Fried Chicken Tray
A Wooden Board
Grandma *(still not really)*
A Dented Soup Can

And last, but not least, the biggest treasure-find-of-them-all: *(drum roll please...)* a box containing a Mermaid Masturbator Pocket Pussy!!!!!

According to the side of the packaging it's "The Best Little Pussy on the High Seas." Yes indeed, a pocket pal; a portable pussy that feels like the real thing, right here by the side of the road at the Ute, Nevada exit.

POSSIBLE CASE SCENARIOS HOW THE POCKET PUSSY GOT TO THE UTE EXIT:

1. After purchasing one Mermaid Masturbator Pocket Pussy, Leo, a disgruntled trucker, flung the product from his window when he became shocked to discover that it didn't feel like the real thing.

2. Unbeknownst to his vacationing Mormon family from Utah, a teen named Quentin purchased the Mermaid Masturbator Pocket Pussy while passing through Vegas. The item was quickly flung from the speeding car window when the acquisition was discovered by his angry, disgruntled father (named Alex).

3. Dieter, a visiting German scientist, was late to give an anatomy lecture at a local University. He purchased said item to use as a visual aid, then became disgruntled and tossed the Mermaid Masturbator Pocket Pussy from his window when he realized his misplaced real, dissected pussy was under the passenger seat, thus he no longer needing the substituted item.

4. A near-sighted grandma (whose loved ones refer to her as "Granny") misread the package and thought she was actually buying a feminine hygiene product. She became furious, not to mention disgruntled, when she discovered her purchase was actually Mermaid Masturbator Pocket Pussy. Tossing-product-from-car-window soon followed.

5. Pascal, a Jeffery Dahmer copycat cannibal killer, was having an unlucky day. Somehow he thought a Mermaid Masturbator Pocket Pussy would do as a placebo for the time being in place of the real thing. No go. Its present locale was the result of disgruntled-ness on his part.

Quick Tip...

Road Trip Budget Lodging

1. HAVE BIBLES SENT TO NOISY ROOMS

If you are staying at budget lodging where the motel walls are very thin and the couple next door is doing the nasty a tad bit too loud, call the front desk (via your cell phone) and say someone stole the Gideon bible from your motel room, and you need a new one sent up immediately. Give the room number of the loud love-makers. Then, sit back in your lonely, lonely motel room and have a good laugh. Treat yourself to a hot fudge sundae (if hot fudge sundaes are available).

CONGRATULATIONS!
YOU HAD A BIBLE SENT TO A NOISY ROOM!

2. CHECK UNDER THE BED

If your motel costs less than $20 per night, it's a good idea to check under the bed before going to sleep. At these prices, you want to make sure the establishment isn't renting out that spot to very quiet Swedish backpackers, claiming that your room is a "Youth Hostel."

CONGRATULATIONS!
YOU CHECKED UNDER YOUR BED!

3. DINING IN YOUR ROOM

Turn your iron into a hot plate by placing it with the handle down on top of an empty tissue box. Make delicious motel room omelets, bacon or flapjacks. Hang your sheet across the light fixtures, and pretend you're no longer in a crappy motel room, but instead, in the middle of the wilderness camping. For dessert, combine the complimentary decaf and regular coffee filters offered for a stronger brew.

CONGRATULATIONS!
YOU DINED SUCCESSFULLY IN YOUR ROOM!

HILDALE, UTAH & COLORADO CITY, ARIZONA

Those Wacky Mormon Fundamentalists

LOCAL MOTTO "Good neighbors."

MY MOTTO FOR THE TOWN "We Practice Pedophilia under the Banner of Religion!"

MEDIUM RESIDENT AGE 13.1 years

PERCENTAGE OF RESIDENTS WITH BACHELOR DEGREES OR HIGHER 8.8%.

FUN FACT The houses in Hildale have more rooms than any other city in Utah. Volunteers from the community were assigned by church leaders to make sure the town's inhabitants were in bed after dark. *(?)*

EXTREMELY USELESS INFORMATION The town's population grew by 43% through the '90's. There have been two major raids on the Hildale/ Colorado City: one in 1941 and the other in 1953. One of the most popular courses offered at the local community college is a GED.

WAY TO GET YOUR ASS-KICKED Say to someone who lives in town, "What you're doing here is wrong and should be highly illegal!"

CULTURAL HIGHLIGHT Avoiding all forms of contact with the outside world, such as modern music, TV and the Internet!

HILDALE/COLORADO CITY IS AN IDYLLIC LOCALE FOR Those who like bachelor parties and wedding gifts.

LEVEL OF CREEPINESS Does this scale go to 11?

What would be a rumpus ride into the aorta of the diseased underbelly of America without a stop off at the largest Mormon polygamy community in the country? Taking Highway 59 past St. George, Utah, towards the north rim of the Grand Canyon, there stands my Shangri-La, Hildale/Colorado City (the Minneapolis/St. Paul of multiple-wives-hamlets).

Set in the red-bluffed mountains on the Arizona border and isolated by a good 44 miles from the next sign of civilization, this haven is the home base of the Fundamentalist Church of Jesus Christ of Latter Day Saints (FLDS). For these residents having at least 3 wives is their straight ticket to heaven. *(Sorry ladies, that's wives not husbands.)*

A FEW WORDS TO DESCRIBE HILDALE/COLORADO CITY:

Creepy!

Spooky!

Eerie!

Here's a little unsavory snapshot. The community has a combined population of roughly 8,000, while the average female age is 14 years old. Mix that with the male population over 50, and you got a pedophile's paradise held together under the banner of religious freedom.

Located relatively near Lee's Pass (named after a Mormon Fundamentalist who instigated the slaughter of hundreds of people migrating West in the 1800s), the big-cheese in these parts is Warren Jeffs – the head of FLDS. Formerly honored with being one of FBI's 10 Most Wanted, Jeffs currently resides in the Purgatory Correctional Facility in Hurricane, Utah. Besides arranging marriages of underage girls *(such as a 14-year-old girl with her own cousin)*, Jeffs has an estimated 90 wives *(how the hell do you keep track?!)*. Man, this Casanova must get laid all the time!

Not sold on the place yet? How 'bout this: FLDS elders, such as Warren Jeffs, are considered living prophets ("I'm a living prophet!") who have God's direct cell phone number. They claim to chitchat with The Almighty, conferring over important decisions. One such example is the "Law of Placing." These so-called "prophets" pull girls as young as 13 out of school and assign them to become, say, some 57-year-old man's multiple-wife. The girls are affectionately referred to by the locals as "poofers" *(they're in school one minute, then "poof," an impregnated, polygamous wife the next).*

With both town officials and the police force FLDS members, this isolated locale is a perfect prison-like atmosphere for any women attempting to escape the polygamous, religious-swinger lifestyle. These "prophets" also have the authority to reassign wives to other men if they feel inclined *(local men remember, don't piss off the living prophets!).*

Needless to say, the religious-sect-citizens of the community hate outsiders – especially journalists. That's why I consider it a hell of a great vacation spot!

FUN FACT

The FLDS elders keep the kids sheltered from such evil "influences" from the outside world such as TV, music, Internet, or anything that would make a 13-year-old child bride realize, "What the fuck am I doing married to a 57-year-old man?" Think of it just like the movie *Footloose,* but only much, much creepier *(and without Kevin Bacon).*

What a glorious shit-hole it is! Tourist attraction-wise, there's not a whole hell of a lot to see. It would be great if a local bar had a wicked Ladies' Night. Instead the town has about 4 businesses: Food Town, a take-away pizza place, Radio Shack *(even people with numerous wives have electronic needs!),* and one restaurant, Mark Twain Restaurant *(because the author of* Huckleberry Finn *would have been tickled by this place),* which also doubles as a motel-with-no-sign-of-usage. California might have Disneyland, but Colorado City has "Babyland," as residents call it. "Babyland" is the local cemetery *(a must see!)* out by the canyon on the outskirts of town, named such due to all the unmarked baby graves.

If You Must Go

Foodtown
30 N Central St.
Colorado City, AZ
(928) 875-2287

Mark Twain Restaurant
1185 W Utah Ave.
Hildale, UT
(435) 874-1030

DID YOU KNOW?

It gets better. Did you know the Colorado City/Hildale area has the world's highest incidence of fumarase deficiency – an extremely rare genetic condition that causes severe mental retardation? Who would have thunk the prevalence of cousin-marriage-inbreeding would attribute to something like that?! Boing!

Amped up on energy drinks – to the point of crack-addict paranoia – I begin to get the feeling that every car behind me is following me *(Is word out that an intruder has entered the city limits?!)*, as I drive through the empty neighborhood streets, comprised of shitty, grey-colored, shabbily-erected houses that still appear under construction due to the numerous additions tacked on *(to facilitate each new wife)*. The dramatic red rock landscape adds an eerie, threatening effect, like we're in Hell-on-Earth and this town is angry with the world. To compensate, I make sure to give a friendly wave to all cars as they pass *(they don't wave back)*.

FUN FACT:

Don't expect the businesses to close on Martin Luther King Day. The cultural diversity of this ruckus place is white, and very white. Maybe it has something to do with such Warren-Jeffs-preaching-nuggets as, "It was necessary that the Devil should have a representation upon the Earth as well as God." And the representative Jeffs refers to: "The Negro." All I can say to him is, "Watchoo-talkin-bout-Willis?!"

This entire community seems to be deserted *(or hiding)*, except for a couple of small boys dressed like elderly grown men from *Little House on the Prairie.* Operating farm equipment, they perform the work of adults, while silhouetted against the setting Mormon sun. Breaking child labor laws must be the least of worries for the youth of Colorado City. Known as the Lost Boys, when FLDS elders feel a competitive-threat for the limited amount of child brides, they'll drive teenaged boys out of town and dump them on the side of the road like a discarded Mermaid Pocket Pussy box at a Ute, Nevada exit.

With nowhere else to go, they often end up becoming male prostitutes in Vegas. So these children toiling in the fields until dusk need to be very thankful for the work; but should also remember to keep their eyes off girls their own age!

DID YOU KNOW?

Did you know when preaching the evils of some contemporary music, Warren Jeffs referred to The Beatles as "pingy-pangy," and provides local residents with a healthy alternative: original music he sings and records!

Ok, I've been to a lot of creepy places, but this has got to be one of the creepiest – EVER! The creepiness is more along the lines of the movie *The Wicker Man (not the crap remake with Nicholas Cage, but the original British version),* where suddenly I'll find myself surrounded by the entire town, as a secret ritual commences to make a sacrifice to Joseph Smith on a blazing bonfire.

I pull up to an intersection in the center of town and things get really eerie. A large white passenger van drives by me filled with a group of identically dressed women; all wearing 19th-century schoolmarm outfits and hair bonnets. This van contains one husband's several wives – it's his tribe! These are the real-life Stepford Wives, groomed and trained exactly to the men-folks' specification. Almost like it's happening in slow-motion, one of the wives – she appears about 16 – looks directly out the van window staring at me like she's just seen a chimpanzee wearing a top hat riding a jetpack. Her face has an expression of both fear and astonishment as the van window makes her look likes a goldfish gaping out of an aquarium beyond her one-corral-castle world. Her eyes widen three times the size they should be in reality, with a combination of awe and *please help me!* I give another friendly, un-responded to, wave.

LETS GO TO FOOD TOWN!

Here's a funny local joke I concocted for the FLDS elders to tell: "Take my wife... please! *(Pause.)* Because I have several, because I'm a Mormon fundamentalist. *(Pause.)* And chances are my most recent wife was raped on her wedding night, when I pulled her out of seventh grade without her consent in order to be my newest bride!"

Ba-dum-dum.

Ah, yes, Mormon fundamentalist humor!

Though the rest of Colorado City seems like a sinister ghost town, Food Town is bustling on Saturday night. The grocery store parking lot is packed almost entirely with white vans. *(If you're going to have numerous wives, you got to invest in a good van!)*

Alas, it's time to meet the Warren-Jeffs-following-polygamy citizens face-to-face. After changing into my standard small town redneck outfit *(so not to draw attention)*, hesitantly I enter Food Town. Nearly turning back, my jaw drops to the grocery store floor; the entire place is filled with all women, dozens of them, slightly on the large size and identically dressed just like those twins in *The Shining*. One rebel wife wears a conventional sweatshirt over her schoolmarm dress – the town equivalent of having a tattooed face.

In groups of roughly five *(are they sisters or wives?)* they shop for their own personal David Koresh, adorned with the same hairdo; braided in back and flipped up like a Jack in the Box *(so ornate you could easily see accessorizing with a small bridge, or Swiss Chalet)*. Each 'do looks as if a painstaking amount of time was needed to prepare. That's one advantages of having several other wives on the team... more detail to hair-preparation.

I don't exactly get a warm reception. I feel like I'm in the middle of the Village of the Damned, and they have the power to read minds. Everyone stares at my every move *(then quickly looks away).* "This is a local shop for local people. You're not wanted here," I expect them all to say in unison, while also trumpeted over the store's intercom system. No matter how low key I try to appear, the entire store watches me like I were Hester Prynne with a huge Scarlet A. A man with a buck knife on his belt, wearing jeans and long sleeve shirts, enters the store amongst the dozens of identically dressed Shining twins. He looks like the type who'd slit your throat while quoting Bible verses, giving me a confrontational look that says, "Are you staring at one of my wives?!"

I'm just going to act natural. You know, like I'm just one of them who has come to Food Town to buy some apples. Yup, just a typical polygamous husband buying apples on a Saturday night. Or maybe I'm a new farmhand whose facial expression says there's nothing weird about being in a store filled with a tribe of identically dressed wives. One apple! Two apples! Three apples! In my attempt to look natural, I actually look so tense it could be misconstrued as great pain.

Quickly moving to the next aisle, acting enthralled with the soup selection, I pass a sign saying all toys are $1.00, noting the mixed message these devices of child-amusement send; from an old school Tic Tac Toe game, to toy farm trucks, and something called The Farming Game. *(Yes, toys to take the kids' minds off of mandatory farming.)*

"Hey look!" I exclaim with delight. The identical dress that the entire woman population of this town wears is on sale, here, at Food Town! So that's where they buy it. How surprising. These modest, ankle-length gowns are stationed right by the cash register as an impulse buy.

All the energy drinks I had earlier have scrambled my brain. "Aaaah!" I cry under my breath, as a small little girl freaks the hell out of me. Dressed and groomed just like the adult women, she pushes around a tiny child-sized shopping cart *(is this to prepare them for early marriage duties?).* I'm sure one of the town's elders already has his eye on her, licking his lips when in a few short years Warren Jeffs can arrange to make her his bride.

I ditch my apples in lieu of another purchase. Waiting in the checkout line with the Children of the Corn, I stand behind a child-bride purchasing four jars of seafood cocktail sauce. You have to buy in bulk if you're one of 90 wives. Obviously you'll run out of seafood cocktail sauce mid-meal leaving some wives cocktail sauce-less.

Maneuvering to the front of the line, it's my turn with the two large women cashiers *(dressed exactly like the others).* Their nametags read "Fawn" *("Let's do Fawn's hair."),* and the other, for some reason, "Giggles and Laughs."

From my shopping cart, I start setting by the register several boxes of feminine hygiene products. "My household goes through soooo many boxes of these," I tell the ladies, hoping they bond with me like a local.

Neither Fawn nor Giggles and Laughs find my jest funny, giving me, instead, a look that could curdle milk. Abruptly leaving without getting my change, I depart Food Town with my five boxes of tampons. Walking hurriedly to my rental car, I expect now is when it will happen; the one man with the buck knife will approach me and say "I think it would be best if you leave town... NOW!" I'll then be driven away by FLDS elders and dumped off on the side of the road like the Lost Boys. Or worse, I'll be stabbed in the parking lot because one of the living prophets just spoke to God and that's what he said was the right thing to do in order to go to heaven.

As I swiftly point my rented PT Cruiser towards the city limits, three of the town's police cars *(most likely the only three police cars)* have pulled over a car on the desolate main street of Colorado City. The red cherry-tops swirl against the pitch-blackness of the isolated, mountain terrain. Drug-sniffing dogs surround the vehicle, as the officers do an extensive search. I'm sure the local police *(Mormon fundamentalist with a past member of the force arrested for marrying a 16-year-old),* surely loves outsiders. If I were pulled over, the dog-sniffing treatment would be the least of my worries to ensure I never come back to Creepy Town. Quickly, I cover up a reference book in the back seat called *The Worst Towns in the USA,* which happens to be flipped opened to the Colorado City page.

As I tiptoe my car past the interrogation, perhaps the severe treatment I'm witnessing is due to some soon-to-be polygamist bride trying to escape town before her so-called wedding night?

If You Must Go

Don't.

FLAGSTAFF, ARIZONA

All The Atmosphere of Wal-Mart In One City

Living in a remote trailer in Arizona is a lot different than living in a trailer in the South. It seems that here it's sometimes less out of poverty, and more like "F.U. Government! I'm going to get rid of my Social Security card and live in a trailer. If you come on my land, I will shoot you!"

After driving past the Grand Canyon *(man, that's a big mother of a hole!)*, through hundreds of miles of Navajo Indian reservation land, only to encounter a town as culturally exciting as Wal-Mart – Flagstaff, Arizona. Though surrounded by the utter natural beauty, Flagstaff has all the charm of a shiny suburban strip mall in Ohio. The town is comprised almost entirely of box stores, chain restaurants, and populated with well-scrubbed white college kids.

But I have no time to ponder that; I'm hungry. Since it's Arizona one would think they could get good Mexican food: and if not good Mexican food at least mediocre Mexican food. When I ask the desk clerk at the Ramada *(right across from the mall)*, she directs me to Chili's. Yes, why have authentic Mexican food, when you can get Mexican food prepared exactly like they do at every single damn Chili's around the country? *(They've learned how to get it right every time.)*

What I love about Chili's is how they train their staff to treat customers like complete morons.

"I'm Ryan and I'll be taking care of you tonight," exclaims my way-too-perky waiter, *(who goes by the name Ryan),* using the same patronizing tone one would if they were about to change your diaper.

"Are *we* ready for another margarita?" Ryan asks me every three damn seconds, from under the bright last-call-drink-them-up lighting they use to create ambiance.

"Can you please not talk to me like I'm a fucking moron," I reply, a bit ornery from my long day of driving. "Okay, Ryan?!"

Later, Ryan sneaks up behind me, practically scaring the fuck out of me – asking about my tortilla soup.

"Are *we* enjoying it?" Ryan says, pluralizing the experience to somehow include himself in the eating process of my food.

"Not too much; we think it's disgusting!"

If You Must Go

Chili's
1500 S. Milton Rd.
Flagstaff, AZ 86001
(928) 774-4546

Diseased Underbelly Road Trip Salute To...

Cities With Funny Names!

1. Intercourse, PA

It has a funny name. Imagine driving and seeing "Next Exit Intercourse." Then imagine laughing. Some of the businesses they have in Intercourse are *(remember no laughing)*, Intercourse Pretzel Factory, Best Western Intercourse Village Motor Inn Restaurant, Intercourse Canning Company, and of course, the Intercourse Swingers Club *(I lied about the last one)*.

2. Happy, TX

The irony here; this is a miserable cesspool of a town.

3. Sweet Lips, TN

This is named such because if you're camping and you run across some of the locals in the woods, this is how they're going to refer to you just before the sodomizing begins.

4. Sandwich, MA

I was kidding about Intercourse, this must be the hometown of America's largest swinger-community.

LAKE HAVASU CITY, ARIZONA

Have A Beer, Have A Screw, Lake Havasu!

POPULATION 41,938

WHAT IS LAKE HAVASU LIKE? Lake Havasu is the kind of place where community college girls go on spring break to try and lose their anal cherry.

EXTREMELY USELESS INFORMATION Located on the white trash Riviera of Arizona, the hottest bar in town has a sign on the wall that says, "Have a Brew. Have a screw. Havasu!"

LOCAL CLAIM TO FAME The transplanted London Bridge.

LAKE HAVASU FUN FACT Property developer Robert P. McCulloch purchased the London Bridge and brought it to Lake Havasu stone by stone. When it opened in 1971, people actually thought they were getting the picturesque Tower Bridge, which has cool hydraulic drawbridge in the middle. Instead they got a grey lump of unremarkable bridge. It's like thinking you're going to see the Golden Gate Bridge and it turns out to be the Dumbarton Bridge.

WAYS TO GET YOUR ASS-KICKED Say to a local, "You can go shove your goddamn London Bridge up your goddamn London-Bridge-loving-ass!"

AN IDYLLIC LOCALE FOR Pouting, disaffected, bored youths in black who stand on street corners, in front of the Acoma Stop & Shop (35 Acoma Blvd.) with that cute look in their eye that says *in mere years we'll have our very own meth lab.*

LAKE HAVASU CULTURAL HIGHLIGHT The bridge, the bridge, the goddamn London Bridge!

THINGS TO SAY WHEN SEEING THE LONDON BRIDGE

- "That's the London Bridge all right. Yes sir-ee!"
- "It's the goddamn London Bridge! *(Pause)* Goddman it!"
- "London Bridge, yes indeed, there it is. Goddamn it, yes!"
- "I'm in London Bridge-heaven! Now that I've seen the London Bridge I can kill myself because the rest of my life will be entirely anti-climatic!"
- "The bees! The bees! Get the bees off me!" *(To be said only if you have a great fear of bees and you feel that bees are surrounding you.)*

If You Must Go

Lake Havasu City Convention & Visitors Bureau
314 London Bridge Road
Lake Havasu City, AZ 86403
(928) 453-3444

LAUGHLIN, NEVADA

For The Old... And The Old At Heart

POPULATION 8,629

TOWN MOTTO "Laughlin – Founded on Fun!"

***MY* TOWN MOTTO** "Laughlin – Speak Up, I Can't Hear You!"

FUN FACT Laughlin is in the Top 5 destinations for American RV enthusiasts. Hurrah!

WEIRD LOCAL SMELLS Mothballs.

EXTREMELY USELESS INFORMATION New Year's Eve revelers are known to ring in the new year in Bullhead City (Mountain Time Zone), and then cross the river into Laughlin (Pacific Time Zone) to ring it in again one hour later.

LAUGHLIN CULTURAL HIGHLIGHT In 2002, Laughlin was the scene of the River Run Riot, a major fight between two rival California motorcycle gangs, the Hells Angels and the Mongols, which resulted in three deaths, plus multiple gunshot and knife injuries! Someone should have told these "tough guys" that Laughlin was "Founded on Fun!"

LAUGHLIN IS AN IDYLLIC LOCALE FOR The old.

What is the deal with Laughlin, Nevada?! It's like Vegas *after* the Apocalypse. The place has the feel of a weird sci-fi movie where a meteor crashes nearby and for some reason kills off all the young people. Or like the movie *Logan's Run,* except in reverse. Everyone here in Laughlin is old! Old! Old! Old! The average age seems to be 100, with fashion styles from rural 1950's. *(Maybe Laughlin is picking up stragglers from Lake Havusu?)*

Ninety miles south of Las Vegas, and a good fifty years behind, Laughlin is a gambling town in the southern most tip of Nevada, set on the Colorado River in the rugged Mojave Desert. Though the more "glamorous and sophisticated" Las Vegas gets all the attention as the destination for decadent bachelor parties, the AVN Awards, and Paris Hilton sex videos, don't underestimate Laughlin; it trumpets such annual events as the Team Roping Finals.

If You Must Go

Team Roping Finals
Laughlin Events Park
Laughlin, NV 89029
(505) 899-1870

Hundreds of cowboys and cowgirls attempt to beat the clock in Laughlin at this annual, five-day November event.

Walking through any given casino, one can be guaranteed to encounter an oldie hooked up to an oxygen machine, still pulling slots. *(What's really the point? The excitement of winning would probably kill them.)* One old guy, with thick-lens stamp collector glasses, examines the operating procedure before taking an optimistic pull of a 5-cent slot featuring "Dick Clark's New Year's Rockin' Eve" *(with an artist's rendering of pre-stroke Dick Clark).*

Even the slot machines are old, as if brought over from Vegas for retirement. The elderly security guards are almost in need of a walker or Rascal, in order to patrol the casino floor.

Whatever gets old in Vegas comes here to Laughlin; it's the end of the casino road, last call, the final spin of the wheel. The old neon cowboy with the moveable, waving arm from Freemont

Street in downtown Vegas, has now relocated to Laughlin *(renamed from Cowboy Bob to River Rick).* He seems to be moving a little slower than in his Vegas glory days; like somehow he too had a stroke. Hotels, like the old Frontier scheduled to be demolished, should be moved and rebuilt here like the London Bridge—surely they would be beloved.

For those who like to shop till they drop *(and no, that's not shopping without the assistance of their wheelchairs)* The Las Vegas Strip has the Fashion Show Mall, with such designer shops as Dillard's, Macy's, and Neiman Marcus, but Laughlin's Horizon Outlet Mall *(on the nearly-deserted Laughlin Strip)* caters to their cliental by boasting such stores as Van Heusen, Casual Male XL, and the Family Dollar Store.

If You Must Go

Horizon Outlet Center
1955 S. Casino Drive
Laughlin, NV 89029-1505

Aquarius Casino Hotel is the local equivalent of the Palms in Vegas. For $29 a night you can stay at the largest casino in town *(the only problem is the last people to sleep in the room, in your bed, are THESE people.)* So not only is Laughlin for old people, but it's for poor old people. Cruising the casino is like a glimpse into your future *(if, in the future, you turn out old and poor).*

The way people look at me, I feel like Sid Vicious circa 1977. So, in order to fit in with the elderly Laughlin patrons, I change into a cunning disguise, with my trousers pulled up to my nipples along with white buck shoes. For some reason I feel like a badass and have the uncanny desire to start a casino fistfight.

If You Must Go

Aquarius Hotel and Casino
1900 South Casino Drive
Laughlin, NV 89029
(800) 270-3574

After eating the $7.99 food at the Café Aquarius, which I saw advertised in the elevator *(the, Café Aquarius has a VIP line!)*, I take in some great Laughlin showbiz entertainment. The strangest acts known to humanity seem to been sent down from Vegas, like former Major League athletes on their last leg now playing baseball in the Mexican leagues; these are the horses being sent out to pasture. Mary Wilson of the Supremes is playing the Edgewater Casino for a mere $30 *(I think that also includes dinner, which I'm sure is cut up into very small pieces)*. There's also the comedy team of The Indian and the White Guy, the Riverboat Ramblers *(featuring two old guys who play banjos)*, and the Ozark Jubilee *(starring some guy in overalls and a straw hat crossing his eyes)*.

Good news! In Loser's Lounge, located in the Riverside Casino, Thursday is Ladies Wet T-shirt Contest Night. Looking at all the grey-hair grandmas, I think now I know why it's called Loser's Lounge.

Inside the sparse-decor of Splash Cabaret an elderly waitress, sporting hair like in Mormon creepy town, clad in a much-too-short skirt, cards me due to the age comparison to the other patrons *(who mostly sit at tables on their own)*. Normally a curly-haired guy with a guitar named Pat O'Brian performs *(whose show boasts "The Excitement Starts Here!")*.

Tonight, a senior citizen is belting out show tunes, such as "The Impossible Dream" from *Man of La Mancha*. She introduces her band, "We first played together in Vegas 20 years ago." Someone requests Barbara Streisand. We all sit alone at our individual tables and listen.

If You Must Go

Loser's Lounge
Don Laughlin's Riverside Resort & Casino Hotel
1650 Casino Dr.
Laughlin, NV 89029
(800) 227-3849

Late night in Laughlin it's very quiet *(everyone goes to bed early)*. In Vegas one can fulfill any vice they so desire. I wonder if the same is true in Laughlin. Time to find the seedy underbelly.

"Can you direct me to the best strip club in town?" I ask a cab driver, being he would be a man in the know.

He frowns: "You have to go over the river to Arizona for that cuz we don't have that here," he says, almost with disgust, making me feel creepy as I once again hear "The Impossible Dream" piped in from inside the casino.

My theory is all the Laughlin strippers have died off, thus the reason why I now have to go over the State Line to Arizona, making me believe that unlike Vegas, the only bachelor parties that come to Laughlin are most likely for widowers.

As they say, "What happens in Laughlin, stays in Laughlin... especially if you die and get buried there."

Quick Tip...

How To Know When You're Too Tired To Drive

Ok, maybe you've depleted your case of Red Bull and think you're still good to drive another 350-375 miles of road. Take precautions; look for the signs to determine that you might be too tired to carry on:

1. You begin to see medium-sized monkeys jumping on your car and they're wearing "funny" large sunglasses and people-clothes.

2. Mr. Haskins-your high school gym teacher-appears hitchhiking on the side of the road every few miles, diminishing in height with each new sighting. He is not wearing shoes.

3. You try to steer with your teeth and are successful!

4. "Hey, what would it be like if your car did a loop-d-loop like on the Duke's of Hazzard?" you ponder.

5. Character actor, and Academy Award-winner Morgan Freeman is sitting in your passenger seat. He is clipping his toenails with a screwdriver.

And lastly,

6. You see and/or want to do things you shouldn't or normally wouldn't do while driving, and attempt to do it due to your fatigued state.

CONGRATULATIONS!
YOU NOW KNOW WHEN YOU'RE TIRED TO BE DRIVING!

AUSTIN TEXAS

BECOMING A MAN IN AUSTIN

POPULATION 718,912

TOWN MOTTO Keep Austin Weird

***MY* TOWN MOTTO** Why does the Rest of Texas Completely Suck Donkey Dicks?

FUN FACT Jenna Bush, daughter of the most powerful man in the world, was cited for underage drinking at a nightclub here.

If You Must Go

Cheers Shot Bar, 416 E 6th St., Austin, TX 78701 (512) 499-0093

WEIRD LOCAL SMELL The smell of Matthew McConaughey smoking weed and playing the bongos while naked.

EXTREMELY USELESS INFORMATION The Real World: Austin was filmed in Austin!

NEARBY CULTURAL HIGHLIGHT A few hours from town is a place called Enchanted Rock, a huge, pink granite exfoliation dome that rises 425 feet above ground.

The Tonkawa Indians believed ghost fires flickered at the top, and they heard weird creaking and groaning. As a popular destination for Austin-ites to go and take mushrooms: those that do claim to hear the same thing (or so I'm told).

AN IDEAL LOCALE FOR Those who like keeping things "weird," or weird-keepers, drag kings, drunk Bush daughters.

DO THOUSANDS OF BATS FLY OUT FROM UNDER THE CONGRESS STREET BRIDGE AT DUSK DURING BAT-SEASON? Yes.

There comes that time on a road trip when a guy just needs to get in touch with his inner-woman-who-likes-to-dress-as-a-man. Taking a stop off from the road in order to pull off one of my greatest acting challenges: I'm going to become a drag king. Follow me on this one; I'm going to be a man pretending to be a woman pretending to be a man. And what better places to pull off being a woman-being-a-man than Austin Texas, which not only has a huge drag king community, but also hosts the International Drag King Festival, an annual event that trumpets the drag king culture of lesbian women trying to pull off being overly macho men.

My goal is twofold. First I'd like to see if I can become a passable drag king. Second, it will be a true test to avoid getting the living crap kicked out of me by angry lesbians who might find out I'm really a man mocking their entire lifestyle.

HOW TO BECOME A MALE DRAG KING

STEP ONE:

TO BECOME A MAN, I MUST FIRST BECOME A WOMAN!

I'm in a small room with what looks like four little boys. That's a first-glance confusion with some drag kings *(are they teenage boys or lesbians?)*. Yes, in preparation I've enlisted a few local Austin drag kings to help me make my multi-layer gender transformation.

"To become a man, you must first become a woman!" explains one of the little boys *(perhaps the leader)* in her *(his?)* living room *(it's already getting complicated)*. Adorned in a tie, he *(she?)* is about to become a drag king Mr. Miagi to my drag king Karate Kid.

"We need to hear him first so that he can be he-she," adds Woody, a drag king with short spiky blond hair and a black muscle T-shirt.

"Him/her/him," I repeat to clarify. Then, "Today I become a man!" I sigh, as my man-breasts are tightly bound with wrap *(to cover my man-nipples)* to give the impression I'm trying to mask women-boobs *(padding actually)* which should give the idea I'm hiding my femininity in order to look like a man *(do you follow?)*.

Steered towards the bathroom, the little-boy-leader pulls out an electric razor and starts shaving off all my arm-hair.

"Aaah! Mommy! Aaah!" I cry.

Satisfied with her *(his?)* work, I look at my newly shorn arms *(arms like that of a teenage girl)*. I now proudly proclaim, "Today I become a woman!"

STEP TWO:
DRAG KING ATTITUDE

Now that I've gotten in touch with my feminine-side, we take an extreme, manly 360.

"It's time for you to man-up!" says one of the little boys *(I think the leader)*, who then hits me in the stomach *(just like a dude would)*.

"You're excited to be tough," the leader theorizes on the drag king psyche. "You're tough with irony. You have underlying uncertainty. And you have a wish to be powerful."

Taking this in, I create a stilted walk that sort of looks like Frankenstein after being hit with a sledgehammer in the nuts.

"Perfect. That's it!" the little boys exclaim. Walk around like that."

"Ok," I mumble. "Got it!"

As a group we emulate the drag king stance *(hands on hips and legs spread slightly apart)* and body language.

"You're kind of making an arrow towards your cock," Woody explains *(just like Pat Morita would if he made inappropriate penile references to Ralph Macchio)*. With fingers pointed in the Thomas Jefferson direction, we slap our hands towards the groin area, then throw out typical drag king sexual innuendoes.

"This stance is hard! *(Pause)* "That's what she said!"

"Let's try it again."

"That's what she said!" I roar again.

The leader goes on to explain, "A typical drag king name is usually a double-entendre, like Big Johnson, Ben Dover...."

"How about Dick Cheney? Or Big Dick Cheney?" I then add, "Or, Ben Dover Dick Chaney?" No laughs.

Instead, I go for a drag king name that sounds like someone trying to be clever but doesn't quite get it right. From Greek mythology, the name I choose: **HIMCULES!**

STEP THREE:
MAN UP!

"You want to know something very interesting, this is the first time I've had my own arm hair applied to my face," I state positively, as the application masks my five o'clock shadow.

Always resourceful, drag kings won't let my newly shorn arm-hair go to waste. Gluing cutoff hair from other parts of their body helps create realistic-looking fake facial hair.

"I knew one drag king who got off by using her girlfriend's pubic hair for a beard," shares one of the little boys. *(I nod and contemplate humorous retorts. The frontrunner: "I'd also like to wear her pubic hair as a beard – while still intact!")*

To further hide my man-ish-ness *(and to look more macho),* I apply a fake goatee.

"I'm looking all Abe Lincoln-ish," I say, resisting the temptation to break into a drag king Gettysburg Address, while applying a fake mustache and sideburns.

A huuuge part of becoming a drag king involves creating an imaginary Johnson, *(in my case, a pair of rolled up socks)*. Yes, time to add "packing."

"When you pack," Woody explains, "Wear two pairs of underwear so your socks don't get sweaty against your vagina."

"Sweaty vagina?" I quip. "That's what *she* said!"

It does make perfect sense though, being I too don't want vagina-sweat on my socks *(wait, now I'm confused?!)*. Opening my outer pair of underwear, I insert my rolled sock like JFK's head at the point of assassination: back and to the right.

Grabbing on to my newly formed package, I now feel complete.

A few drag king extras to top off my look:

1. A bandana tied to cover my Adam's apple.
2. White gloves to cover up my man-hands.
3. A sailor's hat.
4. A tight wife-beater so my bound chest is highly visible.

Adding a black leather vest, I gaze into the mirror at the full production. Yes, I look like a long-lost, rejected drag king relative of one of the Village People.

"Strut like a satisfied tiger that just ate an antelope. Be as sexy as you can!" coaches Woody as we choreograph a lip-synch routine.

Not only am I becoming a drag king, but I'm also going to enter the big drag king lip synch competition. Yes, I'll be shaking my goods in front of 500 drag kings in order to take home the gold!

Making throes-of-passion faces, I wonder if maybe I overestimated my ability. Uncertainty races through my mind. "Question, will I be the worst one there?"

"No," the little boys confirm. "You will be one of the worst, but not the worst!"

"That's what she said!" I add.

They laugh a lot less than I do.

THE ONE-EYED MAN IS KING

Inside bustling Emo's – the legendary Austin music venue, I strut around with my hands on my big belt buckle to accentuate my large "packing." The back patio area is an array of assorted drag king she/hes (as opposed to my he/she/he): a hodgepodge of cowboys, bikers, truckers, etc.... *(You get the idea.)*

Awkwardly mingling, walking like I just got off of a horse, my purposely-visible breast-binding is so tight I can barely breath. Passing tables selling drag king trading cards (collect all the players) and T-shirts that say "Genderfuk," I catch a glimpse of myself in a mirror – my fake mustache is already drooping halfway off. I have sort of a bad feeling about all this, perplexed how real drag kings will actually be fooled *(thus commencing the angry lesbian ass kicking)*. Drinking heavily seems in order.

DRAG KING QUICK TIP #1 — Humiliate One's Self!

If a drag king is being an asshole, I should say something that potentially humiliates myself like, "Do I have any blood on my pants?" being that deep down all kings seek approval.

"Can I get a picture?" asks a photographer from the Associated Press, providing me with a needed boost of confidence. Maybe I was wrong; I've only been here mere minutes and I've already gender-bamboozled the press.

"Sure!" I say in an overly exaggerated husky voice. Grabbing my sock-enhanced package, I point at the camera with a sneer, safe in the knowledge that I'm already the Associated Press face of the Austin Texas drag king community.

"Can you spell your name?" the photographer asks.

"H-I-M-C-L-U-S" *(Whoops, spelt my drag king name wrong.)*

After my photo session, I put some of my newly found drag-king-Mister-Miagi's techniques into action.

"Can I ask you a question, dude?" I say to what looks like a boy in a baseball cap and glasses *(a good ice-breaker is asking someone for help, being drag kings can relate to feeling like an insecure woman)*." Are my sideburns on straight?"

"You look great!"

"But I don't look as great as you!" I retort, applying the drag king technique, *compliment/deflect.*

DRAG KING QUICK TIP #2 — Compliment/ Deflect!

Though I'm supposed to act tough, cool, and entitled, at the same time I'm still a woman (*that's right, I'm still a woman!*). I compliment/deflect since we're all here to make each other feel hot and sexy *(and damn it, with my fake mustache, I feel hot and sexy!).*

"I'm pretty nervous about performing tonight," I add with more compliment/deflecting as I sign up for my spot in the show. "I just hope I don't fall flat on my face."

"You're unique!" she *(he?)* summarizes *(implying there's something different about me than all the other drag kings).* Wow, drag kings are very flirty. But would they still be flirty if they found out I was actually a guy *(with a penis)* who's really just dressed up like a drag king *(who lacks a penis)*?

"Unique? That's what *she* said!" I blurt, utilizing more drag king humor.

Rubbing the little boys shoulder *(since I've been coached to act like a guy when dealing with woman who look like guys),* it's acceptable to touch their shoulder when talkin' to *the ladies.*

Suddenly a woman with dreads starts aggressively rubbing her big booty against Himcules in a gyrating motion.

"What's up booty mama!" I screech *(just because I'm a drag king doesn't mean I can't be a sleazy and hit on the women here.)*

She keeps gyrating against Himcules. I just might score *(which could be awkward).*

"By the way, I wish I had mucho butt," she says, still grinding.

"That's what *she* said!" I quip, letting out a huge, husky laugh, as I spank her ass.

DRAG KING QUICK TIP #3 — Ass Slapping!

Like shoulder rubbing, this is also acceptable.

Unfortunately, booty woman's macho girlfriend suddenly drags her away. This evening, though, just might end with a *Crying Game* experience *("I thought you knew?!").*

IT'S SHOW TIME!

"Austin Texas!" shouts the large drag king emcee, sporting an eye patch and black goatee, who kicks things off from on stage.

"Wooo!" erupts the crowd of 500 drag kings.

"How many people here are wearing facial hair and are on your period?" he *(she)* throws out to the group *(who look mostly like teenage boys).*

"Yeah!" I shriek, turning to what looks like a trucker driver next to me, and share, "How did he *(she?)* know?!"

A parade of little boys take the stage doing all sorts of lip synch acts; from the very elaborate, to just standing there in an outfit and moving their lips. The entertainment gamut runs from a large Elvis with big muttonchops to a grungy punk band that causes me to rock out with a king dressed like Fonzi. I swagger over to receptive little ladies in dresses *(***Fems** *as they're called in the drag king community),* and instigate doing the bump. *(It's becoming fun to be a drag king!)*

After a hip-hop drag king boy band, the large, eye-patched emcee pimps the crowd with, "Our next act comes from Duluth, Minnesota."

God damn! That's me. *(I chose Duluth since there's not a chance in hell that I will run into other Duluth drag kings who could out me as an imposter.)* While in the midst of chatting up one of the teenage boys *(and touching their shoulder),* I abruptly slap one on the ass and sprint across the courtyard to the backstage area.

"Please welcome HIMCULES!"

The crowd is primed. My lip-synch musical selection: George Michael's "Faith" *(with an added surprise, mid-song).*

With my back to the audience and arms outstretched in jazz hands, I take my place on stage in front of the large Emo's banner. "Faith" has the longest musical intro known to humanity, as I hold the pose *(momentarily scratching my neck).* The guitar part kicks in. Screams erupt when I start shaking my butt *(unbeknownst to them... it's an actual man butt).* The drag kings

go bonkers! I go bonkers! I spin around and start working the room. My dance moves are executed like a mad robot of tomorrow. *(I only lip-synch about a third of the words.)* I dramatically grab my package and the drag kings go wild *(if they only knew it was a genuine package?).* Running my hands down the length of my man-body prompts an impassioned drag king to stuff a dollar bill in my pants.

"Faith! Faith! Faith! I got to have Faith!"

Making the sign of the cross over my package, more screams erupt. I truly feel like a drag king rock star!

Suddenly George Michael abruptly stops. Thinking it's a technical glitch, the crowd audibly groans. Wrong! It's my crowd-pleasing ace-in-the-hole. Lynryd Skynard's "Sweet Home Alabama" starts belting out *(a perfect non sequitur segue!).* Mean air-guitaring is instigated on my part.

"Come on! Come on!" I shout, trying to make everyone clap their hands in the air over their heads. "Come on! "You in the back! Come on! Everyone!"

All 500 drag kings clap with their hands over their head. The entire rest of my act consists of this. Mid-Skynyrd, and hand-over-the-head clapping, I abruptly scamper off stage leaving the crowd momentarily confused. Then a huge roar of applause.

"One more time, let's hear it for Himcules!"

"Wooooooooo!"

By no means was I the worst act. In fact, judging by the drag king response, I might just be the best! Not only am I accepted as a drag king, but I've also become a minor drag king celebrity.

"Himcules! Your piece was brilliant," exclaims a girl in a red shirt with short, spiky hair and big smile. "It was the first piece of the night that made me go, 'Yeah, I'm glad I came!' It was just perfect!"

Knocking back a Shiner Bock beer, I feign embarrassment: "I really didn't have a lot of time to practice. And my goatee was a little crooked," I say with a little compliment/deflecting, *(giving my drag king Mr. Miagi a wink)*. "I was nervous because I thought people would think, 'Oh look at Himcules with the crooked goatee!'"

"My socks were knocked off," remarks the little boy with the baseball cap and glasses, who's now touching *my* shoulder *(it's become a regular fans-of-Himcules meet-and-greet)*. "I was screaming so hard my throat hurt."

"I don't think it's about who's best, dude," I harp on a drunken rant. "It's all about community! It's all about bringing together a community of your peers and being part of the community. That's what it is for me," I state, stroking my goatee then rubbing his *(her?)* shoulder. I then add, "My only complaint is my friends bound my breasts so tight, I thought I was going to pass out." She (he?) laughs and pushes at his *(her?)* glasses. "And my packing was making my vagina itch," I add with certainty, getting increasingly drunk. "Worst, I thought I was going to get my period in the middle of my act."

My Mr. Miagi pulls me aside. "You're doing good with the underlying insecurity, but maybe it's time to cock it up a bit. I mean you just performed in front of 500 people and rocked the house. Drag king-ing helps people come to people and find a voice. So I want to see some of that confidence."

"Let's mix it up a bit," I slur, slugging back another beer. "Let's go the other way!"

So that's what I do; cock it up a bit.

"Nailed it! Knocked it out of the park! Yeah, Swinging for the fences. Swinging for the fences," I cry after another fan – a large woman with a Mohawk and nose ring, proclaims, "Himcules, I really enjoyed your performance," *(My reply: "Yeah, it was pretty god damn awesome! Summed up my thoughts exactly.")*

"This is love at first sight!" the Mohawk woman states as she instigates a hug.

"I know it's love at first sight," I cock-it-up reply.

"You're so much fun."

"I *am* pretty damn fun!" And then, "That's what *she* said!"

As we continue to hug *(and the Crying Game looks like it might go down)* my Mr. Miagi approaches.

"Our friend Himcules…" says Mr. Miagi.

"I love him," Mohawk woman professes.

"Do you love her?"

"I love her," she also professes.

"Would you accept her as a her?" she asks *(what is she doing?!)*

"If she wanted to be."

"Did Himcules seem like a normal drag king to you?"

"Himcules made me feel really warm inside," she says with a dreamy look.

"What if I told you that Himcules was on her period?"

"You know I smelled something and it smelled really good," she replies. "And I love that."

What?! Is my drag king Mr. Miagi trying to cock block me with her *(his?)* packing?

Confused. I pull Mr. Miagi aside to ask what the hell she's doing.

"I think we should tell people you're not a drag king," she says, suddenly feeling weird guilt because I'm having too much fun as a he/she/he, thinking maybe they've created a multi-gender monster. As my Mr. Miagi starts to screw up my Crying Game scenario, I'm suddenly accosted.

"Did I hear you're from Duluth?!" shrieks a drag king dressed like a 1930's paperboy.

"What?!"

"That's where I'm from," she erupts, so excited you think her eyes are going to burst out of her head.

"Get out of here!" I shriek trying to emulate her enthusiasm, as she begins to list her *(his?)* favorite Duluth drag king haunts to see, if I too, will shriek with excitement.

"Love those places," I say. "Love them! We should totally start hanging out together."

"You think we'd run into each other, you know, going to the same places," she says with confusion, being there's probably about 5 drag kings in Duluth Minnesota. Then she adds, "Man that was awesome! What I saw was this king is going crazy. It's really refreshing to see a new face, a new energy,"

I puff out my bound chest and state with cockiness, "Yeah, a new face on the drag king scene!"

And then the gender-carpet gets pulled out in front of me. "I'm assuming you're a biological male?" she asks, since she's never seen me around the Duluth scene.

"What?! Me? No!"

"If you are a bio male I think it's fabulous because it's really great to see a male deconstruct George Michael's masculinity," she says. "It's about exaggerating the male persona and gender and it's good to see."

Suddenly all the attention is on me, but not in a good way. To make matters worse, in front of everyone my Mr. Miagi confirms her gender-findings. Suddenly Mohawk woman is no longer hugging me *(where did the love go?)*. The boy in the baseball cap is no longer rubbing my shoulder *(I thought you were my little buddy?!)*.

"What?!" You're a bio male?! What! A bio male?!!"

"That's what *she* said," I spout. Then, not knowing what to do, I pull out my rolled up sock packing and throw it in their general direction in order to create a diversion as I get the hell out of there. In the end, I realize it's hard enough to be a woman, let alone being a man, being a woman, being a man. Perhaps I'm just actually a man trapped inside a lesbian's body!

If You Must Go
International Drag King Community Extravaganza www.idkeaustin.com
Emo's Austin 603 Red River Road Austin, TX 78701 (512) 474-5370 www.emosaustin.com

The Gun-Law Insanity Tour/Austin

When in Austin, why not take the Charles Whitman Murder Tour!!!!! (*Note all the exclamation points!*) Yes, a self-guided tour that will delight, entertain, and astound you with the fact that we have evolved *not one bit* as a country when it comes to our gun laws.

WHO WAS CHARLES WHITMAN?

On a hot summer day in August 1966, Charles Whitman, a 25-year-old student, former altar boy, Eagle Scout, and Marine went to the top of the UT Clock Tower – the tallest building in Austin – and began shooting with astounding marksmanship *(he picked up the skill in the military).*

Quicker than Ted Nugent can scream, "Wang-Dang Sweet Poontang," forty-five people were gunned down and 13 died, culminating at the time in the worst mass murder in a public setting, *(in 1991, fellow Texan George Hennard took Whitman's crown when he drove his pickup truck through Luby's Cafeteria window, in the town of Killeen, leaped out and shot 23 patrons before killing himself),* harking back to a more innocent time before iPods and suicide bombers, when a lone crazed gunman required military training rather than in this modern era of where any fuck-wit can fully arm themselves and live out their ultimate video game fantasy.

Newspapers of the day covered the story using such clever headlines as "Death from Above," "Austin's Darkest Hour," "The Tower of Doom," and "The Clock Struck Murder."

How insanely little have we learned from history?

LET'S GO!

First stop, Charles Whitman's house. In a nondescript, quiet neighborhood lies the very house in which Charles Whitman killed his wife with a hunting knife while she slept. Currently gutted and under renovation, if you peer inside the home, you'll see the original tile still remains intact; tile Whitman must have walked around on that floor plotting murderous details!

Ever wanted to see where a mass murderer took a dump? Though the bathroom's ripped apart, the toilet stands in the middle of the living room (*imagine the plotting that was done on that?)* – or maybe the toilet was already situated in his living room, demonstrating how far gone Whitman was!

End your visit by indulging in a view of the tiny garage behind the house where Charles Whitman constructed a homemade sawed-off shotgun.

Ironic footnote: At this locale, Whitman penned a suicide note and willed his money to be donated to mental health research, saying he hoped it would prevent others from following his route. Way to go Whitman! Even in the swinging '60's crazy guys could easily get guns!

If You Must Go

Charles Whitman's house
906 Jewel Street
Austin, TX 78704-3430

NEXT STOP... SEARS!

Hey-hey! Next there's the Austin Sears store; the very place where Whitman waltzed in and bought a shotgun and green rifle case. Unfortunately for the true Charles-Whitman-Murder-Tour-enthusiast, Sears no longer sells shotguns for prospective lone gunman to purchase hassle-free *(but they do carry a fine selection of quality tea kettles at very reasonable prices!)* Don't fret, Austin still boasts dozens of gun shops.

And remember, in Texas no background check, permit or registration is required!

If You Must Go

Sears Roebuck and Co
1000 East 41st at Hancock Center
Austin, TX 78701
(512) 329-1396

ONWARD TO MARGARET WHITMAN'S APARTMENT BUILDING!

Conveniently situated within walking distance from the UT Clock Tower are the Penthouse Apartments – a beautiful high-rise with an excellent locale conveniently located near a vast selection of fine shops and quality restaurants, situated near the campus' sororities. Charles Whitman killed his mother at this address roughly around 7 p.m. the evening before for his lone-gunman-foray. Push buzzer #505 and find out if the present occupant is aware of this.

Enhance your Charles Whitman Murder Tour with a quick jaunt to a few note-worthy locales, where former businesses used to exist that Whitman visited the morning of his the shooting spree:

- Austin Rental Company (900 West 10th).
  (Whitman rented a dolly to lug his weapons!)
- Austin National Bank (5th and Congress).
  (Whitman went here to cash some checks!)
- Charles Davis Hardware (4900 Burnet).
  (Whitman bought a 30-caliber carbine and ammunition!)

And of course,

- Chuck's Gun Shop (3707 East Avenue).
  (Long before there was eBay, this is where Whitman loaded up on more ammo.)

If You Must Go

The Penthouse Apartments
1212 Guadalupe Street
Austin, TX 78701

A MAN PREPARED

We could all take a page in preparation from Charles Whitman. When he entered the UT Clock Tower, on Aug 1st, 1966, he was prepared, like one would be if they were planning to stay for a long, long amount of time. Besides weapons (he even brought a hatchet), some of the other items he brought with him included:

- 12 assorted cans of food
- Sweet rolls *(Who doesn't like sweet rolls?)*
- Robinson Reminder Notebook
  (Reminder #1: Shoot people from Clock Tower. Reminder #2: Eat Sweet Rolls.)
- Mennen Deodorant *(Just because you're a crazed, lone gunman doesn't mean you have to smell bad).*
- Toilet Paper *(Yes, he was planning to be here a while.)*
- An Alarm Clock *(Rise and shine, it's Day Two.)*

Take in the atmosphere as you enter the UT Clock Tower building and ride the very elevator Charles Whitman struggled with operating, until an employee, Vera Palmer, informed him that it had not been powered, and turned it on for him. He then thanked her.

Did you know Charles Whitman actually took the Elevator to 27th floor, and walked up the remaining stairs to the tower's clock face? If you happened ride to the 27th floor on a weekend afternoon, you'll find it leads to an unattended office where one could easily steal a computer *(I guess computer theft is currently less of a concern with security at the Clock Tower than lone gunmen).*

I once met a guy whose mom was actually the last person to see Whitman alive! She was sightseeing on the deck and encountered Whitman holding a rifle in each hand *(she thought the large red stain on the floor from the dead receptionist was varnish).* Her companion joked with Whitman asking if he was going to the deck to shoot pigeons *(it turned out he wasn't).* When the couple left the room Whitman barricaded the stairway and began his shooting spree on the observation deck *(which just reopened in 1999, after several suicides had it closed for years).* Now a mere $3 will get you a guided tour of the Whitman's shooting vantage points of the scenic UT campus *(though you'll need to go through a metal detector first!).*

Once Whitman opened fire, a good number of students, professors, and other Austinites went for their own deer rifles, and began firing on him from various buildings and other vantage points around campus. Venture to the Pi Beta Phi sorority house and see the spot where numerous men fired away from the sorority's lawn.

Charles Whitman shooting spree lasted 90 minutes, after which he was shot by two Austin police officers – Ramiro Martinez and Houston McCoy. If you look carefully enough, you can still find patched bullet holes in the buildings near the Clock Tower, and then have your picture taken with them!

Yes, indeed, how insanely little have we learned from history!

If You Must Go
Tour of Clock Tower, Information Center Texas Union Building, corner of 24th Street and Guadalupe (512) 475-6633, or 1 (877) 475-6633
Pi Beta Phi 2300 San Antonio Austin, TX 78705 www.utexas.edu

A Diseased Underbelly Salute To...

The Fattest City In America: Houston, Texas

For four out of the last five years, Men's Fitness magazine has named Houston, Texas the Fattest City In America. Here are a few cultural highlights of Tubby Town:

- Houston is served by the Houston Chronicle, its only major daily newspaper with wide distribution, and comprised almost entirely of ads for creamy cakes and buckets of lard.

- Houston has an active visual and performing arts scene. The Theater District is located downtown and is home to nine major performing arts organizations and six performance halls. Houston also has a lot of residents whose feet don't get wet when they take a shower.

- Houston's energy industry is recognized worldwide– particularly for oil – and biomedical research, aeronautics, and the ship channel are also large parts of its economic base. Some of the people who work in these fields must wear overalls because that's the only clothes that can fit them, while their residential mailbox reads "Home of the Whopper!"

CONGRATULATIONS HOUSTON TEXAS!
YOU ARE ONE LARD-ASS CITY!

MAHWAH, NEW JERSEY

Meet The Menimists

POPULATION 24, 062

TOWN MOTTO "Working For You."

MY MOTTO "By Posing as a Sensitive Male I Will Get Laid By A Hot Babe In The Woman's Study Program."

FUN FACT The name Mahwah is derived from the Lenni Lenape word meaning "Place Where Paths Meet." So, I guess the paths meet directly at a real shithole of a town, where the most exciting place is considered TGI Fridays.

MAHWAH CULTURAL HIGHLIGHT TGI Fridays

WEIRD LOCAL SMELLS Jersey Turnpike and Jersey Girls.

EXTREMELY USELESS INFORMATION Former mayor of Mahwah, David Dwork, shot and killed himself in the town's mayoral offices due to personal debt, and not because he was forced to live in Mahwah.

LEVEL OF CREEPINESS Very, very creepy if you find sensitive guys with ponytails wearing a man-dress creepy.

When a guys proclaims, "I'm a feminist!" it sounds like something he'd say just to try and get laid by some girl who reads tarot cards. So do like I do on my road trip, pop in and attend a menimist *(male feminists)* conference, taking place at a progressive liberal arts college *(505 Ramapo Valley Road)* in upstate New Jersey for four long *(I mean looooooooooong)* days. Why? Because not only do I feel for the plight of the sisters, but it will also help me fulfill my goal of posing as such a sensitive and enthusiastic menimist that I actually end up getting laid by some female Woman's Study undergraduate.

Driving up the armpit of New Jersey on Interstate 287, I'm ready to rub elbows with dudes who have no fear of facing their own femininity, as they breakdown gender roles, deal with issues of traditional masculinity, and, of course, are against the evils of porn.

In order to get inside the menimist, you will need a little preparation. Take a few pointers from me:

MENIMIST PSEUDONYM:

Leslie Smalls *(a name that's both male or female and doesn't conform to traditional gender identity).*

MENIMIST DISGUISE:

Sandals with black socks, a murse *(man-purse),* and of course, a man-dress.

MENIMIST OCCUPATION:

Activist to remove sexist content from literature *(also, counter guy at Kinko's).*

MEET THE MENIMISTS

Numerous menimists, mostly adorned with ponytails and sandals, hover around the registration table where the topics of "male" and "masculinity" are on everyone's mind.

"Why do we get trapped with these two words, male and female?" exclaims a guy with really high-cut shorts, while from the other end of the foyer, I hear, "Gay men are hyper masculine because they are untamed by women." It's the kind of crowd who, if exposed to *The Man Show,* their heads would literally explode. Surprisingly, too, a large number of women *(predictably built like fire hydrants)* are present, which offends me—what the hell do these "women" know about what it's like to be a male feminist?! *(What do you even call them; "Fem-menimist?!")*

"I like to challenge traditional perceptions of masculinity," I state, paraphrasing things I found on their website, to a rare, cute women *(meaning not angry-lesbian-built-like-a-fire-hydrant)* behind the registration desk, as I gesture to my man-dress *(unfortunately, no manties, i.e. man-panties).*

"I like your name," the red-haired woman says with a big flirty smile as I slap on a Leslie Smalls nametag. She opens the door to lead me to the conference commencement event.

"Let's go through the door together!" I recommend, pointing out it brings gender protocol issues to the surface, as I lock eyes, letting her take me in with all my menimist glory.

Inside a room filled with 50 menimists, the group's leader, fitted with a bowl haircut, provides the menimist charter, referring to the disease of masculinity. "We turn our backs on traditional male roles of acting somber and serious," he recites. "We, in turn enjoy acting silly and having fun." His big smile turns somber and serious. "We have a commitment to feminism in order to enhance the quality of individual men's lives!"

As a community exercise, we're required to hug someone we don't know and spend a few moments making menimist small talk while holding hands. The red hair girl pops out of nowhere.

"Hellooooo!" I say in a sleazy sort-of male feminist way. We're suddenly hugging *(I hug much longer than she does, slowly rubbing her back).*

"Will you guide me to unlearn large parts of the male gender role," I whisper in her ear.

"She's a celebrity," interrupts her friend, wearing a shirt that reads, *Men Make A Difference.*

"Really?"

"She's the president of the campus feminist club."

With an affirmative nod, she coyly says, "Come visit me later at the table," gesturing to the desk filled with literature underlining faults of males in society. Hmm. I might accomplish my goal very early, and soon we'll be having sex in a kneeling position to avoid gender dominance.

MENIMISTS FUN FACT:

Traditional masculinity includes many positive characteristics, but it also contains qualities that have limited and harmed us.

"Remember there's been a lunch table reserved to discuss gay pornography if you want to talk about that," a guy – with the mullet-ponytail, shorts, and white socks pulled up to his knees – reminds us. "They'll have a card on the table to discuss that topic." (*Sounds great for the digestion process.)* "If you have a topic for lunch discussion let us know and we can facilitate that."

Few takers for my posed topic: Why soccer should be played without goals. Thus, I choose the table reserved for: Why men came to the conference.

Setting my lunch tray down amongst several menimists, we go around the table as we eat.

"I find it hard if someone says an inappropriate joke to call him out and create a discussion about it," expresses a menimist from Virginia, obviously not a fan of irony or the Dave Chappelle Show.

"My partner confronted me by things I did in our sexual relationship that she considered sexist. It made me look at myself!" shares a kid who talks like he has stuffy nose, referring to himself as "a person of privilege," *(a politically correct term meaning he's white).*

"Here's an interesting thing that happened to me this weekend. I was at a barbecue and they had one of those barbecue scrapers and it had a beer bottle opener on it," remarks a fem-menimist. "It was an interesting link to gender roles that says it's masculine to barbecue and drink beer."

"I worked as a Teamster for 25 years," expresses a burly old guy with thick, Archie Bunker-like accent, looking clearly different than the rest of the menimists. "I didn't bring my wife. She's a bit homophobic," he confesses, as the rest of the table shifts uncomfortably. "She says, 'whatever they do behind closed doors I don't want to know about!'" Looking at me a little longer than he should, he adds, "I'd like to correct some of the things I've been missing out on all those years."

"Same here," I pipe in. "I want to un-learn my masculinity. I want to learn to interact with broads differently. Now, I look at broads as my equals!" As things fall tensely silent, I quickly go back to the buffet for a second desert.

MENIMIST FUN FACT:

By rethinking the obsession with winning that so many men are socialized into, we can free ourselves to relate to people in many other, more satisfying and more productive ways.

A wimpy guy lectures the group about Integrating Constructs of Masculinity. "I feel ashamed," he confesses to the group. "Because I'm white, I'm male, and I'm straight."

"First, I hope you feel safe!" a menimist with really high-cut shorts assures him. "But, I want you to appreciate what it's like to be unsafe and maybe learn something from that!"

"Can I sit here?" exclaims the flirty, red-haired president of the campus feminist club, again popping out of nowhere.

"Sure!" I reply, moving my murse *(man-purse)*. I'm her menimist Prince Charming! All I need to do is throw out a few more sensitive sound bites and we'll be non-objectively boning in no time!

A heated discussion undertakes regarding such urgencies as whether men should lead female feminist groups. "Men tended to dominate meetings and decision making, taking on the patriarchal structure of society," the wimpy guy shares with the group, regarding his research.

"It makes my blood boil," the feminist club president remarks.

"Yeah, me too," I say, nodding my head *(noting how I sound slightly insincere).*

She points to the conference program and the workshop on An Examination of Masculinity in Hip-Hop. *(One of four speakers concludes that words like "bitches" and "hos" get used a lot in rap lyrics.)* "I'm interested in that because I just wrote a paper on it," she says proudly about her women-objectifying-actualization about rap music.

"Yeah, me too!" I say, nodding my head *(again noting my insincerity).*

To emphasize her point she quotes a few Eminem lyrics. I shake my head in disgust, then contribute by reciting – perhaps a little too enthusiastically – some rap lyrics from the Ying Yank Twins, throwing out arm gestures and "bitch" a few extra times than needed:

Shake it like a salt shaker,
Tremble like a vibrator
Shake it like a salt shaker, bitch!
Come'on, bitch!

A menimist couple, both with glasses, turns around to shoot me a look. The feminist club president suddenly grows quiet, focusing on an androgynous man in the front row, who comments, "If we had a community of a world where egg and sperm can come together with equality, we'll have a start of a New World."

I put my pen on my chin and act like I'm listening intently, occasionally uttering, "Hmm!" Somehow it doesn't impress her and she abruptly gets up and leaves.

MENIMIST FUN FACT:

Women are still the most universal and direct victims of our patriarchy. Our organization must take a highly visible and energetic position in support of women's struggle for equality.

Inside the Student Union, situated amongst a lot of barefoot people, I nuzzle next to a guy whose T-shirt reads, Men of Quality Respect Women of Equality, ready for a ruckus, knee-slapping evening of politically correct menimist entertainment. A paunchy guy holds a sign up sheet. "I want to hear something from you, be it a song, dance or haiku," he says. In order to impress the president of the campus feminist club *(who is now flirting with a more sensitive guy),* I grab the list and sign up: Leslie Smalls Non-Gender Specific Wordsmith.

Concerned about refreshments, I inquire, "Are you serving any alcohol?"

"There's coffee and soft drinks," a fire-hydrant-built fem-menimist replies.

I nod my head, "Yeah, drinking booze just conforms to the aggressive male gender roles of getting fucked up!"

Without alcohol, this event will shortly become like nails on my feminine side's mental chalkboard.

On stage the guy with a ponytail mullet croons an a cappella number called "The Druid Song." "I am not a tree. A tree is not a man. Oh tree I hear your ancient song in every piece of wood..."

A lanky guy resembling a marionette lumbers into the spotlight. "One of the things I do is write letters to Goddesses." With a sour look and monotone delivery, he segues into a spoken word piece about Abu Ghraib prison, "Women have joined the military—a masculine institution," he recites "Expressing fears of men who might have abused them earlier and eager to please the men who act over them!"

It gets better and better.

"If you have any events where you need a singer against social injustice, please let me know," expresses yet another guy with a ponytail. And then: "I wrote this after a woman's studies class," he says, launching into a song about date-rape.

Almost ready to put a steel spike into my brain, suddenly I hear, "Next up is Leslie Smalls."

Pulling out a piece of paper, I tell the room, "I also wrote this after a woman's study class." What follows is original menimist poetry based on an incident when I accidentally walked into the wrong bathroom.

ONE RACE/ONE SEX
No longer man.
No longer woman
Let's evolve to be humanandwoman!"
Why have a men's rooms?
Why have a women's room?
Why don't we just have a people's room!

I snap my fingers at the end to mild clapping. The guy in the *Men of Quality Respect Women of Equality* T-shirt gives me a hug. I look out into the crowd and the red-haired woman is not present to witness my sensitivity *(what a politically correct tramp!).*

MENIMIST FUN FACT:

By overcoming the traditional male denial of most emotions and feelings, men can have more meaningful relationships, richer and fuller emotional lives and even be physically healthier.

With serious expressions on our faces we menimists look at several canvases featuring full frontal nude portraits of longhaired men with huge knobs, doing things like standing by a refrigerator – none of us are even laughing!

"Can you comment about your work?" asks a menimist adorned in a T-shirt that reads, Resist.

"My paintings explore the cultural constructions of maleness!" expresses an older hippie woman who looks like she's encountered a lot of acid in her day. "Many men have lost femininity in favor of masculinity."

Again, I look at the naked guys with the huge Thomas Jeffersons.

"Did your husband have long-hair?" asks the Resist T-shirt wearer, wondering what he represents.

"They are different men," she replies.

"You certainly have a type."

"What does the penis on the man in the bathtub represent?" I ask.

Confused, she takes a long look. Finally she confirms that the penis is just a penis.

"Ooooh," I blurt, then arrogantly add, "I thought it represented male repression of women in our society as they impose a patriarchal system."

This sparks a brief discussion.

The menimist leader with the bowl haircut looks displeased. Pointing to a portrait of yet another longhaired guy with naked woman, he comments with a sour face, "If I would have seen this without knowing the context here, I would have thought of that painting as pornography!"

There's a momentary uncomfortable silence.

"That's what I see in my sexuality," she argues. *(Close call. If decided it was porn, this whole Men's Issues In Art Workshop could have been shut down!)*

"If you can't masturbate to it," I whisper to my neighbor to clarify, "it isn't porn."

I've developed a constant uncomfortable feeling in my shoulders, as I approach a dinner table where large, slightly balding women is aggressively berating we menimists for not being supportive of her needs. She rants on about how men have done her wrong, blaming the entire male species for the faults of her past relationship. "I'm not talking physical abuse, I'm talking mental abuse," she screams *(while accidentally spitting food)* about her previous coupling *(I try to imagine why someone would want to break up with this piece of work)*. "He loved to control me in the same way our patriarchal society does," she whines. "He works in a very public job. What about exposing him professionally?" she throws out. "What're your opinions on that?"

"You would get a tape recorder and secretly record him," the kid with the stuffy nose suggests.

"Come again?" I ask.

He explains that if you secretly record him, then you could replay it for people he works with. *(In this Bush wiretapping era, it's good to see the extreme left condoning these tactics as well.)*

Her overbearing-nature inspires me to go get more Chicken Parmesan.

"Leslie, don't leave without giving your opinion," she demands.

"Oh, I won't do that," I express.

Upon my return, the balding woman gets immediately confrontational, "Leslie, I want to hear your opinion!"

The red-haired president of the campus feminist club looks towards me for sensitive menimists words of wisdom. Words! Don't fail me now. Come'on words, be eloquent and wise so I can get laid!

(Pause.) "Why don't you just leave him?" I spout. "Clearly it's not working out."

The table looks at me like I just did a bad smell. The balding woman and the red haired girl start yelling in a tirade at how insensitive I am.

"I have to get some chocolate cake," the red haired girl dramatically proclaims as she storms away, along with my chances for some feminist nooky.

"She's all right. That's what the support staff is here for," the balding woman aggressively says, being this is all about her.

Making my excuses I abruptly leave, running into the hippie woman who paints all the nude guys with big knobs. Appreciating my earlier men's-issues-in-art comments, I throw out more phrases like "gender-role challenges" and "powerful." When, I run out of phrases, our conversation segues into geographical small talk about the state of New Jersey.

"I got a map of New Jersey in my car," she exclaims, out-of-the-blue, with excitement. "Do you want to go see it?"

"Sure," I awkwardly reply.

Walking towards the parking lot, she stops in her tracks. "Oh wait, I need to get the keys to my car in my room. Should we go up to my room and get them?"

"Uhhhhh?!"

It suddenly hits me. All the naked guys in her pictures have long hair! I have long hair! If I got to her room, I'll end up painted nude with a big knob, perhaps standing by a refrigerator. Sure my goal was to get laid at a menimist convention, but not by the older hippie lady. Quickly making my excuses, I bolt off to the Men Moving to Create Gender Justice workshop.

MENIMIST FUN FACT:

Men can learn to be good listeners, to be gentle, to be sensitive to other people's needs and feelings, and able to nurture.

THE SHOW — "VOICES OF MEN"

The old guy with shorts-cut-much-too-high corners me and talks way too close. "Is that you?" he asks, with delight in his eye, pointing to the painting of the naked guy in bathtub.

"Noooooooooo!" I solidly reply, as the woman who paints the guys-with-big-knobs gestures for me to sit next to her. (Must-Avoid!)

I'm strapped in for more political correct entertainment hell, this time involving poorly executed celebrity impersonations centered around woman's issues.

The show kicks off with edited film clips from the movie *Rocky*, as the Italian Stallion is made to look like a creepy date rapist as he courts Adrian. The paunchy guy reemerges. With a fourth-rate impersonation, Rocky declares that he will now be more respectful of women.

Then on with the Austin Powers costume.

"Yeeeeeah, baby!"

We're enlightened to learn how Austin Powers objectifies women. His politically correct rendition promises to stop saying

"Yeeeeeeah baby!" and instead, now refer to women by their first name *("Yeeeeeah Cindy!")*.

"Leslie, can I have a word with you," one of the conference organizers says to me, afterwards with concern, *(noting all weekend there's a three-second delay in responding when called that name)*. Not sure if she's found out that I'm only here as part of my road trip destination into the diseased underbelly of America, my mind races for legitimate explanations.

"I heard that the dinner conversation went awry and I'm just checking to see if you're ok?" she says.

"Oh! That!" I exclaim with surprise. "I was a little shaken earlier, but I'm fine now." I remark, adding, "I was shaken, that is, how the patriarchal system stifles women in relationships."

I'm given a hug.

MENIMIST FUN FACT:

Male role demands just one traditional masculine sexual style. On top of his other problems, macho man doesn't have much fun.

"This book is hard to find," stresses the bowl haircut leader, holding a copy of *Against Pornography,* as we sit in a circle with arms dramatically folded. "The author doesn't reprint it often out of fear she'd be sued by magazines like *Penthouse* because she couldn't get permission to reprint the material," he says, regarding unauthorized use of cartoons and article excerpts.

"Good thing *Penthouse* will never know," I perk with an earnest, menimist nod.

"It startles people that the ACLU is on the wrong side of some issues," he trumpets. "It's a front for the industry. One of their buildings was bought by the porn industry, "he adds, theorizing like one would about Bigfoot that the ACLU will sell out their entire civil liberties ideals for a buck. Everything that is harmful is not illegal. Cheese Doodles are harmful," he moronically correlates.

“What about the 1st Amendment?” I throw out, as the red haired girl gives me a strange look, then abruptly walks out of the workshop.

“It’s a fool’s argument,” he assures, regarding eliminating the constitutional clause that protects both porn and Robert Mapplethorpe art shows.

“Yes, a fools argument,” I nod, slamming my fist on my desk, as I act like a total kiss ass.

“James Madison wrote the 1st Amendment. Madison also had 550 slaves. *(Gasps.)* We should be aware of our founding fathers!” I pick my ear as he goes on, “Not all speech is free. You can’t shout fire in a crowded movie theater.”

“Isn’t that to physically protect people from being trampled?!”

(He’s on a roll.) “You can’t burn the American flag! You can’t make bomb jokes at airports. Is it not unreasonable to add one more exception to freedom of speech if there is a clear and present danger?” he adds, already broadening the definition by including banning slasher films like the *Friday the 13th* series.

“If a right-wing person is against murder, should we be for it?” he reasons his position on the other end of the fascist spectrum, in line with the ideology of the Christian right. *(Next time Focus on the Family wants to ban a sexually suggestive Hardee’s commercial, the menimists can lock arms with them on the frontlines.)*

“It is harmful to people to see sex organs in close-ups,” he segues matter-of-factly.

“Your comment came up in the research I’ve done,” states the fem-menimist that scorned barbecue scrappers with beer bottle openers.

“Me too,” I pipe in. “I’ve done lots and lots of research on that topic!”

He throws out the old porn causes men to rape argument. “There’s more significant evidence than the scientific evidence that links smoking to lung cancer!” he assures the room.

"You can add to a pro-rape culture without raping someone," one of the fire-hydrants throws out *(yes, viewers of, say, HBO After Dark are contributors).*

"It's objectification; women become just an object without a name." *(Isn't Jenna Jameson a household name?!)* "If the material is authored by men it's a male fantasy of men." He poses to the menimists, utilizing creepy mime, "Do you really think women like having to suck penises for hours on end?"

"Yours perhaps, but not mine!" I almost blurt. "Cuz mine taste like candy!"

"It wouldn't be hard to shut down a lot of pornography companies by what is going on behind the scenes," the gung-ho pony tailed-date-rape folk singer poses. "Go after them money laundering. Shut them down for other issues." *(Are you listening* Penthouse*?)*"

I help the entire argument: "I know, Salman Rushdie said, 'Porn is the litmus test for defining the bounds of a free and open society.' But we should be aware *The Satanic Verses* is racist towards Muslims!"

FINAL MENIMIST MOMENTS

The closing ceremony is a big new age, male feminist extravaganza, as we form a big hippie-dippy menimist circle and hold hands. The guy with the ponytail-mullet, who last crooned the Druid Song, leads another a cappella classic, "Come and listen to my song. Listen to my song..." The balding, aggressive woman joins in, aggressively showing her vocal range.

"Like other movements unknown to the mainstream, we are standing on the shoulders of giants," exclaims ponytail-mullet guy, as we then go around the circle as each of are supposed to say one word that sums up the four day conference.

"Empowerment."

"Strength."

"Heroic."

As the circle keeps moving, I blurt quickly "Un-laid," before anyone can acknowledge it. We march around the room, holding hands in line, singing, as we're made to stare at everyone's face. When finished, I quickly storm from the building in need of a drink and a baseball game. Then immediately return; I forgot my man-purse!

LAKE OKEECHOBEE, FLORIDA

Kill A Live Animal... With A Gun!

POPULATION 5,376

FUN FACT There is a hell of a lot off hurricanes around here.

WEIRD LOCAL SMELL Swamp Gas and Conservative gas-bags.

EXTREMELY USELESS INFORMATION Lake Okeechobee is locally referred to as Lake O, The Big Lake, or simply The Lake. One local refers to the lake simply as "Cindy."

CULTURAL HIGHLIGHT The Lake, the goddamn Lake!! And let's not forget wild boar hunting.

WOULD WILD BOAR HUNTING MAKE FOR A GOOD HONEY-MOON ACTIVITY? Yes. The website says, "This would be something a newly-married couple will never forget about sharing together, with their friends, family, children, and grandchildren throughout the years."

DIFFERENT WAYS YOU'RE ALLOWED TO HUNT WILD BOAR THAT YOU WOULDN'T EXPECT Handgun, sword, spear, cross-bow, regular bow, and hatchet.

LEVEL OF CREEPINESS 10, if you take on a wild boar without the luxury of "sissy" weapons.

Simply by doing the Google word search: "Wild Boar Hunting Florida," I come across the road trip destination:

Wild boar hunting with dogs that chase, battle and bay up a wild hog is the most exciting hunting adventure a hunter will ever experience in his lifetime. The mere fact of being in close contact with a fierce animal that is charging and attacking the hunting dogs, guides and even the hunter is something that can't be described.

My rental car is already pointed towards the Florida Everglades. If they include an autographed poster of Larry the Cable Guy, and free banjo lessons *(1 of 3 banjo jokes in this chapter),* I'll think I've died and gone to redneck-y/good-ol-boy-ish heaven. I'm sooooo sold! This will be just like Ernest Hemingway elephant hunting in Africa *(if Ernest Hemingway happened to have a rusty car on blocks in his front yard and he played in a jug band).* Most likely I'll be wild boar hunting with very scary people. You know, like the ass-rapers in the movie *Deliverance.* Perhaps Toby Keith? Or maybe the cast of *The Hills Have Eyes?!*

To be prompt for my 7 a.m. wild boar hunting rendezvous, I rapidly drive 2½ hours from Miami, careen down several small roads, past Lake Okeechobee and into the pocket of extreme conservatism – that which is Central Florida.

As the saw grass grows high and the air smells like a mix of gators and escaped prison convicts, I veer off onto a dirt road leading to a rusty gate that reads *No Trespassing.* Undoing the latch as instructed, I expect to hear mild strains of banjo music *(2 of 3 banjo jokes),* continuing towards the Little Lake Lodge hunting camp where a lone trailer sits on the edge off a small lake *(this must be the little lake)* with a large alligator nestled on its shore.

To look the part, I'm dressed in my wild boar hunting costume, (like one about to partake in a small paramilitary operation). My point: camouflage is the fashion word of the day. Parking my rental car next to a large truck with plates that read

Fast Gun, I'm greeted by Cliff – the Crocodile Dundee Of Boar Hunting, adorned with cowboy hat, and paunchy belly, who's loading up a large, red swamp buggy, while the sound of barking hunting dogs permeates the morning air.

"Next time you come hunting, don't wear shorts," Cliff suggests with a thick Southern drawl while rubbing his beard. *(I'm outed as a complete boar hunting virgin.)* "This is in case you do something stupid," he then says with slight indignation, handing me a release form that states if I happen to accidentally shoot one of the hunting dogs, it will cost me $5,000 *(everything has its price)*. Wild boars are much cheaper than dogs; it's only $170 to blow them away.

Looking at my address, Cliff remarks with a sense of wonderment, "You have some crazy people out there in California." Shaking his head, he adds, "I listen to Dr. Dre so I know!"

In turn, I question Cliff if he's ever driven in the General Lee, being I saw the Dukes Of Hazzard movie and that's what I think Southern people do *(he hasn't)*.

Noting I'm from the hometown of Nancy Pelosi, he adds with a laugh, "There's already some gun owner ready to take her out."

Vigorous nodding occurs on my part.

"We had a guy come all the way from Africa," Cliff shares. "He killed every kind of animal on the African continent."

"Did he ever kill a Kinkajou?" I ask.

"I'm sure he has."

(NOTE: Jokes on him. A Kinkajou is a long-tailed, nocturnal mammal from the South American rainforests, not Africa. Ha-ha!)

A fact that makes this boar hunt entirely hellish, unknown to Cliff, is I'm a slight, hacky-sack-playing vegetarian. Not to fanatical proportions *(sure, I'll sometimes eat meat)*, but to the point where hogs slaughtered by gunfire holds the appeal of back-alley dental surgery in Tijuana. Thus, when asked to shoot, I'll say something witty like "I prefer shooting photos, not guns!" *(Yes, I'm so very witty!)*

Following at Cliff's heel, we pass yelping hunting dogs in pens filled with dogshit that has a wafting smell of high, holy hell.

"That's Psycho," he mentions, pointing to one particularly ornery hound *(is he ornery because he has to wallow in his own filth?).* "He will bite and grab the hog by the side of the head." *(More nodding on my part.)* "Then you wheelbarrow the hog, turn him over, put a rope around him."

"Uh-huh."

Grabbing a spotted hound dog named Heavy, we venture back to the swamp buggy, where patiently waiting for the hunt to commence stands a large man with a bushy mustache and a large woman, both of whom are also dressed in wild boar hunting costumes. Both wear matching head-to-toe camouflage fatigues, (the wild boars will never see them coming), looking like extras in the Schwarzenegger movie *Commando.*

"You're going to see a girl kill a hog!" the man portion of the combo boasts with a broad smile.

"Ok," I reply, wondering: are they brother and sister? Husband and wife? Both?! Uh-uh... wrong on all counts. It's a father and daughter combo from Ohio *(tomato farmer and school teacher),* I assume god-fearing people from the conservative heartland who love killing stuff.

"We're a family of hunters," camouflage dad proclaims. He gestures towards his camouflaged daughter *(I hardly see her standing there).* "She shot her first deer at ten and shot a deer every year since then."

"I prefer shooting photos instead of guns," I wittily reply like Oscar Wilde, when he asks my previous hunting resume, nervously letting out what I hope will be a shared laugh, explaining I'm a writer.

"I'm not too much into reading," Cliff snaps with a thick drawl, mocking my "college boy" aspirations *(Come on Cliff! Don't say things like that and sound like a complete Southern stereotype!).*

After Heavy is put into a cage in the bowels of the swamp buggy our motley crew embarks in the large vehicle, which moves at 35 mph across the 1,000 acres of swampland *(adjacent to roughly 32 hidden drug smuggling air strips).* As the early morning Florida sun starts to make its presence known, my mind contemplates possible horror film scenarios that might occur today.

POSSIBLE HORROR FILM CASE SCENARIOS:

1. We get out to the middle of the brush only to be told there are no wild boars. Cliff turns to me and says, "We're going to hunt the most vicious animal of them all."
   "What's that?" I naively ask.
   "Man!"
   And then I'm given a 5-minute head start before they come after me.
2. After a few hours the hunting party turns to me. "Why don't you squeal like a wild boar for me, college boy!" I'm made to wear a wild boar mask, and am then ritualistically sodomized more times than a dozen Ned Beattys, while Cliff plays "The Devil Went Down to Georgia" on the banjo *(3 of 3 banjo jokes).*
3. Cliff turns to me and says, "The lucky ones die first." I'm fed to the gators and then buried in the swamp. Easily it could be made to look like an accident.

As we continue to drive through the bumpy brush, passing patches of saw grass and swamp cabbage, I question the camouflage clothes. Even if the wild boars can't detect us as humans, surely they would see a large, red swamp buggy coming at them at 35 mph.

"Are you calling for advice?" Cliff mocks with distaste after I answer a cell phone call. *(Is he going to start calling me "City Boy"?)* And then: "This hunt you take all your buddies on." (*I note places to hold beers next to the places to hold rifles.)* "Yesterday, Daryl killed 14 hogs." *(Come on, his name really isn't Daryl.)*

"How old was the youngest hunter to shoot a hog?" I ask after Cliff explains that rattlesnakes will eat the baby pigs when they are real little.

"Six years old."

Though that little rascal ended up *blowing the hog away real good,* there have been a few hunting calamities involving other little kids. When an 8-year-old missed a hog 9 times, he was ragged on by his gruff grandfather *(I guess only sissy-boys can't shoot)*. The gruff grandfather, in turn, took 12 shots and then ended up shooting one of the dogs.

Yet, another 8-year-old once shot and crippled a hog. Cliff's buddy put a leg on top of it and told him "Just shoot it behind the ear." The nervous 8-year-old, aimed but moved his hand at the last moment, which threw off the gun. That was the closet someone has come to getting shot; Cliff's buddy could feel the gun's convulsion in his leg. It just goes to show, when it comes to kids and guns, the outcome is always going to be zany!

Venturing deeper into the brush, and further into the heart of darkness, Cliff presents us with several killing options. "Are you going to hunt with a gun or knife?"

"I did bring the buck knife," proclaims camouflaged dad.

"I had one guy who wanted to do it with a knife," Cliff shares. He's referring to a hardened WWII vet. He walked into the bush with his knife out. After a big tussle, he then walked out with a dead hog and a bite mark in his leg. "That was a trophy hog!" *(Now that's pure love of hand-to-hand combat killing.)*

Also optional is Ted Nugent-style bow-hunting. But there have been some mishaps. "Daryl got stuck with an arrow once. He was running through the woods in front of a bow-hunter and suddenly stopped. The arrow stuck into him this far." Extending his hands out in measurement, Cliff adds, "That's why I have life insurance."

Already trigger happy, camouflage dad points at a large water cow with horns, and asks, "Can you shoot that thing?"

"It's $1,200 to kill that thing," Cliff replies *(everything has a price)*. "I just bought it yesterday." He puts a hefty pinch of chewing tobacco in his mouth. "Gators are good for nothing! It's $300 to shoot that." He then gives me – the college boy – a condescending look. "I shouldn't while a writer's around."

"Why?" I reply.

"It's illegal," he says with a sly grin like a cat that just ate the canary.

"Is it okay to bring your own animals to hunt?" I question.

"Depends on the animal."

"Would I be able to hunt a monkey wearing people clothes?"

A line is drawn... monkeys wearing people clothes are flatly denied.

Cliff stops the red swamp buggy to give us the boar-hunting skinny. I lean forward, listening attentively while playing a game called "Replace The Word "Hog" With Any Racial Minority."

"We'll ride around and see if we see something moving. If we don't find one, I'll let the dogs loose. Once he finds a hog, he'll start barking at it. And he'll stay barking at it until he stops. Then I'll say 'Get on the Hog.' That will mean safety off, finger on the trigger, and aim dead on at the hog."

"Warthogs are nasty," the camouflaged girl *(translation Wart-Asians are nasty)* who sits back drinking a Mountain Dew (*this is a product endorsement),* says while holding her camouflaged camera bag.

"Do not shoot until I say, *'Shoot or kill!'*" Cliff explains, "I had a guy a few weeks back whose buddy was saying, 'Kill him! Kill him! Kill him!' and he started blasting away. I finally had to take the gun away from him and said 'Y'all done!'"

Yes, sometimes tough love is needed when it comes to wild boar hunting.

"I don't think nothing's around so we'll put the dog down." Heavy's let loose. Cliff elucidates the same wild boar we'll be hunting once bit off one of the dog's legs. "We've had a rash of dogs getting wiped out lately. I can't afford to loose another one."

Cliff then starts up the swamp buggy and almost accidentally runs over Heavy *(so that's how the dogs have been getting wiped out).* Heavy then runs off wildly, disappearing into the brush. Suddenly, there's mad hound dog barking. "He's found a hog right there!" Cliff turns to the group. "Ok, which one of you is ready?"

The camouflaged girl *(I can hardly see her)* sets down her

Mountain Dew and loads her rifle.

"She won the Miss Annie Oakley award for her high school," brags camouflage dad *(making me feel sad my high school didn't have an Annie Oakley award)*, at her shooting proclivities.

"We got something like that here," Cliff quips while bullets are being loaded into a rifle. "But it's who can shoot the most while drunk!" *(Footnote: Drunks-with-guns humor is one of my favorite types of humor!)*

The temperament changes. Suddenly a hog with long tusks frantically runs out of the brush with Heavy close behind.

"That hog's a hairy one isn't it?"

Miss Annie Oakley, from about 50 yards away, *gets on the hog*. Still seated, one shot fires out. BAM! The dog barks louder. My ear hurts. She practically shot over my shoulder *(good thing she's Miss Annie Oakley)*, hitting the hog in the back.

"He's going down." And then, "That hog's dead."

After the beast is loaded into the buggy like a sack of potatoes, Cliff remarks in a more reflective moment: "That Slimfast, it ain't bad, but it ain't good either," he says dipping into his chewing tobacco. *(Clearly this is the weirdest thing I hear him say all day.)*

Our little Sunday tea party abruptly comes to a close: "Heavy's got another one!"

Cliff turns to me and asks, "Do you want to shoot?"

Camouflaged dad and Miss Annie Oakley's face light up with hope.

Ok, so this is the part where, once again, I'm supposed to say the witty, "I prefer to shoot photos not guns," and then everyone laughs. But somehow I don't. With only mere, minor peer pressure I suddenly find myself holding a 30/30 Winchester – and given brief instructions on how to shoot things – as I'm told to *get on the hog.*

"Don't shoot until I tell you."

"So shoot whenever I want?" I ask, wondering why the hell a gun is in my hands.

"Keep the gun level," screams Miss Annie Oakley.

I nod my head, still not knowing why I'm still holding this damn gun.

In hot pursuit, Cliff yells, "There's three of them! Shoot the one on the left right between the eyes."

When he says those words, it makes me realize exactly what I've gotten myself into.

"Look at the neck on that thing. That hog weighs more than you!"

I fire a shot, purposely not *getting on the hog,* in fact I'm rooting for the hog to get away so we never see him again and I don't have to shoot anymore.

The hogs run into the brush. Cliff jumps off the swamp buggy chasing after it. He disappears into the brush as well. The dog barking grows louder.

Cliff runs back. "Good shot. You broke its leg."

What?! How can that be a good shot? I wasn't even pointing the gun at the beast.

"I kept Heavy on the front hog," he says, giving an update. "Come on. You got another in the chamber."

At any point I could have Miss Annie Oakley tag me out and finish the job. But instead, I find myself running through the brush with Cliff in front of me, swamp vegetation hitting me in the face; scratching my bare shorts-wearing legs. I'm scared shitless.

Will the enraged hog charge and gouge me with his tusk for shooting him? Will I get a big chunk of my leg bitten off like the WWII vet with a knife? I want back on the swamp buggy.

"Don't worry, he'll eat me before he eats you," Cliff assures.

"I got you covered," says camouflaged dad holding up a buck knife at waist level.

"If it comes running at you, be sure to run side to side."

"Come again?"

"Don't run in the same direction if the hog comes out you."

"Huh?!"

The last bit of advice: "When you shoot, do it through the head."

No longer do I want to be a big, tough hunter; instead I want to be eating ice cream on Santa Claus' lap, as the camouflage dad and daughter coax me on.

"That's his back legs!"

"How do I not shoot Heavy?" I ask, *(remembering it's $5,000 if I do)* as the dog bites at its head. *(Would they be sad if Heavy went down too?)*

The wild boar growls and makes a run towards me. I shriek like a little girl crying for her mommy. *("Aaaah!")* Somehow I fire off another shot in the frenzy *(I hope I didn't hit Heavy)*. The wild boar makes a loud noise and takes off running.

"You shot him in the gut in the far side."

I'm stunned how easily I succumbed to peer pressure. It makes me question if I were in Nazi Germany would I shoot at Jews with such little prodding. Why didn't I say my witty, "I shoot photos not animals?" Why?!

We get back on the swamp buggy. Heavy has the hog trapped, still biting at its head, as we park the vehicle almost directly over it.

"Shoot it right in the head!"

Even with my eyes closed, I end up unintentionally shooting the hog execution style in the back of the head. There wasn't a chance in hell I could miss... I'm directly above it.

"That's a good shot."

This has become more like Dick Cheney hunting from the window of his Cadillac. I now somehow respect the old WWII vet who hunted the boar with a knife; at least the hog had a fighting chance and got a swipe in by biting his leg.

Cliff gives an aw-shucks laugh, shaking his head as he says, "He moved around pretty quickly with a broken leg. Let's let him finish off dying real quick."

Venturing off the swamp buggy, we stand there, as the hog lies dead in a puddle of blood still kicking its legs like they were powered by a motor.

"His last thoughts were run, run, run," Cliff jests, as the former hog occasionally growls even after death; drool froths out the side of its mouth. Do I no longer know the difference between good and evil? Is my excuse, "I was only following orders?!"

"He's dead. That's what matters in the end."

The moment is immortalized; it's picture time!

"Put your legs against it and lift its head," Cliff instructs, as we stand besides the smelly corpse. "Lean up against him like that and hold its ears."

"Do I have to?" I say with shame, as The Smith's "Meat is Murder" reverberates through my head.

Not only did I kill this poor, extremely ugly, animal, I now have to degrade it in death by straddling it. As I lift the dead animal's ears, I feel like one of those Abu Ghraib prison guards madly grinning it up in front of a pyramid of Iraqi genitals. I look

towards the camera like I've just witnessed a packed school bus burst into flames.

"That's a big 'ol pig." Cliff remarks as blood drips out of its mouth. "He was tough, he didn't want to die."

All I can think is I'm going to go to hell for this. Satan will ride in on a giant wild boar shooting me in the leg. I gag at the hog, which smells like a cross between moldy carpet in a dilapidated crack house and rotten egg salad. Again, I find myself doing something I don't want to, simply because I'm given orders.

As we head back to camp, camouflage dad tells a dirty joke about a Wal-Mart greeter *(something to do with tampons).* I don't really follow because I've fallen into silent contemplation. Cliff requests to tell a dirty joke, but doesn't want to do so in front of a lady.

"Don't worry. She's all boy but the plumbing," he says referring to his daughter, who, apparently is all boy but the plumbing. *(Does that mean she's a lesbian?)*

GUTTING

I shamefully shift back and forth, glancing at boar blood – the victim's blood – smeared on my leg. The smell of dead warthog permeates my hunting costume.

"We had to twist your arm real hard," Miss Annie Oakley mockingly says back at camp, referring to how easily I folded to peer pressure when it comes to killing a living thing. She presents me with the bullet shell I used to kill the boar... a proud reminder.

"Your wife, how come she didn't come?" yells Cliff as he hangs the pair of hogs like two Ed Gein victims waiting to be made into human lampshades.

"She rather shoot with a camera," camo-dad replies.

Damnit! That's what I should have said and it would have been all right *(but I didn't),* and now I harvest this terrible secret for the rest of my life!

Dad and daughter gather together by the swinging hogs to take a proud family photo.

"Eeew Jenny, he's leaking," camo-dad notes, as blood pours out of the bullet hole.

"We'll move the other one so it doesn't look so little," Cliff cracks. *(Ah... wild boar hunting humor.)*

"I shot a baby," Miss Annie Oakley says, commenting on the size of the hog she killed compared to mine.

"I shot a baby once," I share, looking down in horror without explaining further.

"Lean against it like Lee Harvey Oswald," Cliff says before snapping the shot. Then, like David Copperfield, he pulls a long string of intestines out like they were streamers magically produced from someone's ass.

As he continues to yank out the hog guts quicker than a zombie in *Day of the Dead (third in the George Romero series),* camo-dad offers me homemade deer sausage made from the innards of one of the deer from a recent hunting trip.

"That's deer summer sausage," he says while all the hog's internal organs are being removed and thrown into a cart.

"Hey, thanks!" I hear myself saying, again simply amazed how easily I succumbed to peer pressure. Not only am I breaking the vegetarian code by now eating meat, but also it's deer meat eaten in front of a hog whose innards are being ripped out as blood sprays. I've never eaten deer sausage but I assume this is under the most unappealing circumstance. *(Again, why do I keep following orders?!).*

As the hog swings from a cable, steam rises from the animal. The once-charging boar is now reduced to a pile of meat. The head is still intact and attached to its long spine, *(maybe to be worn later by Cliff as he dances nude under the full moon in honor of the owl god Moloch).*

If it were a cuter animal, I'd feel worse *(as it stands, it's so ugly I only feel like the embodiment of pure evil).*

"Do you have a cooler?" shouts Cliff slicing off the hog's hooves and snout with an electric knife. Cliff wants me to take my slaughtered hog back to San Francisco.

I say "no," hoping they don't start tying it to the roof of my rental car. My elderly Jewish Miami relatives I'm visiting later would absolutely freak if I arrived for dinner with a dead pig dripping blood all over the vehicle.

The others jump in with possible solutions regarding how to bring the flesh back on the plane in plastic bags.

"Pack it up and put it in your luggage."

"Yeah. I think you could have up to 50 pounds."

I draw the line and stand up for myself – not a chance in hell am I going to pack fresh dead pig flesh in my carry-on suitcase.

Before leaving I go inside the trailer and, like Lady Macbeth, harshly wash my hands to get the blood off. And it just won't come off, so I keep washing and washing and washing.

As I put the keys into the door of my rental car, Cliff runs over.

"What do you think?"

"Pretty cool," I find myself mumbling at least twice.

Cliff has a gift. He presents it with a huge smile. I'm handed a plastic bag filled with blood and large bloody boar teeth.

"When you get back to San Francisco, just boil it in water. You could make a necklace out this."

I stare at it.

"That could do some damage," he adds.

(Pause) "Thanks," I say, already calculating the amount of miles I'll drive from this place before I toss it from my window.

I speed across the swampland countryside faster than Burt Reynolds in *Smokey and the Bandit.* The plastic bag filled with bloody pig teeth in addition to a bullet shell sits on my passenger seat, making me feel like a serial killer with trophies from his victim. Seems like if I got pulled over by a Florida State Trooper I could easily be framed for some murder I didn't commit. As I race down the rural Floridian roads, I promptly toss the evidence out my rental car window. *(Remember kids, it's not cool to litter).*

If You Must Go

Ron's Guide Service
Beck's Food & Tackle Store
Moore Haven, FL 33471
(863) 946-1742
www.ronsguideservice.com

BELLE GLADE FLORIDA

AIDS, Muck, and Crime!

POPULATION 14,906

TOWN MOTTO Gateway to the Everglades

***MY* TOWN MOTTO** Gateway to Catching AIDS

BELLE GLADE FUN FACT The US crime index is 330, while Belle Glade is at 1,285. The local paper arrest reports are a good solid page long. It's even longer than what you'd find in the San Francisco paper *(mostly domestic abuse and cocaine sales – but lots of them!).*

HEADLINES OF LOCAL PAPER *Virus Means No Horses Here.* It's a precautionary measure due to the current equine herpes outbreak – yes, there's a massive herpes outbreak amongst the horse population of Belle Glade.

GOOD NEWS ABOUT BELLE GLADE It's really great place for fishing and catching the "Big O," *(a wide-mouth bass, rather than a sexually transmitted disease).*

BELLE GLADE –AN IDYLLIC LOCALE FOR if you sell "muck," or like living in a mosquito-plagued hellhole.

LEVEL OF CREEPINESS 10 without a condom while sharing needles.

How can I cleanse my palate of this whole bloody- innards-pulling-wild-boar-killing debacle? I know, I'll have a lunch in the AIDS capital of America! Yes, this little vista, tucked away in Florida's hurricane country, Belle Glade, Florida has more cases of AIDS per capita than any other city in America! They even trumpet this fact on the Chamber of Commerce web page. Chances are if you have sex with someone in Belle Glade you will most likely die!

The drive to Belle Glade along the unremarkable Lake Okeechobee is, as the Dutch would say, spectacular, as I encounter a large orange sign that in most places would say "Men at Work." Instead it reads "State Prisoners Working." Giving a friendly wave, I pass a modern-day chain gang clad in prison jumpsuits doing roadside work, while *the-man-with-no-eyes* looks on from a nearby car.

I know I must be getting close, as a local Belle Glade radio station plays a commercial for a restaurant called, Dixie Fried Chicken. The ad stresses that the chicken is prepared in a new spotless, sanitized kitchen, which makes me ponder what were the conditions like before the need for this statement?

After stretch after stretch of dilapidated mobile home parks, boarded up buildings and rusty cars on blocks – like you hear about in those lame Jeff Foxworthy jokes – I approach my little tragic Shangri-La. Entering the city limits, a large sign doesn't read "Welcome to the AIDS Capital of America – We're #1!" Instead, it boasts, "Her Soil is Her Future." I guess the *"Her"* the sign refers to is the town of Belle Glade. (And chances are *"Her"* has AIDS.)

The name Belle Glade literally means Beautiful Glade. I crane my neck in hopes of a glimpse of these beautiful glades, but instead only see a child care building sign that has lost a few letters and now reads " HI D CARE," and another down the block that reads, *Muck For Sale.* Questions arise: Is muck-sales a cottage industry in Belle Glade? Is muck expensive or reasonably priced? Do people say, "Honey, we need more muck!"

Stressing health standards seems to be a theme running throughout the town – as if they want to prove America wrong. Manny's Meat Market boasts, "Seafood is Our Prescription to a Healthy Life." *(Not to mention contributing to the healthy factor: condom use.)*

All and all, I got to say, AIDS or no AIDS, Belle Glade is a glorious cesspool of a community.

Time for a little culture. The town's only statue *(530 South Main Street)* captures an entire family running and fleeing in terror; their hands twisted, outstretched over their heads. *(Are they running from the town's AIDS epidemic?)* Reading the plaque the statue commemorates the 1928 hurricane that almost wiped out the entire place the same year the city was incorporated *(more good news).* Adding to Belle Glade's joyous misery, this fleeing-in-terror-family icon pop up numerously throughout town – a constant reminder of both fleeing, terror, and, the desire thereof.

I venture inside the only museum in town, the Lawrence E. Wills Museum, located inside the town's tiny, almost empty, public library *(also at 530 South Main St.).*

"What do you want?!" the large woman behind the front desk demands with extreme suspicion. *(Maybe it's because I'm still dressed in my camouflage wild boar hunting costume?)*

"I'm here to see the museum!" I chime like a little kid about to enter Disneyland's Magic Kingdom.

"Get the key from her," she grunts barely, moving her mouth. Excellent. I've been to numerous museums *(the Smithsonian being one),* but this is the first museum I get to unlock by myself!

"What do you want," barks another large woman behind the book checkout counter.

I once again express my anticipated thrill of seeing the museum.

"She said I could get the key from you." I joyfully state.

"I can't give you the key but I can unlock for you."

We walk silently side-by-side. Once unlocked *(not by me)*, I get free reign of the darkened museum *(pretty much a tiny room inside the library)*.

Here's what I gather from the Belle Glade Museum:

- A hurricane happened here in 1928 and one of the families, fleeing in terror, would later be immortalized in statue-form.
- A bear trap was once used in Belle Glade. *(To curb the AIDS outbreak?)*
- In 1947 there was a parade in Belle Glade, where, at one point, citizens lined the streets.
- Mrs. Homer "Dolly" Hand was a bearer of the Olympic Torch on behalf of Belle Glade *(I think I see her in the library)*.

Museum tour over!

An old man stands outside the Town Star Gas Station holds a Scratch and Win game. He looks at the card with a glimmer of hope and starts fiercely scratching away. Judging by his reaction, he didn't win. Shaking his head, he wanders off down the road as the afternoon sun casts long shadows on the streets of Belle Glade.

If You Must Go

The Lawrence E. Wills Museum
530 South Main St.
Belle Glade, FL

Diseased Underbelly Salute To...

The Most Polluted City In America: Aberdeen, Maryland

Aberdeen is home of US Army Medical Research Institute of Chemical Defense, and is the most polluted place in America! Due to the years of production and testing of chemical weapons, this site is contaminated with the various agents and plagued with buried non-stockpile chemical weapons. Forty non-stockpile munitions, including sarin, mustard and phosgene were unearthed in 1994 and four of them were detonated in the open just a few miles from the local population and boaters on Chesapeake Bay. Thousands eat fish and crabs from the Bay, thus ingest toxins such as dioxin.

Go figure – Aberdeen has one of the highest rates of cancer in the country with a reported 193 deaths per 100,000.

CONGRATULATIONS ABERDEEN!
YOU'RE THE MOST POLLUTED PLACE IN AMERICA!

If You Must Go:

US Army Medical Research Institute of Chemical Defense, 3100 Ricketts Point Road, Aberdeen Proving Ground, MD 21010-5400 (410) 436-2230 ccc.apgea.army.mil

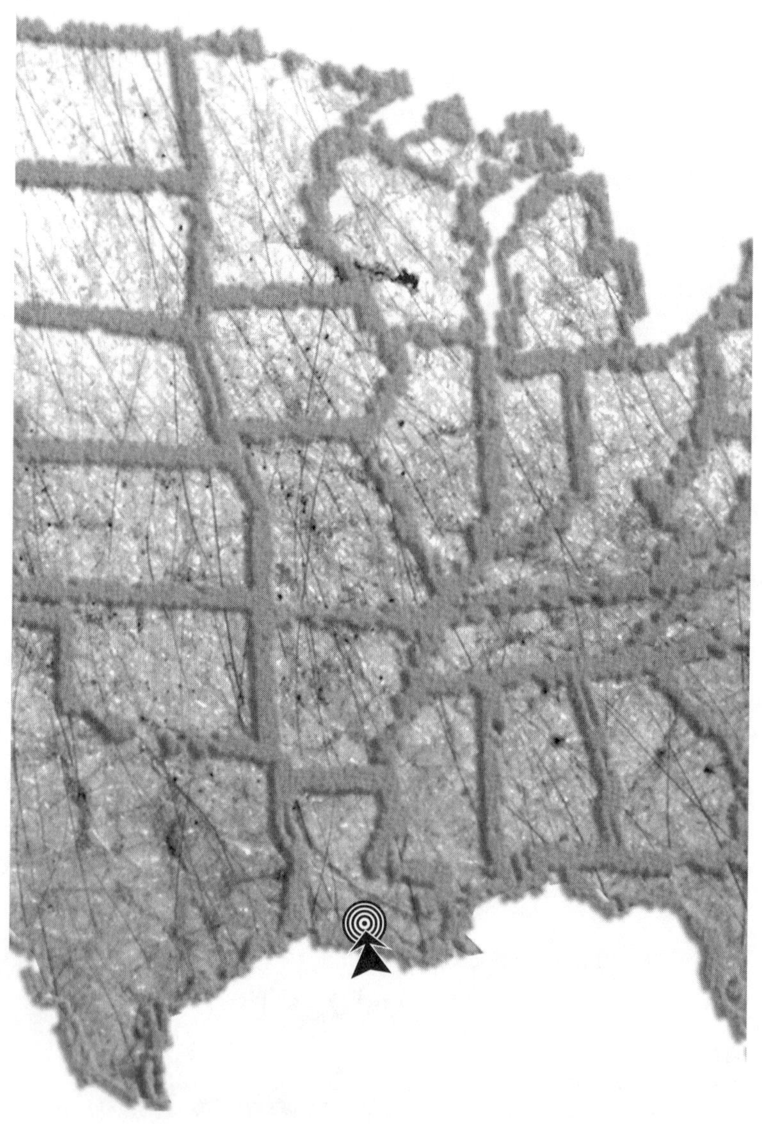

ST. MARTINVILLE, LOUISIANA

"It's Our Heritage, It's Our Tradition." Cockfighting in St. Martinville

TOWN MOTTO "Where Cajun Began"

MY MOTTO FOR TOWN "We Cut The Throat Of A Pig In Front Of A Crowd Of Children And Old People!"

POPULATION 6,989

WEIRD LOCAL SMELLS Segregation and Animal Cruelty.

ST. MARTINVILLE FUN FACT Willie Nelson has been arrested twice in St. Martinville!

EXTREMELY USELESS INFORMATION Tabasco sauce is made just outside St. Martinville. Currently, the contents of my refrigerator consist entirely of barbeque sauce, salad dressing and Tabasco sauce. Tabasco sauce is packaged in 22 languages and dialects (the bottle in my fridge is labeled in English). In Finland, Tabasco sauce is popular on pizza.

WAYS TO GET YOUR ASS KICKED Approach a large Louisiana man and shout, "The Confederate flag is racist, you big, stupid swamp-hillbilly!"

HISTORIC MILESTONES When the French Acadians were driven out of Canada in 1755, many settled on the muddy banks of the Bayou Teche in St. Martinville. Much later on, the French made a journey too far when they found Jerry Lewis funny.

CULTURAL HIGHLIGHT Cockfighting, Confederate flag-waving, sticking to your own race.

LEVEL OF CREEPINESS 10, if you're a rooster, or pig whose throat is about to be slit in front of a crowd of children and old people.

The horrors of humanity flock to New Orleans for Mardi Gras. It's amateur night packed with weekend warriors, girls gone wild, frat boys, and middle-aged housewives drunk on Long Island Ice Tea. But if you venture further into Louisiana, horrors of a different variety can be found.

Louisiana is the last State in America where cockfighting is legal. For those not in the know, cockfighting is a centuries-old blood sport where two gamecocks are placed in ring and fight it out to the death.

In Louisiana, chicken homicide is considered family-orientated entertainment. Game clubs are populated with good ol' boys, their rug rats, and first-cousin spouses, who cheer on the proceedings and place bets on the winning cock *(insert your own cock joke here).*

To ensure bloody carnage, the birds are outfitted with Freddy Kruger-style claw spikes, and sometimes injected with crystal meth to increase aggression *(if you've ever been the victim of meth-head panhandling, you know how that goes).*

"It's tradition. It's our heritage!" is always the rally cry when the majority of society wants to abolish something that is either:

A) Violent.

B) Racist.

C) Violent and Racist.

Sure it's their tradition, but there's also the sadistic kick these swamp hillbillies get seeing one animal tear another to pieces, and should perhaps go the way of such other great Southern traditions as slavery, black-face minstrel shows, and lynchings.

Fortunately, this might be cockfighting's last hurrah. The Senate has introduced a bill called SB10 to legally ban chicken-on-chicken action. That's why St. Martinville in Southwestern Louisiana is an ideal road trip destination for their annual Les Grande Boucherie Des Cajuns. Known as the birthplace of Cajun culture, St. Martinville is Louisiana's third oldest city, which boasts both gothic, Southern charm and a racially segregated population, not to mention family-friendly cockfighting (that phrase rolls right

off the tongue). Also, pot-smoking country hippy Willie Nelson has been arrested twice in St. Martinville *(coincidence?).*

During Mardi Gras, the black people in town have a wicked-ass parade with booty shaking dance lines and funky high school marching bands. The town's white folks, on the other hand, hold an event that features along with cockfights, the "Squeal like a Pig" competition.

Venturing from New Orleans on Highway 10, you cross a long bridge over swampland of which I've heard two tales:

1. Corrupt cops will slap a $100 per mile ticket if you go over the speed limit while crossing the bridge. And if you "don't look right," they have the tendency to seize your vehicle on the "probable" cause of wrongdoing.
2. Piss off one of the other locals and you'll find yourself tied to a tree in the middle of said swampland, where you'll never be found again – well, at least not by humans. The gators, however, will be happy to make your acquaintance.

All in all, I think it wise to adopt protective coloring for the cockfight. My cunning disguise includes a camouflage hunting hat, newly grown muttonchops, aviator shades, and a string of Confederate flag beads.

Parking my car in St. Martinville, I walk a couple of miles from town, with beer in hand *(drinking in public also is legal in Louisiana!)* to a locale down by the river. Coming to a park where Confederate flags wave high and proud, I know I'm in the right place when I come across a jeep in the parking lot with a dead chicken tied to the grill like a hood ornament.

"I saw you liked the chicken," a drunk guy at the gate remarks with thick Cajun accent. "We're going to have the chicken fights in a little while. *(Pause)* You can't beat a good cockfight!"

"That's what I say all the time," I reply.

"It's just a bunch of nice people having a good time," the drunken guy adds, while I note that black people seem to be excluded from this specific good time.

Making my way towards the revelry I pass people clad in overalls. A Cajun Zydeco band, the Who Dat Kings, features my favorite instrument – the washboard *(I have a theory that all it takes to be a washboard player is to own a washboard, and how many of us claim that?)* is on stage performing songs in French, while assorted couples dance real close. *(I know it's a Southern stereotype but a lot of those couples are not just missing teeth, they're missing front teeth.)* Though camouflage hunting hats seem to be very popular, I'm pegged as an outsider *(maybe it has to do with the airline tag on my camera bag?).*

"This beer is on me," says the beer guy handing me a Bud Light, then adds with a slightly sinister-tone adds, "Y'all be safe, you hear?" I hope that doesn't mean I'm going to end up tied to a tree waiting to be snack for alligators.

The locals' Cajun accents sound like unintelligible garble when mixed with good old-fashioned drunkenness. It sounds like Boomhauer on *King of the Hill* – I can barely make out what people say.

I HEAR:

"It's all about livin' off the land out here. I'm running a catfish farm… Catfish this big…" exclaims a local with a cigarette dangling out of the side of his mouth. *(I continually nod while his vernacular grows increasingly confusing.)*

I ALSO HEAR:

"They got sarsaparillas and big ol' jungle bunnies swimming across the bayou… He might have a sniper rifle on you right now. He might be up in that tree. He's a big old gorilla monkey…." *(More head nodding on my part.)*

"After we play this song, we'll be butchering a hog!" announces the guitar player from the zydeco band. If that isn't enough fun for people missing eye teeth, he adds, "Then we're going to have the cockfighting. So put your money down on your cock!" *(Optimum place to insert another cock joke.)*

Cock fight *and* pig slaughter – will the merriment never cease? I've gone my entire life without seeing a hog gutted, and now this is going to be the second one in less that a month. But no time to press. I now must – with sincerity – utter a phrase I've never said before in my whole entire life: "Do you know where the pig slaughtering is?"

After more drunk garbled talk, *("The sarsaparillas over yonder…")* I'm pointed in the right direction. Passing kids jumping in one of those inflatable moonwalk jumping-things, who shriek with childhood delight, I make my way over.

A huge, 257-pound pig lays in a cage with a "comical" sign hanging over it that says "Bacon for Sale." Little kids with big smiles run over to pet the soon-to-be-sliced animal.

"I don't want to eat that!" remarks a small boy wearing an Iron Maiden T-shirt. "They take its guts out." As I lean in, the in the small boy sticks a toy guy in my face, makes shooting noises then runs away. A little girl tenderly pets the Charlotte's Web-looking pig who will soon be cheered on by the crowd when its death becomes a spectator sport. A very cunning ploy giving the pig a false sense of security by letting little kids come over and play with it. With all this attention, the pig must think this is the best day ever! He must think he's been awarded something special that he can later brag about to all the other pigs back at the pen. *(Little does he know, he's just been sent off to the camps!)* Peering in closer, the look in the pig's eyes – laying there lethargically –reveals he knows he's going to get whacked!

"Grab it now!" somebody suddenly yells.

Moments later four large men wearing blue aprons are in the pen holding down the fighting pig – you know the one that was just being petted by children.

A crowd of about seventy people has gathered, mesmerized, with cameras poised.

The large, mustached leader, the largest of the crew, sits directly on top of the swine while the others hold its feet. "Put 'em up," he yells, giving the audience the perfect photo-op as he reaches for a knife. Immobilized, the pig bucks its head back and forth.

"Woo-hoo!" some man yells with thick Cajun accent. "You get dat boy!"

"I can't see it," says a small girl of about six.

Her mom holds her up. "Look," she says, bringing her tiny daughter in for a better view. The awestruck crowd of kids and old people looks on. People lean in real close, smiling with their cameras wanting to capture the moment of death. The still-fighting pig, kicking and squealing as hard as it can, fighting for its life, lets out a netherworld-squeal as its throat is slit. Almost slapstick, blood splatters everywhere spraying the crowd like they were in the front row of a Gallagher show and he just smashed a watermelon with a mallet *(except it's not a watermelon but pig's blood).*

Fun Activity: Wear a white tee-shirt in the front row of a pig-sticking and create your own unique splatter-spray design!

"Oh my god!" I hear myself uncontrollably uttering out loud, with the pig making one last elongated noise that sound like a baby hysterically crying. Blood starts flowing freely, like spilt grape juice, turning the green grass below crimson red. The large mustached man takes a hearty swig of his Bud Light as the pig lies dying, with pats on the back and hearty laughs filling the air along with the pungent smell of death.

"It's still wiggling," exclaims a little girl in – I kid you not – a pink frilly dress, standing near the "comical" Bacon for Sale cage, which is now caked with cartoon-red blood.

The four large men to carry away the 257-pound pig by each leg, laying it on a table near a pot of boiling water.

The enthusiastic man next to me cries, "He's going to shave him! He's going to gut him! That's when the shit hits the fan!"

The leader wipes blood off his hands, ready to get to work, to the sounds of knives being sharpened and buckets of water being poured on the hog. Kids watch in fascination, as the shit hits the fan, while others have arms folded with unmoved broad smiles. The leader works in a frenzy, slicing away, occasionally swilling Bud Light, sweat dripping on the hog, blood pouring out of the wound in his neck.

"Oh look!" a child proclaims.

A Cajun baby starts crying and a girl runs from the table when they cut the pig's head off with an old-school hacksaw. In the end the pig head lays alone on a table. Someone adds a cigarette in its mouth making it a popular photo-op.

Afterwards, with cans of Bud Light in hand, the mustachioed leader and one of his almost equally large assistants look exhausted.

"How did this compare to other hogs?" I ask.

"This one was hell. It didn't want to die," the leader stresses. "I don't know. It fought the hell out of ya," he confesses. "It just kept going. It didn't want to die. *(Pause.)* Hear me out!" *(Not wanting your throat slit as an enthusiastic crowd cheers is one great reason to, maybe, fight the hell out of ya.)*

"He's the man, he is the man!" his assistant adds with a finger point. "This is just what our ancestors did back in the day; we're doing it now – legally! But we just try to keep it going. That's what we do!"

"When I was a little boy. I use to get off the school bus and my dad would be waiting at the oak tree with a pot of water boiling," the leader explains. "That meant we had to go kill a hog." He then gestures with his hand what I assume represents hog-killing. "If we wanted to do anything, we had to do that first. That's how I learned."

For those still with an appetite, the pig's blood *(which is everywhere)* is mixed up to make boudin *(Cajun blood sausage).* While that is frying in a large pot, a girthy fella stirs a pot of cracklin'. "It's pretty much the belly of the pig," the assistant explains. "It's only fat." He pats his own paunchy stomach, adding, "Not good for you at all. But people love it!"

IT'S TIME FOR MORE PIG SQUEALING!

A pair of chubby men, who look as though lots of cracklin' is under their belts, stand on stage in front of the crowd.

"We got two contestants for the squeal like a pig contest," announces the guitarist from the zydeco band. "We got two squealers. *(Looking at the contestants, someone should inform them its squeal like a pig, not look like a pig.)* "If you can squeal like a pig, line up and we'll get going!"

Wow! You don't have to make these people squeal like a pig; they'll volunteer to do it themselves. A bunch of little kids, fresh from hog-throat-slitting, join the pair in the stage lineup. First up, one of the chubby men lets out a loud effort that sets back Southern stereotypes a good 50 years.

"Squeeeeeeeeal!"

"I think Kenny's calling all the pigs from across the bayou there. That's a good one!"

Though impressive, Kenny's contribution can't compare to the horrific, netherworld pig-squealing we just heard from the real thing at its moment of death.

In the end the squeal-like-a-pig-crown goes to 3-year-old Dane. "That's the youngest contestant ever!" the announcer declares. "You're our pig squealing champion at only three years old!"

I think he won because he's three years old and appealed to the crowd's pig-squealing-sensibilities. The three-year-old winner holds up the trophy, which is much bigger than him, and almost topples over.

FIGHT TIME

I got so caught up with pig squealing and throat-slitting I nearly missed the cockfights.

Excitement's in the air as people of all ages gather around the fenced individual pens where large, multi-colored roosters with long, sharp claws manically pace with frantic head gestures, occasionally letting out a crack-of-dawn cock-a-doodle-do cackle. Under the hot Louisiana sun, hardened men holding beer cans closely inspect the birds.

One of the gamecock trainers, a squat, pudgy fella with a fighting cock blazoned on his baseball cap, and adorned in a T-shirt that says, "My Hobby Is Cockfighting. Who Gives A Shit– What's Yours." *(Where do you get T-shirts that say things like this?! My T-shirt choice would say: KEEP YOUR LAWS OFF MY COCK!),* cradles his prize bird like a beloved pet, gently petting its feathers, while a guy wearing Confederate flag beads *(like mine),* passionately tells the trainer, "You got to keep this going. You got to keep the gloves on and keep this in the State!"

The wearer of the Confederate flag beads *(like mine)* – a cockfight fan since the age three – provides a little background on the blood sport that started centuries back. "It was just something do to pass the time. You know, people betting on two chickens fighting. That's what it comes down to. It's just a pastime." He elaborates on the different variations of the pastime: "They can fight them with razors. That's when they put razors on the chickens *(one-inch spurs).* Then they got something called short-knife where they can puncture 'em and hurt 'em, but it don't kill 'em. The long knife *(one and a quarter inch)* will actually kill the chicken!"

I look over at the pudgy trainer, who is putting a yellow apparatus around the leg of the rooster. "They put the covers over the gaffs *(boxing gloves over legs in cockfighting-speak)* of the chickens so they don't stab the other chicken," he says, explaining today we're going to see family-friendly cockfighting *(again, rolls nicely off the tongue),* where the roosters won't kill each other. No... they'll simply torture one another. "There's nothing else you can do with these chickens because they are born and bred to fight."

For true blood-spurting cockfighting, he recommends the Sunset Recreation Club; it's located right down the road, one of Louisiana's largest cockfighting venues with fights year round, amassing crowds of up to 1,000.

"It's big stuff," he declares. "Depending on how many entrants they have, they'll start on Friday and run around the clock." Bets on the big fights bring in up to $20-30k. "Somy chickens are worth $12k. It's like a racehorse. With a good breed you get a bunch of champions."

From his car, the pudgy cockfighter gets his last rooster, a large, menacing bird with yellowish white feathers, out of a cage.

"Is he a winner?" I ask pointing to his cock *(insert joke here).*

"Oh yeah, many of times."

(Holds up bird on the palm of his hand.) "This cock right here has fought 11 times and 11 times he wins."

"So he's a killer!" I state.

Giving me a good look, he gets confrontational, "First let me ask you. Are you for cockfighting or against it?" *(He pegs me for "not from around these parts.")*

Embarrassingly, I scratch my muttonchops, hoping he doesn't sick his bird on me. Quickly, I work through my brain which answer will get him to open up. *(Think brain, think.)* "For it!" I blurt with confidence, and then point, again, at his cock. "What's its name?"

"He doesn't have a name."

"How come?"

"We don't name 'em."

"Why's that?"

"I name some of them." He shares a story, "I got a daughter that's three months old. I got a chicken named after her. Right. Some of them I do name. *(The rooster lets out a cackle and tries to escape).* "Think about it now," he says getting philosophical. "You eat chicken at Popeye's?"

"Love it," I reply, fueling his momentum. "They also have some killer red beans and rice."

"You love it right. *(Holds up bird and smiles proudly.)* That chicken got 45 days to live. A gamecock has two years to live before he has a chance to fight for his life. Right? Think about it. Huh? *(Proud.)* He's got a 50/50 chance in two years to fight for his life." *(Twisted logic, yes, but this is not about me, it's about him.)* "These birds get better taken care of than a human being!" *(The bird jumps out his arms.)* "You got a girlfriend? If he goes and talks to your girlfriend would you be mad?" he inquires, then points to a man who looks like Larry the Cable Guy. "Would you want to fight him?"

"It depends on my relationship with my girlfriend," I reply. "And our level of trust." *(Not the answer he was looking for, though great insight into how little one has to do to get beaten up around here.)*

"Rooster is just like a human being. They are going to fight over a female. This rooster right here is going back to breed. He is going back to his girlfriend. *(Pause.)* Think about it now. You're protecting your land. Wouldn't you fight for your land?"

"Yeah, sure," I say, wondering if a one-bedroom apartment counts, and how I'd feel about a crowd getting off on my fight to death for it, and my couch for instance.

"That's what a rooster is doing. He's fighting for his territory." *(Pauses to make point.)* "A lot of people don't realize what cockfighting is all about. George Washington fought chickens. Not just him, but other presidents of the United States. You got senators, you got governors in each and every state that fought chickens *(chicken jumps out of his arms)*.

"Right!" I contribute.

Growing tired of our conversation, the pudgy trainer starts warming up his fighting bird, setting it on the ground, holding its tail, and letting it lunge forward. A large crowd, mostly large good ole boys in baseball caps, has gathered around the fighting pen. Little kids grip the fence, pressing their noses against it for a better look. Some are on their father's shoulders, holding yellow balloons.

"They're just warming up," the man in the Confederate beads (like mine) remarks. "Without the gloves, they'll kill each other!"

The two trainers hold their cocks (insert own joke here) and have the two birds touch beaks (you can say, we see two cocks touching) throwing their heads together to rile them up, making them pissed off – known as pitting the chickens against each other *(in cockfighting-talk)* – with loud flapping from their wings. The roosters, momentarily pulled apart, are set down and let loose.

"Oh, it's going to get real now!" someone yells out from across the pen with expected excitement. "Here we go!"

They spring at each other jumping up, making contact mid-air, with flapping wings sounding like a helicopter blade upon contact. A distressed woman abruptly walks away, but the rest of the crowd cheers and screams at the fighting bird melee.

EXAMPLES OF THINGS YELLED:

"Damn, look at those feathers fly!"

"He's got some spurs on, watch him!"

"Not one dead yet!" *(Screamed with disappointment.)*

These birds want to kill each other, demonstrated by their feathers standing up like a peacock's. I try not to look horrified, because when I do, people come up to me and ask why, so I keep a fixed smile on my face, while zydeco music blares from beyond, and cock-a-doodle-dooing erupts from birds in their separate pens. Multi-colored feather fly everywhere.

The yellowish-feathered rooster flies again through the air, jumping over its opponent's head like a bird version of Jet Li. The 11-time-killer then pounces on top of the other bird instigating a fowl-body slam, rendering it helpless, immobilized on the ground, twisting its opponent's body in unnatural positions.

"Uh-oh!" shouts a little girl. "He's going to peck him to death. The poor thing! He's tearing him up!"

"If they were fighting with knives blood would be flying all over," a chubby girl in shorts, wiser than her pre-teen years, shares with her friend.

Yes, the rooster with the yellowish feathers now has the other bird on its back and begins pecking him in the face. The crowd goes wild with sadistic excited pleasure. The bird keeps pecking the helpless creature's face-area. Cheers erupt as the momentum of the feverish pecking increases.

"Ah, he don't want anymore," remarks the chubby girl. "That white one's murdering him!"

Overhead the Confederate flag waves boldly, while the pudgy trainer looks on with pride.

Feeling the other bird has been sufficiently tortured, he pulls his bird off, clearly victorious, safe in the knowledge that the other bird would be a Popeye's chicken McNugget platter if they were fighting with knives. To think that fun booty shaking is going on in the other part of St. Martinville, while the town's white people indulge in the joys of cockfighting and animal throat-slitting.

When he's good and drunk, I catch up with the pudgy trainer, who's now putting his finger between the bird's beaks.

"What are you getting out of its mouth?" I ask.

"Feathers and dirt." He looks down at the bird and frowns. "He broke his beak," noting that the bird's intense pecking of deadly intent ended with self-inflicted beak-damage.

(Pets his bird.) "If I didn't have a real job and just trained roosters I'd spend all day on them. If the world wasn't about money, it would be about game fowl. *(His bird tries to escape.)* "If somebody came and gave me $1,000 I wouldn't even take it. These birds are my life."

"How do you feel if your prize bird gets killed or something?"

(Holds up bird.) "This rooster right here is like a pet. I'd feel sad like if a pet got killed." *(Pats the bird then looks down at it with seriousness).* After a pause, "Hey do you want to hold him?"

"No!"

"You can hold him on your arm like this," he says, demonstrating. "It's not going to peck or nothing."

"It kinda scares me."

Moments later, I now have the rooster on my arm. The bird flaps, raising its bright Halloween orange and red tail feathers like a puffer fish.

"My great grandfather did this when he was a young boy. My grandfather did this for over 60 years, which he passed on to me. I'm 27 years old and I've been doing this for 27 years *(he smiles, pausing between statements).* "My first memory was going to a rooster fight and my grandfather named a rooster after me. *(Proud.)* That rooster was named after me and he won many a derbies. That's all the rooster fights I've ever seen and that was with a rooster that was named after me." *(I wonder how he felt when his namesake eventually got pecked/clawed to death?)* "If they make it illegal it's still going to go on. Dog fighting, they made it illegal, right. It still goes on. *(He also raises pit bulls).* Like I said I have a three-month-old daughter. Hopefully when she gets old enough to see stuff like this, it's still around, you know." *(Big smile)* "I'm in love with game fowl. 27 years. Passed on to me from my great grandfather!"

As the day drags, Bud Light cans litter the landscape while drunk Cajuns stumble to-and-fro; all to the beat of zydeco. Suddenly a drunk blond woman attaches herself to me by grabbing my waist and not letting go. She's about 25 and a drunk mom of four, wanting to drive me to a bar in town. After I politely decline, she accuses me of "Playing for the Pink Team." *(I think people around here get married at around 19, thus these very flirty girls must have jealous spouses close by ready to attack me like a angry gamecock in a pen.)* I talk her less-drunk friend *(also a mom of four)* to drive her car instead. *(Drunk moms of four don't end up tying you to trees in swamps, do they?!)*

Things get awkward when the drunken-mom-of-four keeps massaging my leg while at the same time disciplining her kids over her cell phone. I sure hope her husband isn't the town's sheriff!

If You Must Go:

La Grand Boucherie
Magnolia Park
N. Main St.
St. Martinville, LA
February, Sunday before Mardi Gras
(337) 394-9426

At Robert's Town Tavern the tiny bar is packed with elbow-to-elbow drunken revelry.

I ask the drunken-mom-of-four about the noticeable racial segregation. "How come there aren't any black people in here?"

"We just don't mix," she casually responds.

"So they never come into this bar?"

"There ain't nothing for them here!"

I end up dancing with old Cajun ladies to yet another zydeco band *(is it me or do all zydeco bands sort of sound alike).* A large, drunken blond woman starts dirty dancing with me. She's like the drunkest person in the bar.

"What do you do here in St. Martinville?" I ask, trying to get out of her grasp by boring her with small talk.

"I'm the deputy sheriff," she slurs with the language of drunk, gyrating away. She then makes a few sexual innuendos involving me being handcuffed. Yikes! I'm dirty dancing with a drunk, off-duty deputy sheriff of a small town in Louisiana! She's the living embodiment of Officer Clemmie on *Reno 911 (only larger).*

"I heard the cops down here are corrupt," I blurt, feeling she's warmed up to me.

"Yeah, me and another guy are the only ones who aren't," she replies with a drunk smile and a nod of her head, then goes back to dirty dancing.

If You Must Go:

Robert's Town Tavern
402 South Main St.
St. Martinville, LA (419)586-6891

WHERE TO STAY: CYPRESS TREE INN

This budget motel is conveniently located right next to the Lafayette Airport—literally. Only a fence separates the motel from the tarmac. All you'd have to do is climb over, and there you are – you know, the airport where the planes land. *(Surprisingly, not a single cypress tree to be found on the premises of the establishment.)* Though only about three people are staying at the motel, it seems, for some reason, twenty people are working here in order to renovate the place to recreate a glory day that never was.

I think I could have talked the toothless woman *(I know, another Southern stereotype, but it's true)* working the front desk down from $60 to $10 a night and she would have gone for it, but I'm much too tired to barter *(I think I got the "You're not from around here" price.)*

Fun Activity: Count the Stains in you Hotel Room!

1. The top of air conditioner has a residue that looks like hardened spit.
2. Chair has black blotches on the fabric.
3. Bed sheets have assorted darkened spots.
4. Bathroom wall has peeled wallpaper, with yellow stains as well.
5. Carpeting has hand-sized blotches.
6. The bathtub is discolored with hairs on the tile wall.
7. Dresser looks like beer was spilled on it and it stained the wood.
8. The hangers are rusted.
9. Mattress looks like something the color of coffee stained it.
10. Box Springs have various shades of yellow stains.
11. When you pull the case of the pillow, it looks like it was dipped in an oil spill.

And don't get me started about motel bedspreads. I once saw one of those A&E true crime documentaries, involving a murder that took place in a motel. A forensic scientist came in and did a test of the bedspread, and said he found 57 different semen samples, and here's the kicker, none of them matched the victim. Eeeeeeeeeeeuuuuw! Throwing the bed spread off the bed is the first thing I always do when I check into a motel. I don't even want to imagine what a forensic scientist would find in this vessel of filth known as the Cypress Tree Inn.

In the morning, after checking out I stand in front of the motel and snap a few photos of the Cypress Tree Inn motel sign *(so I'll remember this shithole forever).*

A large guy with a mullet, wearing a wife-beater, comes over to my car and taps on my window. He's frowning.

"I see you taking pictures. Is there a problem?" he says with thick, Southern accent, not so much as a question, but more like interrogation where I better have a damn good reason for doing such things.

I expressed to the large, mulletted man that I just stayed at his fine lodging establishment and want to remember it forever.

"How was everything, then?"

"It was just great!" I hear myself saying, not knowing why. "Just great!"

You know a place is a shithole if someone taking pictures of the motel's sign makes the establishment's owner paranoid that somehow the photos will be turned over to the Board of Health.

If You Must Go:

Cypress Tree Inn
2503 SE Evangeline Thruway
Lafayette, LA (337) 234-2000
Rooms start at $56.95, plus tax.

Road Trip Lodging Quick Tip...

Play Amateur Forensic Scientist At Budget Motels!

Budget motels can be both money-saving and educational! Why not use the opportunity to play amateur forensic scientist! That's right, you can have your very own CSI Miami, right there in your motel room right off the Interstate!

THINGS NEEDED:

- Tweezers!
- A Magnifying Glass!
- A Black Light!
- A keen sense of wonderment!

Like a super-sleuth, or regular self-imposed Hardy Boy's mystery, start snooping around your room for hidden clues of past occupants, then make logical deductions.

EXAMPLE:

> "Judging by the blood stains on the towels and the curly red hairs left on the pillow, the last occupants of this room were... Vegans!"

With your black light, have a little fun with the bedspread and discover what kind of shapes you can make out of the stains left behind. See if you find Abe Lincoln or the State of Delaware!

CONGRATULATIONS!
YOU NOW READY TO BE A MOTEL FORENSIC SCIENTIST!

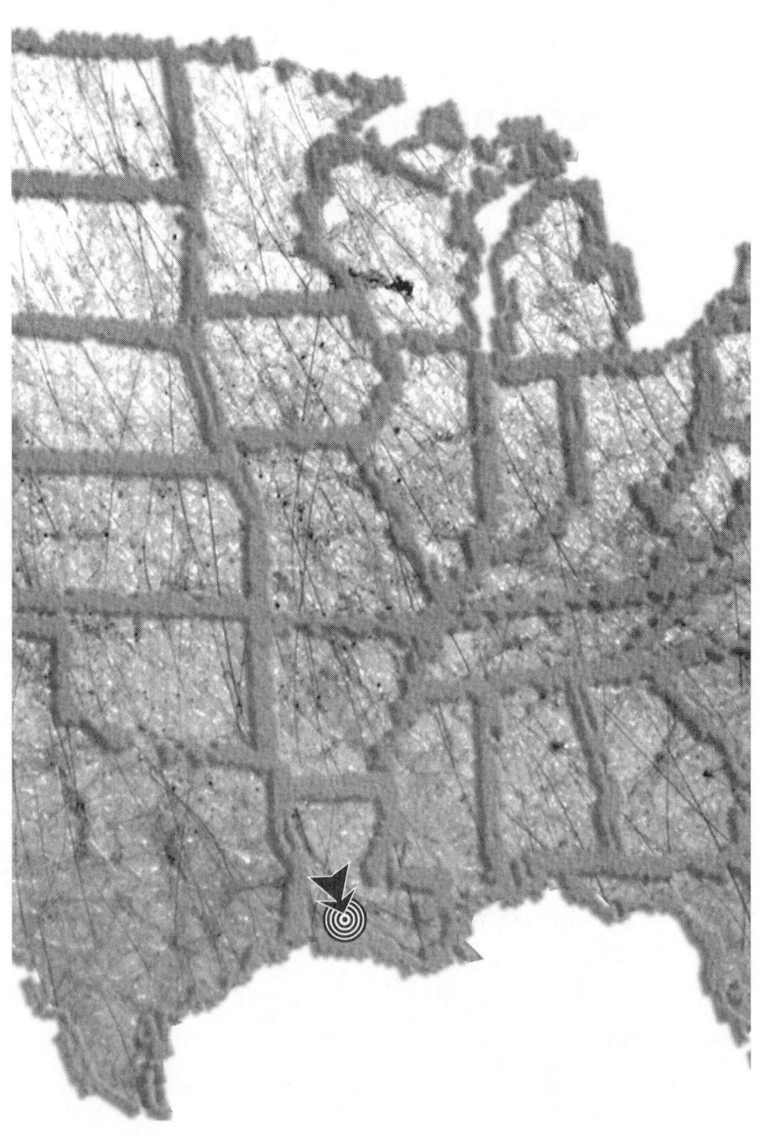

EUNICE, LOUISIANA

Fun Before Death

POPULATION 11,499

TOWN MOTTO "The Prairie Cajun Capital of Louisiana!"

MY MOTTO FOR TOWN "Falls-off-of-a-Mardi-Gras-Float-Resulting-in-Death Capital of Louisiana!"

FUN FACT In May 2000, a chemical freight train derailed in Eunice, spilling numerous hazardous chemicals and causing about 15 tank cars to explode and burn; approximately 3,500 residents of the town were evacuated for five days. Whoops!

TOWN HISTORY Eunice was founded in 1893 when C.C. Dunson drove a stake into the ground and said "On this spot, I will build a town and name it for my wife Eunice." If his wife had been named Nancy, then this would be a different town altogether.

EXTREMELY USELESS INFORMATION Eunice is the kind of Southern town where matronly women working at cafes call you "Babe," and the local police scare the living shit of you.

EUNICE HISTORIC CULTURAL HIGHLIGHT Locals speak of the '50s when the white folks in town would stand by the railroad tracks and do what they called The N——r Twist. If any black people would try cross the tracks, they would shoot them! Of course they got away with it because who was going to arrest them?

EUNICE IS AN IDYLLIC LOCALE FOR Corrupt cops, people who like screaming the N-word in public, those who have the desire to play the washboard as a musical instrument.

A man in St. Martinville said if I came to Eunice, I'd experience people riding in on horses with hoods on their heads. Am I being set up to witness a Klan rally? He assured me its part of a traditional Cajun Mardi Gras celebration. *(I make sure to double-check this information.)* Driving I-10 from Lafayette, passing a billboard with a man's face and the words, "I Was Murdered Here," and a stand selling both fresh shrimp and children's bikes, I trek towards Eunice. Veering off on Highway 13, where Spanish Moss drips from the trees like, say, Spanish-Moss-colored Cheez Whiz and the crawfish fields are filled with an abundance of traps *(messing with someone's crawdaddy trap will quickly get you tied to a tree in the swamp).*

Turning right at a Pawn Shop where a rotund fella in wife-beater walks out counting a handful of bills, I reach the edge of town and suddenly there's scores of drunk people on horses. Yes, literally hundreds and hundreds of costumed horseback riders. For the most part they *do* look like the KKK (if the Klan wore a multi-colored scheme created by Ringling Brothers). Almost the entire town of Eunice seems shit-faced—and it's not even noon!

Under the gray sky, thrown-together floats pulled by pickups through farm roads, carry drunken Eunice citizens. A green Port-a-Potty is the main fixture of the party-vessel *(like a crazy-astronaut-lady-speeding-across-Florida, there's no time to stop and let people pee)*. Revelers throw beads in my direction, looking like they're about to fall off the sides of the floats.

"They usually have 10 deaths during the parade," a local woman watching the festivities shares with a big smile.

"What?!"

"I almost got ran over last year by the trailer," she adds like it's the most normal thing in the world.

Suddenly, the sound of sirens permeates the small Louisiana town. Moments later an ambulance zooms by.

"See!" the woman proclaims, almost with pride. "Someone just got ran over!"

What? Already?! *(A 4-wheeler flipped on top of a Mardi Gras reveler.)* But the party loses no momentum. Drunk guys now stand on top of their horses see how long they can do such. More wasted people in colorful Klan outfits clop by with beers in hand. One fella' out-dresses the Klan-gang; he wears blackface and fake afro *(is that still popular in these parts?!)*. Others hang dead chickens wrapped in Mardi Gras beads from their neck.

"Do you want to see me eat a chicken?" a drunken lady in witch outfit asks, with a live chicken in her arms.

(Pause.) "Ok." I respond.

She then puts the bird's head into her mouth.

"Leave that poor chicken alone!" shouts her friend, who then lets the fowl drink from his can of beer.

Spotted, again, as a complete outsider (it's my lack of colorful Klan-attire), I'm invited to ride on a float by someone whose dad is a bigwig in town. Pulling up a bale of hay, people now jump from floats to ride on horses.

"I grew up a mile down the road that way," shares a trashed man in a Grand Wizard hat, lifting his yellow, veiled mask to drink his beer. And then, "Hey! It's a damn n—— standing over there.

That's a damn n——!" he starts yelling, spotting a black person in the crowd, not in a malicious way, but in the same manner like he just saw a living carnation of the Easter bunny. "This is white shit, no n———." He then takes another sip of his beer and stumbles backwards into the Port-a-Potty. "Why aren't you drinking?" he asks me."

"The cops scare the shit out of me," I respond, needing to keep my wits about me here in swampland.

"For good reason. They will literally beat the shit out of ya. They will beat you so hard that the shit will literally be running out of ya!" (Why isn't it difficult to image police doing that to him?)

"Chicken run!" a man on a horse suddenly declares. He holds a chicken over his head. A dozen or so drunk men jump off floats and join him in an open field.

"Stay here until I say go," he commands. Then, "Y'all ready?"

Taking off trotting, he then tosses the chicken overhand in the air. The bird lets out a loud squawk. The large men run after it, with bells and beads loudly jangling. They dive for the fleeing bird. Only one emerges victorious, bird-in-hand!

"It's my first time!" declares the winner; a chubby guy in a patriotic red, white, and blue Mardi Grad costume. Holding up the bird, he plants a kiss on its beak. "I got this baby!"

As the afternoon wears on, drunk people start falling off horses with more frequency. More ambulance sirens go off. More dead chickens swing from people's necks. A cop holding a beer whizzes by on 4-wheeler.

"Do you know those people who live in those houses?" says the guy who was spouting the N-word earlier, pointing to two guys who just jumped into a sewage ditch. "That's their shit-ditch," he astutely remarks. I now see why Britney Spears went to rehab—she's from this stock of people.

The parade concludes down the main street of Eunice. Thousands of people with arms outstretched stand behind police barricades, screaming, "Throw dem beads! Throw dem beads!"

making me feel like the Beatles or the first man who landed on the moon. *(They're just beads, get over it!)*

"Throw dem beads! Throw dem beads!"

The key is to throw beads at waving people you like, or throw at people not looking, that you don't like.

"Throw dem beads! Throw dem beads!"

In the end, I'm not sure if the day was considered a winning season; the total casualty rate failed to top last year.

"I heard at least 6 people got ran over," I remark to a man who directs me to where I parked my rental car.

"At least," he replies, sharing that one person got their head run over. In a more reflective moment he replies, "That ain't bad!"

EUNICE NIGHTLIFE

Upon arriving at the Dugout Bar – a dark dive of a place in downtown Eunice – I'm greeted by a drunk good-old-boy who aggressively wants to buy me a shot, utilizing that drunk friendliness that could somehow turn ugly at the drop of a hat.

"Last night 12 people got arrested here," a woman at the bar shares about the Dugout.

"Why?" I ask.

"Cuz the cops didn't like the way they looked!"

Quickly looking in the mirror, I try to determine if the way I look *(big muttonchops, military hat)* would be liked by local Eunice, Louisiana police *(who will literally beat the hell out of ya.)* I imagine the arrest scenario:

"I don't like the way you look, boy!"

"What?"

"Are you eye-balling me, boy?"

"Excuse me?"

"Put your hands behind your head, NOW!"

The drunk good-old-boy-who-insists-I-do-a-shot staggers backwards, then falls into the cop manning the door knocking over his table. The cop just laughs *(apparently he has no problem with how the drunk guy looks).*

"He knows his daddy," the woman at the bar explains, pointing at the large local cop.

"In the '50's, the white folks in town would stand by the tracks do what they call 'The N—— Twist,'" she further enlightens about Eunice law enforcement. "If black people would cross the tracks into the white part of town, they would shoot them!"

"Wouldn't they get arrested for that?" I naïvely ask.

"Who was going to arrest them?" she states

Another woman tries to aggressively flirt with every man in the bar. Maybe it has something to do with courting in this Catholic, Southern town. I'm told, "On her fourth date she got pregnant. She came home to find her parents, their priest and her boyfriend. They married them on the spot." *(Pause)* "The marriage didn't really work out," she says. I note the woman gyrates on yet another cowboy.

"I heard if people around here don't like you, they will tie you to a tree and leave you in the middle of the swamp," I ask to confirm this fabled scenario.

"Not only will they tie you to the trees," the woman confirms, "But they'll come back and take pictures!"

The trashed married woman staggers over to my area. She makes an enticing offer that could only happen in Eunice, Louisiana: "We could go back to my daddy's farm and ride 4-wheelers in the mud and jump in the pond!"

Enticing, but I decline *(I don't want the picture-taking-while-tied-up-in-the-swamp scenario).*

The woman at the bar ends up giving me a lift back to my shithole lodging at the Eunice Inn. I notice something in her back seat.

"What's in the trunk?" I question.

"Stuff," she quickly replies.

"What kind of stuff?" I press.

"Stuff from Germany. From the War."

"Really? What kind of war stuff from Germany?!"

"Nazi paraphernalia. *(Yikes!)* It's historical," she legitimizes. "My grandfather was a collector."

"You can let me off here" I abruptly blurt. "I'm fine walking the rest of the way."

If You Must Go:
Dugout 206 S 2nd St. Eunice, LA 70535 (337) 546-0510
Eunice Inn 1151 E Laurel Ave. Eunice, LA 70535 (337) 457-4274

DINING IN EUNICE

Mama's Fried Chicken has the restaurant catchphrase, "Eat at Mama's!" *(I think I see Mama, right there in the kitchen.)* This hole-in-the-wall diner serves up some great gumbo. But what's really weird about this tiny Louisiana eatery is a small wooden booth in the corner, only able to fit roughly one person, designated for playing gambling devices *(to keep video poker discreetly out of view by popping into the wooden box).*

A sign on the swinging doors reads, "If you or someone you know has a gambling problem call..." *(One sign of a gambling problem might be gambling inside a wooden booth at Mama's Fried Chicken.)* Right below, another sign that reads, "ATTENTION Do **Not** leave children unattended while playing Gaming Devices!" You know this scenario has happened numerous times before. *("Daddy, please come out of the booth! I want to go home! It's Christmas!")*

If You Must Go:
Mamas Fried Chicken Of Eunice Inc. 1640 W Laurel Ave. Eunice, LA 70535-4018 (337) 457-9978

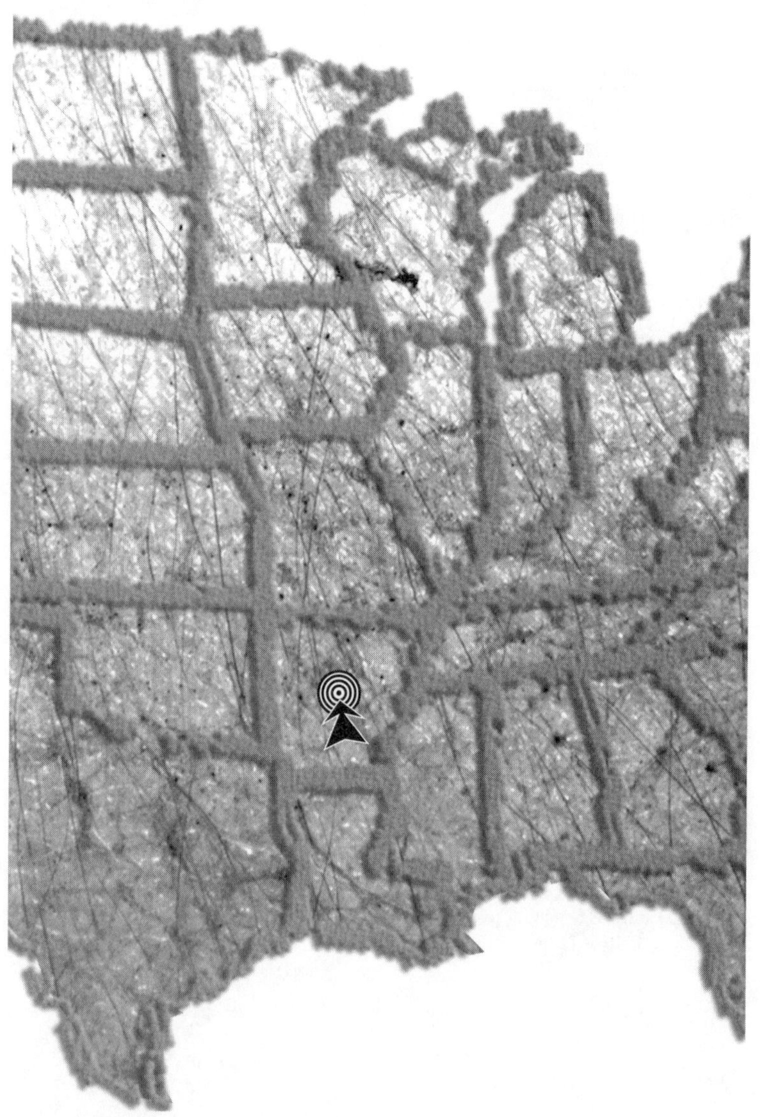

ARKANSAS

The Throwing Crap Out On Your Lawn State

STATE MOTTO The People Rule, *or* The Natural State

***MY* STATE MOTTO** The Flea Market State, *or* The Jesus is Very Popular With Us State *or* The We Live in the Woods and Have Our Own Country State

Arkansas {ahr'-kuhn-saw} was the 25th state, admitted to the United States in 1836. The name Arkansas is derived from a Quapaw Indian word meaning, "Downstream People," *not* the commonly mistaken "Down-Syndrome People."

PERCENTAGE OF ARKANSAS POPULATION THAT'S CHRISTIAN 86%

PERCENTAGE OF ARKANSAS POPULATION THAT'S LISTED AS "OTHER RELIGIONS" 1%

FAMOUS PEOPLE FROM ARKANSAS Bill Clinton, Chelsea Clinton, plus over 7 others!

NUMBER OF DRY COUNTIES IN ARKANSAS 42 counties in Arkansas forbid the sale of alcoholic beverages! Well sodomize me with the festering stump of a crusty sailor with scurvy!

Crossing the Louisiana border into Arkansas, you go from swamp hillbillies to backwoods hillbillies. The billboards start reading things like "Jesus is Real," followed by "Jesus and Mary Loved Me," followed by "People Let You Down/God Doesn't," followed by "Jesus Died for Your Sins," and of course, "He Said, She Said, God Said!" *(What does that even mean?!)* I'm starting to spot a reoccurring Arkansas motif. I've never seen so many churches in all my life. The creepiest – such as in a town infested with trailer homes and reeks of moonshine and incest – is when there's simply a sloppily, hand-painted sign that reads "Jesus My Lord," leading to a dirt road into the woods. Now I see why Larry the Cable Guy is the #1 comedian in America as I pass service stations with tons of hubcaps lying around everywhere, cars on blocks, and a little shack in the woods with a big cross and American flag in the front yard – and I hope neither of them are going to be burned!

If you tune into either the AM or FM you'll get all Jesus radio – all the time!

The radio shows have managed to sign legions of talk show hosts sincerely convinced that man and dinosaurs walked on the planet AT THE SAME TIME *(merely a few thousand years ago)*! No, seriously!

One Christian radio show spews on that the reason archeologists find dinosaur bones is because the dinosaurs died during flood made famous in that *historical* Noah's Ark escapade. Well fuck me sideways! At the Creationism Museum in Kentucky they say they'll prove this point by showing anamatronic dinosaurs walking alongside anamatroic men. *(I hope the men took advantage of this by riding atop of the dinosaurs like giant ponies.)*

"It's the *account* of Noah's Ark, not the *story* of Noah's Ark," the radio host clarifies, being if it's refered to as a *story*, then it implies that Noah's Ark – you know, where two of every animal from around the globe were put onto one handmade boat – is a fable *(which it is)*, and not a historical event *(which it isn't)*. Which begs the question, why weren't two dinosaurs invited by Noah for that ark-cruise?

The answer: dinosaurs were sinners!

If You Must Go:

Creationism Museum
2800 Bullittsburg Church Rd.
Petersburg, KY 41080
(888) 582-4253

"In order to know the truth, you got to look at who was there; Scientists or God!" reasons the radio host.

Yes, I have officially entered America's Bible Belt!

To avoid any unnecessary police harassment, I've slapped one of those Jesus fish-things and a *Support Our Troops* magnet on my rental car.

The Arkansas State motto is The Natural State. I think they should change it to The Flea Market State. Flea markets seem to be most residents' main source of income. What people do is put all the shit in their house out on their front lawn and porch. Then they hang up a large sign that says "Flea Market." Yes, one man's crap is another man's treasure.

Valero Supershop (*next to the CB Shop),* in Conway Arkansas has a sign outside that reads, "Pray for Diana." *(Wow, these people still haven't gotten over the Lady Di tragedy.)* Browsing amongst their selection of beef jerky, the store also sells baseball hats that say philosophical things like: *DON'T BOTHER ME WHILE I'M DRINKING UNLESS YOU'RE BUYING!* which sits directly next to hats with born-again Jesus sayings, begging the question; does one hat lead to the other? It's kind of the whole dichotomy of the Bible Belt; what is hidden beneath the surface. For example, the graffiti in the bathroom stall reads: *GO JESUS! JESUS LOVES EVERYONE THAT'S COOL.* That's right below graffiti reading *PUT YOUR LIPS ON MY WARM COCK!* Which came first?! I end up buying a bag of Brims packaged cracklin' *(in order to compare it to the fresh variety I had back in St. Martinville).* The cracklin' has a Bible verse written on the bag – a different Bible verse on each one – cuz the Lord wants you to eat packaged fried pig fat *(that's how Jesus got those washboard abs).*

If You Must Go:

Valero Super Shop
Hwy. 64 & I-40
Conway, AK

Road Trip Quick Tip...

Ways To Stay Awake While Driving:

Perhaps your supply of energy drinks has run-eth dry, and yet, you have a good 600 miles to drive before turning in for the night. Here are a few tips on how to stay awake.

Have a near fatal car crash!
Yes, almost careening into a freeway underpass will not only jolt you awake, but also you won't be able to sleep for days afterwards

Think of all the people who might bury you in a shallow grave if you pull over to sleep at the desolate rest area!
Yes, this list will include: drifters, disgruntled truckers up for days on amphetamines, hooker serial killers, and Canadians.

Wear very constricting Victorian underwear!
The more uncomfortable and binding the better!

Chimps Wearing People Clothes!
Pull out a funny picture of a chimp wearing people clothes, especially if the chimp is in the middle of doing a person activity such as answering the phone while wearing a business suit, or cooking while wearing a chef outfit. This will make you laugh so hard, you wont even have time to think about falling asleep.

CONGRATULATIONS!
YOU NOW KNOW HOW TO STAY AWAKE WHILE DRIVING!

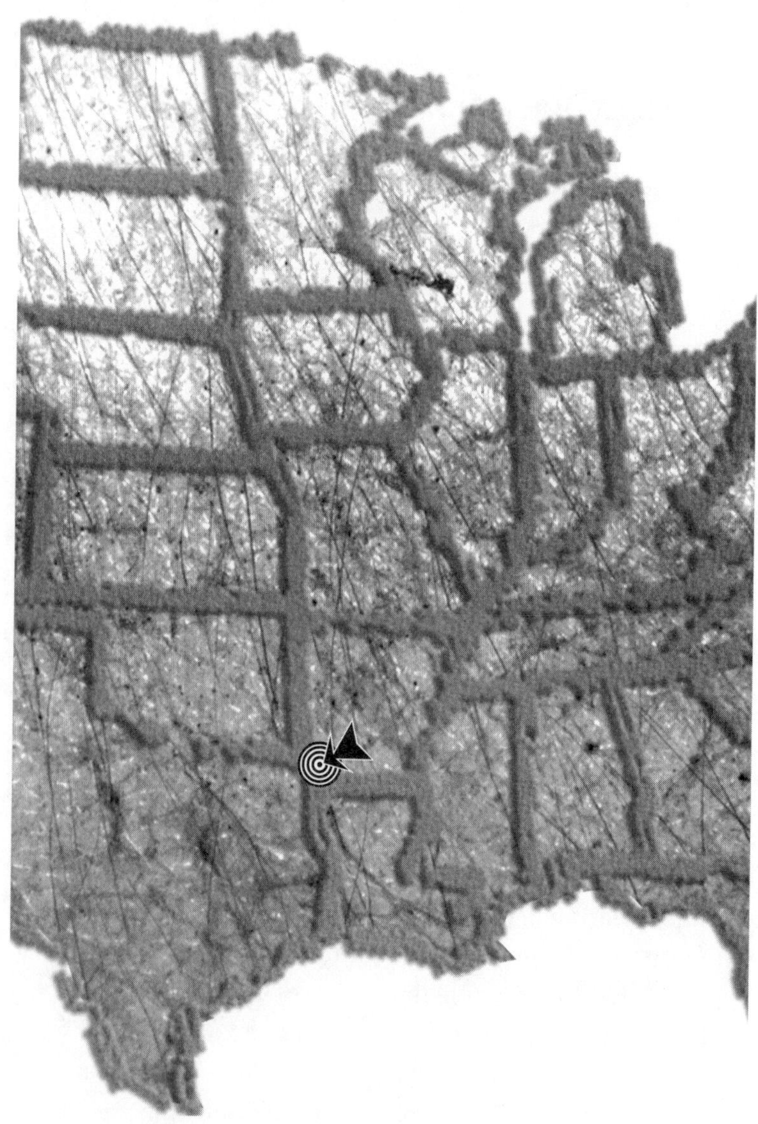

TEXARKANA, ARKANTEXAS

Where Jesus And Crime Prevail

POPULATION 132,846

WOULD TEXARKANA MAKE FOR A GOOD LOCALE FOR A HONEYMOON? No! Texarkana is a cesspool of a community, reeking of church-going and crime. You feel like residents are either going to rob you or pray for you. A flippin' church is on almost every corner, yet the convenience store has bulletproof glass, while a correctional facility greets you as you enter the town,

WEIRD LOCAL SMELL Despair, mixed with the aroma of past lynchings echoing through the eerie silence of the boarded-up ghost town – with huge Confederate War monument – which they call downtown.

FAMOUS PEOPLE FROM TEXARKANA Jeff Keith, lead singer of the 80's heavy metal band Tesla, Ross Perot, and one or two others.

TEXARKANA FUN FACT Texarkana's big claim to fame is the town is located directly on the Texas/Arkansas border. Go directly to the State border and take turns jumping from side to side, while declaring, "Now I'm in a Texas hellhole! Now I'm in an Arkansas hellhole! Now I'm in a Texas hellhole! And once again I'm in an Arkansas hellhole!" *(And so on, and so on, and so on...)*

EXTREMELY USELESS INFO In 1946, Texarkana was the site of one of America's first widely publicized serial murders. Dubbed the "Texarkana Moonlight Murders," the only description of the killer, in this unsolved case was that he wore a plain pillowcase over his head, with eyeholes cut out – you know, just like, well, the Klan.

LEVEL OF CREEPINESS 8. 9 if you believe in the reputed Boggy Creek Monster that is said to inhabit the, well, local boggy creek.

Directly across from the downtown post office is The Arrow Bar – "Texarkana's Oldest and Finest." This drinking hole *(and only drinking hole downtown)* is the only sign of life in the vicinity... well, sort of.

The place is like a vacuum of despair, a joy killer for any happiness that might currently be lingering in your soul as you enter. Seven people sit in the darkened bar; old cowboys with walkers, a gruff man with jailhouse tattoos sharing drinks with a crack-ho, etc., drinking in stony silence as somber country music plays. Life's regret and failure are welled-up in people's eyes. Not recent regret, but regret that happened long ago and weighs heavier, and heavier the more time goes by.

It feels like a needle being pulled off a record as I belly up to the bar. Sure, the Arrow Bar is the waiting room for Purgatory, but hey how can you complain when 2 beers run ya $3.50!

"Must not sleep!" I mumble to myself in order to fit in. "Must not sleep!"

THREE THINGS TO SAY IN THE ARROW BAR IN TEXARKANA THAT WILL GET YOU BEATEN UP:

"John Wayne was a Queer!"

"You never worked a hard day in your life!"

"Anyone up for a game of hacky-sack?"

Looking at the restroom doors, I'm not sure which applies to me as they read SETTERS and POINTERS, corresponding with the Men's and Women's Rooms. *(Fortunately, I choose correctly with POINTERS.)*

"Don't you forget the party on Friday," the ancient cowboy with the walker says, speaking awkwardly into a microphone, while the old guy with jailhouse tattoos plays with his dentures. I'm not sure if he really has a need for a microphone. "Don't forget about the party," he says once again, as everyone falls back into silence. Wow, the fun-and-giggles this so-called party must offer.

"Must not sleep!" I mumble again. "Must not sleep!"

Clearly these people at the Arrow Bar need a hearty dose of Jesus... which can be found on every damn street corner of Texarkana. Or at least that's what I tell the bartender before leaving.

If You Must Go:

The Arrow Bar
112 E 5th St.
Texarkana, AR
(870) 772-1171

A Diseased Underbelly Salute To...

The Worst (Or Best) Bar In America!

Alary's in St. Paul, Minnesota (139 7th St. E.) is either the *worst* or *best* bar in America – depending on your skewed, Americana perspective.

The whole place is filled entirely with men – large men in groups with a standard-issue haircut, and something vaguely familiar and asshole-ish about the crew that makes you feel slightly on edge – like you're about to be busted for doing something wrong, or going to be riddled with authoritative sarcasm akin to the time you were pulled over for speeding.

While the Hard Rock Cafe mounts autographed guitars on the wall, denoting a rock music motif, Alary's hangs dozens of police squad car doors from the ceiling, autographed by each force, while walls are designated to police force patches and other law enforcement memorabilia – creating a relaxing police motif.

It gets better; almost all the patrons are off-duty cops, drinking it up, doing shots... who might just get all liquored up and whip out their pepper spray for laughs, or put you in the chicken chokehold to huge guffaws. Uniform police officers on the beat occasionally come in to share a laugh with their drinking buddies.

What mad visionary, what Renaissance man, concocted this place and thought it might put the average drinking Joe at ease, where you're constantly reminded of the people who can arrest you, while drinking elbow-to-elbow with those out of uniform who can instigate the arresting.

Not yet sold? The female bartenders, *(the only women in the place)* look about 17 and wear the standard Alary's uniform; short-shorts *(something between a bikini bottom and thong underwear – making me again question health-code standards),* along with a T-shirt that vaguely only covers the mammoth breast area. *(Their website has photos of one of the staff in naughty police outfits in sexually provocative poses, which makes you chant "USA! USA! USA!")*

The girls look penned in and trapped working behind the enclosed bar area while middle-aged off-duty cops make loud, crude comments like "I like her dimples," referring to their barely covered, chunky, cellulite posteriors. *(Remember, this is St. Paul, Minnesota not L.A.)*

"They made that one wear jeans." I say to myself, noting one hefty, big-breasted Midwestern gal somehow not permitted to wear the ass-crack-revealing short-shorts *(she must know),* while I sit under my designated squad car door and patrons continue to salivate over the almost under-aged looking scantily-clad drink-slingers.

Alary's is a fascist police-state version of Hooters, with all the atmosphere of a cold jail cell floor. We like sports. We like Cops. We like woman who are hired here to wear practically nothing and serve us. I can only imagine the crowd here rooting for the LAPD, if the large TV screens that beam in every imaginable sports game, suddenly showed the Rodney King beating.

Yes, Alary's the worst *(or best)* bar in the country – depending on your perspective.

If You Must Go

Alary's Bar
139 7th St E
St Paul, MN 55101
(651) 224-771
www.alarys.com

HARRISON, ARKANSAS

"It's Klan-tastic!"

POPULATION 12,152

TOWN MOTTO "The Perfect Climate for Business and Pleasure."

***MY* MOTTO FOR THE TOWN** "Harrison, It's Klan-tastic!"

HARRISON FUN FACT The racial makeup of the city, 97.24% white!

WEIRD LOCAL SMELL The stank odor of White Power and intolerance.

EXTREMELY USELESS INFORMATION The Golden Goblin, Harrison High School mascot, is considered one of the most unique in the state of Arkansas. Well, fuck me sideways!

WAY TO GET YOUR ASS KICKED Be black and express interest in moving to Harrison with your hip-hop record label and clothing line.

CULTURAL HIGHLIGHT Cross-burning crossed with small town charm.

AN IDYLLIC LOCALE FOR Non-African Americans, Non-Jews, Non-Latinos, Non-Catholics, Non-Asians, and meth addicts.

LEVEL OF CREEPINESS 7, when no crosses are burned. 10, when crosses are aflame.

Shooting up Highway 65 through the Ozark Mountains, a billboard beckons me, "RELOCATE: Retire in Harrison – You'll Love It!"

Interesting sentiment. Considering that if you love Harrison, you probably hate minorities, because Harrison is the hometown of the KKK. You know, the Grand Wizard, the Knights of the Ku Klux Klan, all that crap. Set deep in the scenic, but creepy-backwoods-scary Ozark Mountains, the largest and most active Klan faction operating in the nation today has its headquarters in Harrison.

As if that weren't enough, like metal shavings to a magnet, or flies to shit, other, more up-to-date bigot organizations have been drawn to Harrison by its KKK rep. For instance, Christian Identity, an emerging supremacist group for the racist who loves Jesus, but eschews the silly pointed hood. Their theory being that in the 21st Century they don't have to wear hate on white sleeves, as long as they keep hate in their hearts.

Tired from driving all day, and worn down by hours of relentless right-wing talk radio, I finally spot a sign that promises: Harrison, 32 Miles. I've never said this before, but I say it now, "Thank God, I'm almost in the hometown of the Klan!" Smoke seems to billow down from the mountain slope: I hope it's not a cross! Only thing worse would be if a tornado touched down sending all the mobile homes I've been passing flying in my direction.

"Klan-rific!" I exclaim, finally arriving in Harrison. The town has an isolated, insular, small-town charm, cut off from the rest of the world, as though the calendar had been flipped back to the 1950s when drinking fountains were labeled "White" and "Colored," and residents tried to protect their kids from evil jungle music like Bill Hailey and the Comets.

I'm disappointed there are no sheet-clad goons goose-stepping down Main Street, but if you squint and look at it from an obstructed angle, the logo for North Arkansas College somewhat resembles a swastika.

K-K-K-Harrison abounds in contradictions. Although there's no Martin Luther King Drive, there is a Chinese Restaurant, which doesn't make supremacist sense *("We ingest the food of the White race, unless the Yellow Horde delivers Mushu Pork and egg rolls.")* But it seems apropos that the local tanning salon is going out of business.

Harrison is the epicenter of hypocrisy: smack dab in the middle of a dry county, which means you can't buy booze for your Beige Power rally, but local meth labs conveniently dot the countryside.

With a close look at the city's paper, *The Harrison Daily Times,* all I have to do is read between the lines of the news stories to find the hidden racism:

> **EXPLOSION, UNEXPLAINED**
> Residents reported they heard a loud
> explosion about 10:15 p.m. Wednesday.

Hmmm? An *unexplained* explosion? I'm in town five minutes, but I could come up with an explanation double-quick, and even make a stab at the location *(behind the Chinese restaurant, perhaps?).*

I base my assumptions on town history: Harrison was an early innovator in ethnic cleansing. During the "Race Riots" of 1905 and 1909 the Harrison uptight whiteys drove all citizens of color out of town by burning down their houses, after shooting out the windows, and other un-neighborly reverse-Welcome Wagon efforts. Thus creating a lily-white community, and making Harrison what they call down South "A Sundown Town" *(so named for supposed city limits signs reading, "N——, Don't Let the Sun Go Down on Your Ass in ___!").*

I try to picture what the few assorted people around the town square would look like with hoods on, as I pull into Sonic Burger for a cheeseburger.

I park my car next to several pickup trucks full of very white people, and when the blond teenaged girl comes with my order, I say, "Thank you my pure Sister!"

Later on when she asks, "How's your burger?" I give her a thumbs up and reply, "Klan-tastic!"

Journeying to Town & Country Cleaners & Laundry I ask the church-hair lady behind the counter if they can take care of a special order.

"Can you handle large loads?" I inquire.

"How large?" she asks.

"Around 100 sheets to be dry-cleaned."

"We could," she replies "But it would be very expensive: $6-$8 per sheet. Is this for a place of business here in town?"

"Not exactly a business, more like a local organization."

"Would you need the sheets folded and pressed?"

"I don't think we need them folded, because they're going to be worn." I then add, "By the way, can you get blood out – Jew blood?"

If You Must Go:

Town & Country Laundry & Cleaners
217 S. Cherry St.
Harrison, AR 72601
(870) 741-5857

Venturing into the Harrison Tourist Center, I'm surprised there isn't an informational pamphlet on "Today's Klan!" featuring smiley Klux men and women bungee jumping in Martha Stewart sheets from K-Mart.

The bubbly yet reserved woman working at the office pushes the local caves and caverns. Noting that Harrison supports roughly 70 churches *(practically one for every three town citizens)* I ask, "Are there any synagogues in the area?"

"No," she answers curtly.

We share an awkward silence. I page through another brochure on hiking trails, and then ask, "How about tours of the Ku Klux Klan headquarters?"

"No!" Her mood has turned snappish; she retreats behind her desk and pretends to arrange things.

If You Must Go

Harrison Tourist Information Center
3391 Hwy. 65
North Harrison, AR 72601
(870) 741-3343

Despite the large-as-life KKK presence in town, the Information Center is also devoid of Klux paraphernalia. But what's the point of being a tourist in Harrison, if you can't bring home a souvenir glazed-ceramic robed Klan statuette with eyes that light up! *($28.95, xenophobes rejoice: no shipping charges in the U.S.)*

If You Must Go

Ozark Craft
6377 Lead Hill Rd.
Harrison, AR 72601
www.puttroopsontheborder.com

Luckily, I found the info on Klan kitsch at the local library, as well as the address and phone for headquarters. Much to my surprise, *Mein Kampf* isn't prominently displayed in this library *(although there are two copies in the stacks),* but the front room is stocked with a goodly assortment of teen romance novels.

If You Must Go

Boone County Library
221 W Stephenson
Harrison, AR 72601
(870) 741-5913

I call the Klan's phone number and wait for it to be answered: "Ku Klux Klan, how can we help you harass the mud people?" Instead, a recorded message says, "Hello, you've reached Christian Concepts. If you'd like an information pack, send $3 and a self-addressed, stamped envelope." Three dollars for an information packet? Man, the Klan is a bunch of cheap bastards!

I drive to the headquarters on the edge of town, and know I've arrived when I spot a sign that reads, Soldiers of the Cross. *("Providing it's burning," I think.)*

Several small, non-descript buildings sit on roughly an acre of land, one of which the casual viewer might mistake for a poor country church, if they didn't know it was the clapped-out Kluxer headquarters.

Looking at the place, my reaction is, "Man, the Klan has got to get their shit together. This place is a dump!"

I expected a KKK Dollywood, with simulated lynching rides and white cotton candy, and what we have here barely qualifies as a low-rent David Koresh compound.

Hoping for a glimpse of Kluksmen in 200-thread count, I get out of my car for a quick peek. Perhaps there are Klansman gardening, airing out the laundry, or maybe a big Ku Klux volleyball game and limbo contest out back. But no go.

"Klan? Where are you?" I yell. "Come out and play."

The Ku Klux Headquarters is a pathetic disappointment. Judging by the dingy complex, the KKK is a sad throwback bunch, like '80s bands such as Flock of Seagulls, who attempt to keep it going long, long, long past the glory years.

The Klan is a eugenicist dinosaur!

If You Must Go

Really? No, I mean, ***really?*** Are your affairs in order, have you made out a will? My mother is happy I'm home. If this is a hipster doofus move on your part, you should know that hate groups are notoriously irritated by the tongue-in-cheek gawker.

If, on the other hand, you worship Harrison as the mothership of your (twisted) ideals, be aware that Civil Rights legislation has empowered victims of hate groups with the ability to sue. Just ask the African American mother of one victim, a nice black lady who has been handed the keys to a former KKK headquarters.

If you're a bigot, perhaps it's best to continue getting your hate on by shouting along with Fox News, lest you lose both the portable and the trailer through some Kluxing screw-up.

Don't say you haven't been warned:

Ku Klux Klan National Headquarters
P.O. Box 2222
Harrison, AR 72601
(870) 427-3414

Road Trip Quick Tip...

Utilize Fast-food Playrooms

Burger Kings and McDonald's have great playrooms on major highways. Pull over every now to then and burn off some road-energy and alleviate some of those pent-up aggressions. These playrooms will most likely be filled with tiny, little children, but don't let them intimidate you. Make noises like a mighty bear, raising your hands like they were powerful claws in order to claim the playroom for your own personal use. "Grrrrr!"

CONGRATULATIONS!
YOU HAVE UTILIZED A FASTFOOD PLAYROOM WHILE ON YOUR ROAD TRIP!

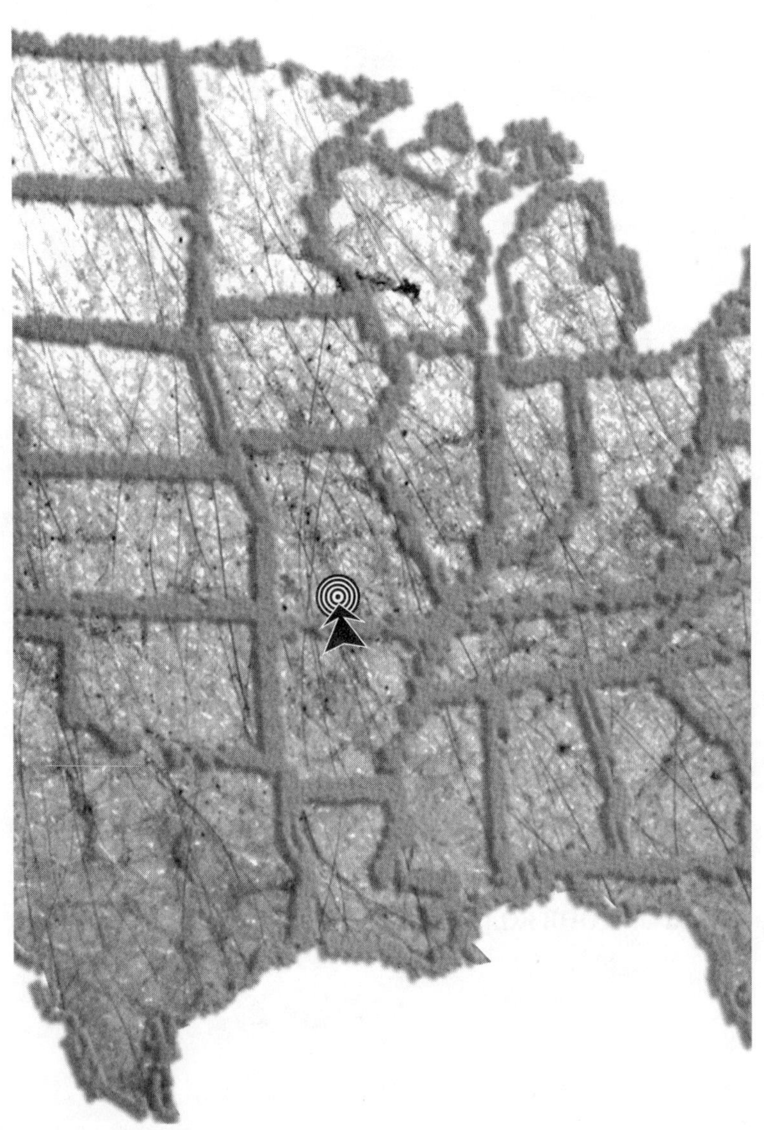

BRANSON, MISSOURI

The Land Where Yakov Smirnoff Is King

POPULATION 6,050

TOWN MOTTO "The Live Music Show Capital of the World."

***MY* MOTTO FOR TOWN** "What the hell is a Baldknobber?!"

WEIRD LOCAL SMELLS Like thousands and thousands of Larry the Cable Guys.

BRANSON FUN FACT The racial makeup of Branson is 0.84% African American and 0.71% Asian.

EXTREMELY USELESS INFORMATION Branson's named for Rueben Branson, postmaster and operator of a general store in the area in the 1880s. He was rumored to have a large collection of human teeth and had a daughter who has a hermaphrodite. Well, f**k me sideways!

WAYS TO GET YOUR ASS-KICKED Sing the French National Anthem while wearing a yarmulke.

BRANSON IS AN IDYLLIC LOCALE FOR Patriots, flag-wavers, gray-hairs, white supremacists, corrupt cops, mad-with-power magicians, meth-heads, fans of Christ and country music, unfunny Russian comedians.

LEVEL OF CREEPINESS 10. You will crap red, white, and blue with a Jesus chaser.

When someone mentions Branson, two words come to mind: *Yakov* and *Smirnoff*. Yes, not only does Russian "funnyman" Yakov Smirnoff perform in Branson, but he also has his own goddamn theater! *(The Yakov Smirnoff Theater.)*

On Highway 65, right over the Missouri State border one is greeted with a huge Yakov Smirnoff billboard as they enter the Show Me State. But his comedy comes with a warning:

All, I can say is, "*What a motherfucking country!*" All State borders should be required by law to have portraits of Yakov Smirnoff greeting motorists entering their region. But sadly they don't – only here where it matters!

Branson is the Las Vegas of Christian, Pro-America, Country Music. They call it "The Live Music Show Capital of the World," trumpeting 40 theaters with over 100 shows. A place that promotes "family values" entertainment; where you can get steaks the size of a baby's head! Branson is what every Saturday night would be like, *everywhere*, if Bush won a third term.

Las Vegas has the Vegas Strip, Branson has W. Country Blvd; an endless parade of budget motels and shabbily-constructed venues, resembling elongated tin sheds with movie studio façade fronts that look thrown together in roughly an hour of construction time.

Mad-with-power celebrities, the rest of the world has never heard of, construct theaters in their name. Magician Kirby VanBurch has the Kirby VanBurch Theater. Japanese bowl-cut-haired fiddle player Shoji Tabuchi *(advertised as one of the greatest musicians in the world)* performs at the Shoji Tabuchi Theater *(he's also the only minority found in Branson).*

If You Must Go
Kirby VanBurch Theater (417)337-7140 www.kirbyvanburch.com
Shoji Tabuchi Theatre 2709 State Hwy 248 Branson, MO 65615-2130 (417)334-7469 www.shoji.com

Driving towards Shepherd of the Hills Expressway, a reoccurring Branson motif is spotted, passing The God & Country Inspirational Gardens *(with a big 10 Commandments replica perched in front),* Dentures billboard, the God and Country Theater, The Good Shepard Inn, and of course, the American Presidential Museum.

If You Must Go
The God & Country Inspirational Gardens 76 Country Music Boulevard Branson, MO 65616
God & Country Theatre 1840 W Hwy 76, Branson, MO, 65616 (417) 334-6806 www.godandcountrytheatre.com
Good Shepherd Inn 1023 W. Main St. Branson, MO 65616 (417) 334-1695
American Presidential Museum 2849 Gretna Rd. Branson, MO 65616 (417) 334-8683 www.americanpresidentialmuseum.com

Sauntering in to Branson Gifts, you can tell a lot about a place by the T-shirts they sell. It's good to see you can still buy a T-shirt with the Confederate Flag right next to T-Shirts that say FREEDOM blazoned with a large eagle and Old Glory. My purchase is a chemise designed like the 7/11 logo that says *"Twenty-Four-7... Jesus is with US ALWAYS.*

If You Must Go

Branson Gifts
3315 West State Hwy 76
Branson, MO 65616
(417) 339-2271

Stopping off for an Egg McMuffin, McDonalds has piped in Christian music. *(Who is this "Jesus" guy? I'm beginning to think he's very popular!)*

If You Must Go:

McDonald's
76 Country Blvd.,
Branson, MO 65616
(417) 335-2505

I'm in the belt-buckle of the Bible belt. Billboards for church services are alongside those for the Beatles Liverpool Legend's Show, trumpeting, "Take Time to Think How Great God Is." *(Does that apply to church or faux Beatles?!)* Vegas has quickie wedding chapels; Branson has Jesus Chapels for those who spontaneously want to become born-again. Branson boasts roughly 60 churches *(sorry, no synagogues or Buddhist temples).* With only 40 theaters that's more than one church for each Branson headlining act.

If You Must Go

Liverpool Legends at The Caravelle Theatre
3446 West Hwy 76
Branson, Mo. 65616
(888) 222-8910
www.claycooper.biz

During peak season, with smug ironic detachment one can gawk at the entertainment stylings of such has-been oddities as the Osmond Brothers, Bobby Vinton, or Andy Williams. For pure fear and loathing, the best time to visit Branson is during the winter months when the place is practically deserted and half the shows aren't even running. Branson is spooky without people, making a generally creepy place even much, much creepier.

For my evening entertainment, I, Mr. Big-and-Clever, will seek out the worst show in all of Branson. Sure it's easy enough to mock Mel Tillis, but I want a show that's truly bad and offensive – on so many different levels! Where to start? "Celebrate America" sounds promising *(Mansion American Theater)*; almost like something on The Simpsons. It boasts, "A portrayal of the courage, creativity, tenacity, and heart of what it means to be American!" done with musical numbers, heralded by a cast of children and old people perched in front of an American flag. "The Road to Rock" has the hard-ass tagline of "Any Questions?" *(Question: at what point did these musicians completely sellout doing the same damn show 6 nights a week in Branson, Missouri?)*

If You Must Go

Celebrate America at Mansion America Theater
189 Expressway Lane,
Branson, MO 65616
(866) 707-4100

The Road to Rock at Branson Showcase Theater
(inside the Branson Mall) 2206 W. Highway 76
Branson, MO 65616 (417) 339-3939

The "Baldknobbers Jamboree" has me at hello – I'm sold on the name alone! What you get from Baldknobbers is:

- Classic Country
- Hilarious Comedy
- Patriotic
- Gospel
- Family Entertainment

Baldknobbers offers all that, along with a name that sounds like the tip end of someone's penis! Confirming the show's hilarious comedy the flyer merits two guys in overalls with fake bad teeth crossing their eyes *(if the show wasn't "funny" then eyes clearly would not be crossed!)*. And, let's not forget such offerings as "The Promise" *(Mansion American Theater)* centering around

Jesus in a musical-entertainment extravaganza that would make any sane man go, "Oh Christ!"

If You Must Go

Baldknobbers Country Music Theatre
2835 West 76 Country Boulevard
Branson, MO 65615
www.baldknobbers.com

Then there's the King himself; Yakov Smirnoff and his Explosive Laughter *(that's laughter not diarrhea!)*. Clad in traditional Russian garb and waving an American flag, his brochure merits some sort of patriotic-flag-waving-isn't-America-great comedy debacle. *(Like Cher before him, Branson-ites refer to him simply by the one name: Yakov!)*

Sadly, his theater is closed for the winter. *(In Russia, he would be forced to perform year round!)* Yes, the shit-of-Branson-shit unfortunately is on winter hiatus.

If You Must Go

Yakov Smirnoff Show
470 State Hwy 248
Branson, MO 65616
(800)728.4546 www.yakov.com

That's why I settle for Grand Jubilee, featuring Branson's Best Quartet, New South – four guys with creepy, fake orange tans, looking like they've had a Crest Whitestrips mishaps on their teeth. Unlike the rest of civilization, singing quartets are really big in Branson. Their flyer shows the Fab Four with big smiles in matching shirts.

"What a nice group of clean-cut boys," your average Branson patron would say while looking at their photo. In San Francisco, we'd look at the photo and go, "Come on! These guys are soooooo gay – to Lance Bass proportions! Who are they fooling?!" The show also includes a man in a funny orange suit and bow-tie, who "Keeps you absolutely doubled over in laughter." This is Branson's Reigning Comedian of the Year *(Yakov is #2 to this guy?!)*.

Grand Jubilee looks more painful than botulism. I'm soooo there!

To avoid paying $27 for this crap, I call the theater 40 minutes before the showtime and ask for the PR person.

"Yes, I'm from a Canadian TV show. We're shooting in Branson and I'd love to do a segment on New South." After minor coaxing, it worked; a comp ticket awaits I... of Canadian TV fame.

Inside the Grand Country Music Hall, I make my way past a gift shop that sells "What Does Freedom Mean To You!" quilts, towards the wall of Army patches, near the box office.

I'm quickly learning that the family-friendly moniker toted by Branson, means no fucking *(pardon my swearing)* booze. Anywhere! None of the 40 theaters serves it! All the better: I have to endure this sober!

I also learn the show that "satisfies any age," tonight mostly satisfies the age of 80 and up. A long line of thrilled, overweight gray-hairs careens around the corner. Though I'm in disguise *(cowboy hat, bolo tie, Twenty-four-7 Jesus chemise),* an old man, whose T-shirt says, "We Rock Hard for the Lord!" stares directly at me like I'm wearing a g-string and pumps, because I have earrings. The staff, on the other hand, is thrilled that I – of Canadian Travel Show fame – have arrived *(fortunately my lack of crew and $300 camera aren't questioned).*

"Canadian TV is really tickled to be here!" I exclaim to the woman at the ticket booth, assuring her, "This show will be broadcast throughout Moosejaw," adding for further thrills, "And even in parts of Halifax!"

Entering the 500-seat theater, roughly 90 gray-hairs are ready for a squeaky-clean show with material not to offend.

Anticipation builds. Under colored lights, the MC emerges, adorned in a sparkling sequined jacket *(these are very popular in Branson).* He kicks things off with the guy wearing the funny orange suit, doing corny Hee-Haw humor you can see coming a mile down the turnpike *(mostly involving eating fiber or seeing the doctor).* Even though they do 12 shows a week, the pair crackup at their own jokes.

"I was having a dream of about me and Ann-Margaret."

"That sounds great."

"The only problem, I was Liberace!"

- Big laughs -

(FOOTNOTE: The humor lies in the fact that Liberace was a gay man who died of complications due to AIDS.)

The brochure said I'd be doubled over in laughter, but in fact it's making me double over in pain. When the doubling-over dies down, it's time for Branson's best quartet, New South, a poor man's Oak Ridge Boys, *(of course they do "Elvira"),* whose country music is fortunately without all that Johnny Cash hard-livin'. The sequenced-jacketed MC introduces the quartet, specifically expressing that each member is a good family man and very active in their church. Something, though, is a little fishy when he introduces the "bachelor of the group."

"Now ladies we're going to help Scott out," he says, pulling him aside, then requesting all the grandmothers and mothers in the audience to pull out pictures of their granddaughters and daughters. "Take them to Scott at intermission and maybe we can make a love connection, huh?" The Lance Bass of New South has been found. *(I think this is a subtle way to say, ladies and gentlemen, he's gay. Please pray for him in the name of Jesus Christ!)*

Fun Activity: If you're a woman (or a man) ask the bachelor of the group out, and watch him squirm!

A costume change occurs. New South reemerges wearing matching, sparkly red, white, and blue sequined outfits. I get the feeling something's going to happen, and it's going to be patriotic!

"Ladies and gentlemen, here at Branson we are proud to celebrate God and country every single day!" proclaims New South's miniature lead singer. "This is a song that has a beautiful message. Listen as we sing, 'In God We Still Trust!'"

Big hoots and hollers. The lighting shifts. The singer croons, "You put your hand on His Bible...."

A video flashes on the large screen with Old Glory waving and kids doing the Pledge of Allegiance in a classroom.

"There is no separation, we're one Nation under Him."

This is either the worst or the best music video I've ever seen! Images of Mount Rushmore, eagles flying, fireworks over New York, fill the screen, along with kids praying, crosses perched on top of mountains, inter-cut with shots of Old Glory.

"Here in America, In God We Still Trust."

This show has it all: patriotism, Christ, and country music! Actual enthused whistling and cheers erupt – this is what the crowd loves. *(I imagine the same response if New South sang, "Here in America, let's get creationism in public schools and kill those towel-heads...")*

Firemen stand with their hands over their heart *(a subtle or not subtle 9/11 reference),* cross fading to wide-eyed children. Wait, yes, I have to say, THIS IS THE BEST MUSIC VIDEO EVER!

"He's the one to turn to, He's the source of our strength, Here in America. In God we still trust!"

Huge applause from these God-fearing-elderly-folks-from-the-heartland who optimistically dream of the day when church and State can finally be one.

The guy in the funny suit then comes out. We think he's going to cleanse our palate with comedy. Instead, he sings a song – a serious one. It's as if to say, "Hey, I'm know I'm wacky and wear funny suits, but I have a serious side – I'm a multifaceted person!"

Smoke machines spew as New South now wears matching white suits. This time it's not about patriotism; it's strictly about Jesus. People in the audience spontaneously put their hands up in the air in a stick-em-up pose, feeling Jesus-magic. Some break into prayer position as the chorus reigns, "Oh Lord My God is awesome..." To be brutally honest, it's pretty weird. Branson is such a bunch of bullshit.

Saved by a mid-show intermission *(I guess to give the audience a colostomy-bag change break),* it also allows New South and its band to hawk CDs *(each member has their own individual CD to sell).*

"The second half really rocks," confirms the teenaged girl working the ticket booth to I... of Canadian TV fame. "We usually sneak in there and rock out."

"Canadian TV can't wait to rock out as well!" I reply.

That's my cue to get the hell out of here and far away from New South – quickly!

If You Must Go

Grand Jubilee at the Grand Country Music Hall
1945 W 76 Country Blvd.
Branson, MO 65616
(417) 335-2484

BRANSON NITELIFE: Booze and Bible Trivia

It's absolutely rare to find a place to get a drink in Branson which leaves a bar called Waxy O'Shea. What an oasis to cleanse my palate of patriotism and Jesus, in my quest for the seedy underbelly of Branson. Nestling up to the bar with one of my best friends named Guinness, I've made it just in time for Waxy O'Shea's weekly Pub Quiz Night.

"According to the Bible, who was the world's first baby?" the quizmaster asks the bar crowd. I almost do a spit take. "That would be Cain," he states, as those who got the correct answer go, "Yeah," and high-five. "In the Bible how many days did Jesus fast in the wilderness?"

What the... ? In Branson if drinks are involved, does the Bible have to be as well?

Fun Activity: Answer every question in the Bible Quiz, "Satan, or one of his lesser minions!"

"Are you in one of the shows?" I ask the man sitting next to me who sports a fake tan and white teeth *(just like New South)*, hoping he's the fourth wheel of a power quartet.

"No," he responds. "I'm a timeshare salesman." The orange-skinned man then adds, "You should come back in 3 months, then you can see what Branson is all about."

“No,” I reply as another Bible question is thrown out to the crowd. “I think I see what Branson is all about right now!”

I try to act interested in the Bible questions when the timeshare salesman navigates the conversation to the topic of his favorite sexual positions.

“This is the second-biggest county in the country for meth production,” shares his buddy who just spent 2 years in prison for possession of 2 ½ pounds of weed. “I’ve seen people that made 20 pounds of it in a week and sold it,” he adds as the Bible questions continue to fly through the air.

“What’s it like growing up in Branson?” I ask, glad to no longer be talking to the timeshare goofball.

“Very boring,” he replies in a groggy manner, being he’s on a mix of assorted chemical imbalance drugs such as Ritalin and Xanax. “Very right-wing conservative. I’ve been stopped by people while on my skateboard and preached to.”

I buy the guy a drink in hopes he’ll ‘fess up some more Branson dirt.

“They advertise Branson as the country music capital of the world, but I would call it Americana. Like the Presley’s Country Jubilee wear these awful hideous sequin suits with American flags on the back to harp on people’s sentiments, even though half of them are gay cokeheads that don’t believe it.”

“Come on, give me some real dirt on Branson,” I further coax, buying him a shot as well.

“Jim Stafford’s a cokehead,” he blurts about the man with the 70’s hit Spiders and Snakes *(OK, the alcohol is working)*. “Shoji, he’s a real asshole. He has a pool table in his bathroom.” *(This is getting better.)* “New South, the one on the left on the billboard is gay.” *(The bachelor of the group!)* “Kirby VanBurch had his ears surgically altered to look like Spock. That’s why his hair is always covering the top of ears.” *(Ok, that’s plain weird.)*

My medicated prison-friend tells me of a time when the award-winning magician who makes a unicorn disappear on stage, went mad-with-power. “I was in jail when he got arrested for a DWI. He was threatening the cops, saying, 'Do you know who I am!?' They were like, 'Shut the fuck up, we know who you are!'"

As the Bible pub quiz wraps up, a rambunctious participant, either filled with alcohol or Jesus, goes outside and starts hitting the hanging lights. Immediately the police appear.

"The local cops are corrupt," the guy-who-went-to-prison explains, claiming he used to go out with the sheriff's niece. "I bought guns from the evidence room from the sheriff. They confiscate meth and sell it back." Mentioning the guards at jail are the ones who bring in drugs since they only make $6.25 minimum wage, he adds about his arrest for weed, "I think they took it and smoked it."

Wanting to show me the seedy underbelly of Branson, the guy-who-went to- prison offers, "I could show you the junkies in Branson!"

"No, that's all right," I reply. "I know what junkies look like."

"Do you want to see the hillbillies?" he throws out, suggesting a bar across the river named Dillon's Pub. "You might go up there and see a fight!" he adds. "One of my friends goes up there all the time, I could call him. *(Pause.)* I don't agree with him since he got into the Aryan Nation."

(Pause.) "Oh really?!"

"Yeah they're kind of strong here. He has two lightening bolts on the back of his neck, which means he's a 2nd lieutenant and has done a lot and has a little bit of power." The guy-who-went-to-prison adds, "They're all pretty crazy but they're nice."

Great! Nice Nazis and hillbilly fights in Branson?

I'm there!

If You Must Go

Waxy O'Shea
253 Branson Landing Blvd.
Branson, MO 65616
(417) 348-1759

HONKY TONK HIDEAWAY

Though I'm offered a ride to Dillon's I decline, being I don't want the cops to mistake me as an accomplice to the guy who just went to prison for 2 years. Instead, I take a cab.

A large cab driver takes me to Dillon's where hopefully I'll see hillbillies fighting! Disappointment crosses my face when the parking lot heralds two cars *(thus, if there were fighting, the odds are it would involve me!).*

"You should go to the Hideaway," offers the cab driver. "I was planning on going there later."

The Hideaway it is. We pull up to a dive bar located far from the tin-shed theaters, behind a motel that's being renovated. The large cab driver even comes in to have a drink with me. This is the place where country music dreams go to die! The bar is filled with out-of work hotel and restaurant staff, who've come to Branson to make it big, and are spending the last of their money until the season starts.

The front wall, adorned with autographed country music headshots from twenty years ago, rests alongside a sign reading, "Shirts and Shoes Required... Bra and Panties Optional," while every CD in the jukebox features someone wearing a cowboy hat *(except the Grease soundtrack).* I take a place at the bar next to my cab driver and an out-of-work motel housekeeper, while a handful of people dance to country music karaoke *(songs I've never heard before in my life, but everyone else seems to know them).*

"Being an American citizen is one of the greatest gifts in the world!" a drunk ex-marine starts spouting within my personal-space zone. He starts aggressively telling me tales of being a sniper in Iraq, and chopping off suspected terrorists' heads while videoing it. He moves in closer. "They say the first person you kill... you lose your soul. I don't give a fuck!"

(Pause.) "Ok."

Branson is becoming much scarier than the hometown of the Klan. The drunk marine then presents a challenge.

"I bet I can do more pushups than you!"

(Pause.) "How 'bout this," I offer as a compromise, "Why don't *you* do the pushups and *I'll* count?"

The drunken marine drops to the grimy floor of the Hideaway in a prone pushup position. I start counting *(1,2,3...),* while the large bald bouncer takes to the karaoke mike and sings with intensity, "I don't have you anymore..." He's doing karaoke for keeps. During the instrumental break, he slow dances with a woman from the crowd with his eyes closed.

The big-bottomed bartender takes a turn belting out another country tune. These are the down-and-out country music wanna-bees. Laid off and broke, from states like Oklahoma, Kansas, and Iowa. This is their Hollywood, where they go with big with stars in their eyes, now facing the reality; singing country music karaoke with the cab driver waiting on deck and a drunk marine doing pushups *(37, 38, 39...).*

For every Kirby VanBurch and Shoji, Branson has rooms full of these folks.

"That girl sings her heart out," my large cab driver comments about the bartender's karaoke performance on the way back to my motel. "Lovely voice. Too bad she's too large to make it in country music," he adds about Branson's cutthroat truth.

If You Must Go
Dillon's Pub 136 Carter Road Branson, MO 65616 (417) 334-9651
Honkytonk Hideaway 448 St Hwy 248 Branson, MO 65616 (417) 339-2000

Before leaving town, I venture to the Harold Bell Wright Shepard of the Hills Museum.

This museum is thee place to:

- Learn the history of Harold Bell Wright
- See his antique gun collection and original manuscripts.

"One ticket for the Harold Bell Wright Museum." I tell the old man behind the counter, who looks surprised to see someone requesting admission. After paying my money, I ask, "And, who is Harold Bell Wright?"

"He wrote the second-biggest book of the Twentieth Century," the old man says pridefully.

"What's the first?"

"The Bible!" *(Hmm? With thesecond-biggest book of the Twentieth Century, you think I would have heard of him.)*

"That ticket's good for all day!" the old man stresses.

You have to walk through a Toy Museum to get to the Harold Bell Wright Museum *(I don't really see the connection),* where they pipe in subliminal Jesus messages. While I stare at Star Wars toys, I hear, "I will be with you in times of trouble. I will be with you in salvation..."

This is becoming like military psy-ops torture, where they play the Barney the Dinosaur theme over-and-over again for Iraqi prisoners in metal shipping containers.

Okay, I get it. Branson is all about flag-waving and Jesus. It's not funny anymore.

Surprisingly, I have the entire Harold Bell Wright Museum to myself. I see Harold Bell Wright's glasses. I see copies of his book *Shepard on the Hill* in several different languages. I see a video reenactment of his early days selling furniture polish.

"Remember, that ticket's good for all day!" the old man stresses again, as I leave, having my Harold-Bell-Wright-fill.

Driving north, instantly out of town, from the highway the final thing you see leaving Branson is one last sign, beckoning you: *Yakov–Exit Now!* You can never leave Branson – it will always stay with you. I've hit an All American Wall, suffering from a bad case of Red State Madness – like a hangover but without the drinking, as I shit red, white, and blue with a constant dry taste of Jesus in my mouth, amidst bad entertainment, bad food, fat, old Americans and utter lack of culture. As they say, "What happens in Branson stays in Branson, especially with Our Lord Jesus Christ looking over it."

If You Must Go

Harold Bell Wright Museum
Mutton Hollow West Highway 76
Branson, MO 65616

Diseased Underbelly Salute To...

Cheshire, Ohio

The entire town of Cheshire was wiped off the map in the span of two or three years by the massive James M. Gavin coal-fueled power plant just a few hundred feet away from city limits. For many years blue sulfuric clouds escaped from the plant's smokestacks and passed over the town, causing problems ranging from a sooty residue on houses to milky chemical fogs, while white droplets of acid rain fell from the sky. Some of this came from AEP's attempts to remedy other contamination problems; anhydrous ammonia was used to clean the smokestacks' exhaust, but the side effects of this process included those sulfurous clouds that caused eye and skin irritation, as well as headaches, sore throats, and lovely white burn marks on the lips and tongue. The final straw for Cheshire residents was a report that stated local schools would have had about six minutes to evacuate in the event of an anhydrous ammonia tank leak.

So instead of fixing the problems, the power plant paid $20 million for the 221 residents to move out by the end of 2002 (though a few elderly citizens still remained). Now the homes are boarded up and deserted, as blue clouds still linger in the sky.

CONGRATULATIONS CHESHIRE OHIO!
YOU ARE A TRUE AMERICAN DISEASED UNDERBELLY TOWN!

Highlights Of Driving Through Southeast Missouri:

The monotony of the road kicks in on long windy stretches of Missouri *(all the small towns begin to look alike).* Out here, American right-wing talk radio begins to make sense; wearing on me like nails on a mental chalkboard, corroding my soul with conservative ideology and screamed argument debate points. Ok, I get it – it's all about Jesus and patriotism. I can't even laugh any longer with smug ironic detachment.

- I almost accidentally drive off a two-lane road, scared shitless, as an angry right wing talk show host screams about the Wussification of America. "You've lost your Man Card," the talk show host declares. "You've committed a Man-Code violation!"
- Dozens of huge billboards dot the landscape of southeast Missouri, advertising a restaurant/gift shop called Hillbilly Junction, *(apparently capitalizing on that big backwoods hillbilly craze).*

"Do you know where Hillbilly Junction is?" I ask the woman working inside Hillbilly Junction.

Standing under a large banner that reads Hillbilly Junction, she thinks for a moment, then replies: "This is it!"

I look confused for a moment. "Are you sure?"

If You Must Go

Hillbilly Junction Restaurant
Hwy. 60/63 E
Willow Springs, MO
(417) 469-4296

- Willow Springs is home to maybe the worst museum in all of America, "The Soda Pop Museum." Hot damn, a whole museum dedicated to soda pop. All I can say is, where do I cut off my right nut in exchange for admission?! A sign taped to the door, reads, "No Open Containers ALLOWED!" I guess if you bring in your own soda pop, they wouldn't be able to tell if you're stealing from the collection *(this must have happened numerous times before).*

If You Must Go

Antique Fire Truck, Automobile & Soda Museum, Business Hwy 60/63 East, Willow Springs, MO (573) 469-3158

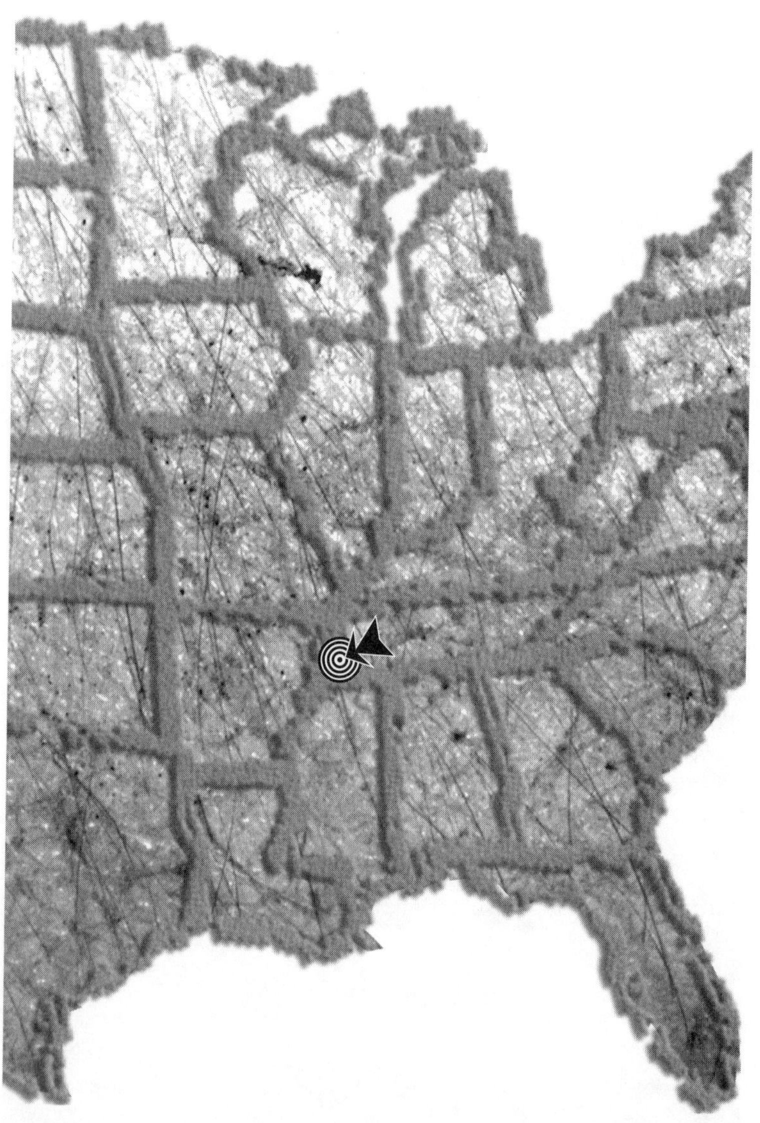

MEMPHIS, TENNESSEE

Elvis Died Here On The Toilet

POPULATION 1,260,581

TOWN MOTTO I don't know, but Elvis is from here.

MY TOWN MOTTO "Motherfking Elvis is From Here!"

MEMPHIS FUN FACT Residents of Memphis contend with the nation's second-highest violent crime rate. In addition, the rate of robbery and burglary are among the nation's highest.

WEIRD LOCAL SMELLS Elvis

EXTREMELY USELESS INFORMATION Did I mention Elvis is from here?

CULTURAL HIGHLIGHT Elvis, Elvis, and Elvis *(he's from here, you know).*

AN IDYLLIC LOCALE FOR Elvis, Sonny and the boys, teenaged girls wrestling in their underwear for Elvis, TV sets to be shot out by Elvis.

Crossing the Tennessee border, you immediately move on to more of your Boss Hogg-type Southern rednecks. Memphis is the Birthplace of Rock and Roll. I know this cuz everywhere in the city tells me so. Another thing I never knew until coming to here; Elvis Presley lived here. Have you ever hear about this? It's true. The most famous person to ever die on a toilet called Memphis home. Good thing I came here to learn this fact, which is posted on almost every nook-and-cranny within city limits.

Beale St. is like Mardi Gras – all year round! *(I mean that in the worst sense of the word.)* The experience is like tagging along with a really bad bachelorette party scored by blues music. Every large city has that one area where all the tourists must flock like lemmings, and Beale St. is it, where drunken amateurs spill out into the streets with their multi-colored drinks and weekend warrior attitudes. With its musical history you'd think Beale St. would be cool, but it's so not; it's like Fisherman's Wharf, if you gave everyone at Fisherman's Wharf three Long Island Ice Teas.

Though there's great blues music at places like B.B. Kings and Wet Willies, I try to find the restaurant with the worst music and atmosphere. It's the Rum Boogie Café where while dining you can enjoy the music of Pam & Terry; a husband and wife team on guitars who, every weekend, play much-too-loud classic rock hits such as Eagle's covers *(complete with witty husband-and-wife playful banter between songs).* It's an act that would fit in perfectly in Branson *(you can never leave Branson).*

I get an outside table at Rum Boogie Café so, while eating Memphis-style barbeque ribs, I can loath the sea of drunken humanity floating by *(it's a much more horrible dining experience that way).* The waitress sort of rolls her eyes when I request attention, making me feel as unwelcome as a fresh outbreak of stinging herpes.

A middle-aged woman, looking like the numerous puffy-haired Bible belt church ladies I encountered in Arkansas and Branson *(I can spot "the look"),* suddenly makes direct eye-contact from the street, extending her arm, reaching out towards me. Uh-oh! What's going on here? Is she going to hand me some Bible/Jesus literature saying man and dinosaur walked on earth together a mere few thousand years ago? Is she going to literally grab Satan right out of me, shaking my body back-and-forth?! Wrong on all counts; she wants a napkin off my table. How freaking odd! Okay, I'll give church-lady a napkin. Wait. The look in her eye doesn't say, "I want a napkin," instead it says, "Help Me!" The church lady suddenly starts puking into her cupped hand. Walking slow motion towards me like in the Mummy movies, she pukes again, this time trying to shove it back into her mouth *(as if that will somehow make it okay).* As she continues making direct eye contact I attempt to eat my Memphis-style rib dinner. The puking church lady starts grabbing napkins off my table. I'm too stunned to stop her. She pukes one last time directly in front of me *(almost causing me to puke),* continuing again to shove it back into her mouth. She then tries handing the vomit-filled napkins back to the jaded, unfriendly waitress *(who, for some reason, is nicer to her than she was to me).*

This whole scenario begs the question; is the puking lady an alcoholic and this is the moment she realizes she needs Jesus? Or has she lived a completely righteous, church-going life, and has just been smitten down by Satan? As classic rock hits are being performed by the husband and wife team of Pam & Terry from inside the Rum Boogie Café, all I know is my Memphis-style rib dinner is finished!

If You Must Go

Rum Boogie Café
182 Beale St.
Memphis, TN 38103-3714
(901) 528-0150

GRACELAND

Elvis Presley lived on Elvis Presley Boulevard. I wonder is if it was named that before he set up home at Graceland, thus and that's why he moved there? *(Kind of like when you wonder if a Lou Gehrig's Disease existed before Lou Gehrig contracted it – which came first?)*

Graceland is located by KFC, Sonic Burger, McDonald's, Dodge's Fried Chicken, and some fast food restaurant named Checkers. I imagine Elvis stopping at all of them before pulling his pink Cadillac into to the gates Graceland, where he'd later shoot out a TV set, watch underage girls wrestle in their underwear, or whatever-the-hell-else he did in his leisure time with Sonny and the boys. Besides TV sets, Elvis also once shot up his refrigerator, his stereo, and poor little Lisa Marie's slide. But that's his prerogative, being Elvis received a special agent badge for the Bureau of Narcotics and Dangerous Drugs from President Richard Nixon, making him Special Agent Elvis.

Looking down the squalor that is Elvis Presley Boulevard, I'm surprised some entrepreneur hasn't opened a string of Elvis tie-in establishments in this area. Sure there's the Heartbreak Hotel *(Guess what? They play Elvis movies in every room)*, but where is the Don't Be Cruel S&M gift shop, or the A Hunk-a-Hunk-a Burning Shish Kabob kabob shop, and so on, and so on, and so on…

In the parking lot across the street from Graceland stands Elvis's private jet. He named it the Lisa Marie *(again, was the jet or the daughter named that first?!)*

The best time to go to Graceland is around 11 p.m. at night, when it's lit up and the only people standing outside the musical gates of Manor D'Elvis will be you and maybe some British tourists. Leaning towards the British tourists, I point towards Graceland and explain, "That's where Elvis died on his toilet!" *(Blank stares.)* And those sentiments are exactly what I write as my entry on the long Wall of Love that extends down the block: "Elvis Died a Greasy Fat Fuck on this toilet." Because only in a place like America can we both celebrate Elvis while at the same time our idol-worship is what killed him.

I know what you're thinking: *don't be cruel!*

If You Must Go
Graceland 3734 Elvis Presley Blvd. Memphis, TN 38116 (901) 332-3322
Heartbreak Hotel 3677 Elvis Presley Blvd. Memphis, TN 38116-4105 (901) 332-1000

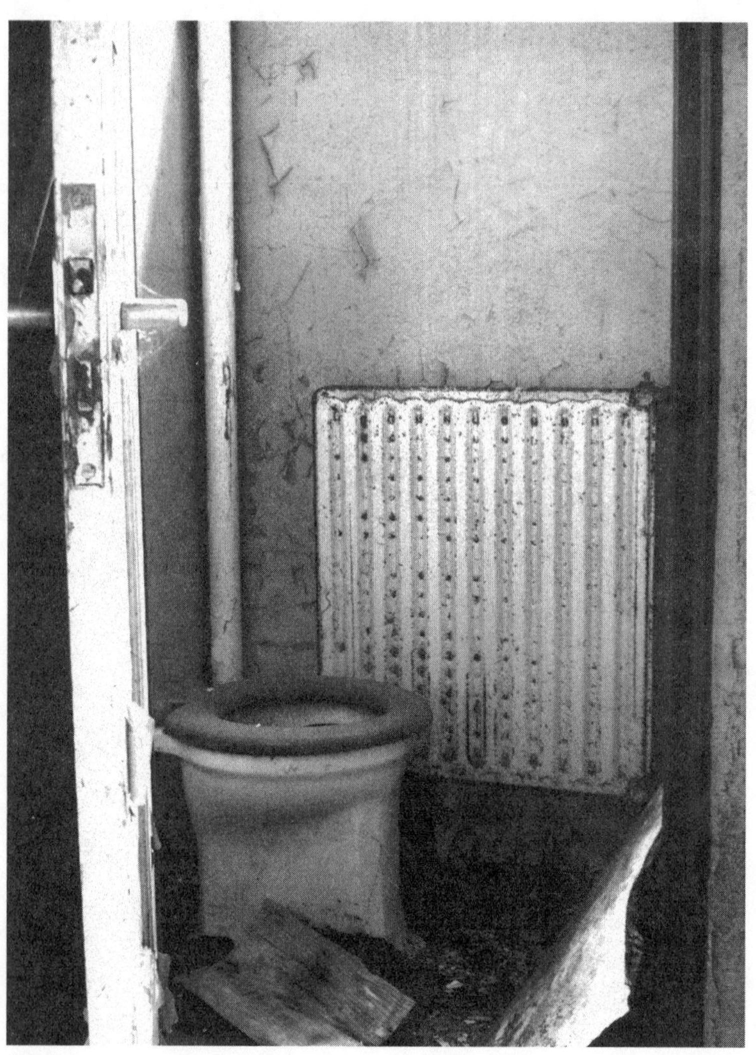

Road Trip Quick Tip...

Clean Up At Gas Stations

When on the road, you can easily turn a gas station restroom into your own personal day spa. First, lock the door. Place your head under the sink and use the push-soap as shampoo. Pull off your t-shirt and use it as a towel to dry off. Once dry, use the damp T-shirt as a washcloth to clean other areas of your body. When people start knocking on the restroom door, be sure to snap back with a snotty tone, "Excuse me! But *someone* is in here!" Treat yourself to a hot fudge sundae afterwards!

CONGRATULATIONS!
YOU HAVE CLEANED UP AT A GAS STATION!

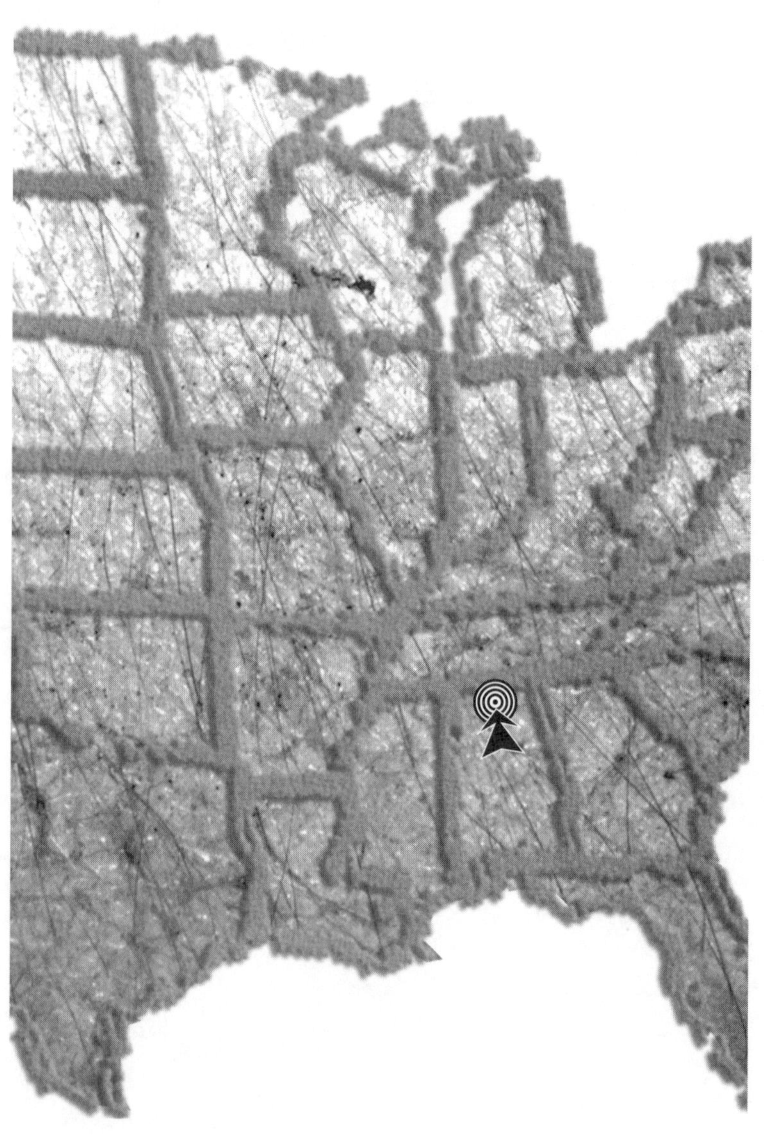

HUNTSVILLE, ALABAMA

An Adult Stops Off At NASA's Space Camp For Kids, To Save The Planet!

LOCATION U.S. Space & Rocket Center, Huntsville, AB

FOUNDED 1982

FUN FACT The 1986 movie *Space Camp* was partially filmed at Space Camp in Huntsville. Look for a cameo from a young Joaquin Phoenix, who later on went on to be Johnny Cash.

ANY NASA ASTRONAUTS DONE SOMETHING WEIRD LATELY? Yes. One wore a diaper and drove across Florida to kidnap a rival.

I've seen those summer blockbusters like *Independence Day, Men in Black,* and *War of the Worlds.* Let me tell ya, space aliens are out there, ready to swoop down on Earth, for the sole purpose of:

1. Putting us humans in human space zoos!
2. Using us humans in lab experiments to test out the safety of their alien cosmetic products.
3. Kicking our human butts and then simply laughing that smug alien laugh of theirs *(a laugh only dogs can hear).*

That's why I need to **protect the world from an alien invasion.** They're not going to destroy my Earth. No sirree! Sneaking over OUR intergalactic borders, taking OUR intergalactic jobs, and messing up OUR neighborhoods, while playing their loud extraterrestrial hoochie music – not in my backyard, they don't! We need to preserve the human race, especially the American humans. Chant with me: HUMANS-OF-USA! HUMANS-OF-USA! HUMANS-OF-USA! That's right, we're No. 1, we humans *(of the USA, of course)!*

Already there are clear-cut signs that aliens are messing with our species. How else do you explain Tom Cruise freaking out about Scientology on the *Today Show*? Do you want what happened to Tom Cruise to happen to you? *(Damn you, aliens!)* Nothing good comes from an alien invasion *(unless it's the oft-mentioned "alien anal-probe").*

Just as most of us routinely have fire drills in our homes, we humans need to have alien drills, to be ready for an invasion by those shifty-eyed, E.T.-looking, towel-headed space aliens.

Through a Google search, I find a listing for MUFON, the Mutual UFO Network, with a phone number you can use to give your babbling report of a UFO sighting to a "Field Investigator." This is great; it will give me a little practice for when we're at full intergalactic Amber Alert. The MUFON site says that UFO field investigators not only have references from the UFO community, but also have experience in UFO cases, animal mutilations, or UFO government cover-ups. These are my kind of people!

But let's test the waters to see if they can handle a full-on, War of the Worlds invasion.

As my rental car speeds across the Alabama countryside, I make a cell phone call to a UFO field investigator who is located in Mobile, Alabama. His name is Clay. I give him the full scoop.

"UFO Reporting Center," says UFO Field Investigator Clay.

"SON OF A BITCH! SON OF A BITCH!" I exclaim to indicate the frazzled state I'm in as a result of my recent sighting. Besides, the swearing adds to my credibility. "I'm spooked! I'm kind of spooked! Son of a bitch!"

"Calm down, sir."

"I would like to report a sighting!" *(Pause)* "I am not a crackpot!"

"Let me turn off the TV." *(Sound of loud TV being turned off)*

"Son of a bitch! Son of a bitch!"

"Ok, tell me what you saw."

"It looked like a goddamn giant woodshed with lights, that hovered, then shot straight up like a goddamn bullet! Son of a bitch! Son of a bitch!"

The best that MUFON Field Investigator Clay can do is take down all the information concerning the incident, while I graphically describe the alien anal-probe I encountered, after which I give him the phone number and address of my ex-girlfriend, in case he needs further information.

If You Must Know

Mutual UFO Network
(970) 221-1836   www.mufon.com

But it soon becomes clear: If they just take notes in Mobile, field investigators like Clay offer little hope to the human race. And I need to hit the aliens where they live. So that's why my rental car is pointed towards Huntsville, Alabama and U.S. Space & Rocket Center in order to attend NASA Space Camp for kids – as an adult! To take action for the good of mankind. To prepare for space. To get one step closer to an alien anal-probe.

(Aahh, an alien anal-probe!)

Sure, I know what you're thinking: This all sounds like a craaaaaazy Jack Black movie waiting to happen. Can you see it? Jack Black as a chubby, hung-over, way-over-the-top substitute Space Camp instructor who must whip a ragamuffin crew of kids together to become space cadets. Then, due to a series of mishaps, he accidentally ends up launching himself and the kids into outer space, causing them to bond together to get the craft safely back to Earth. But here's the ironic twist: They all end up tragically dying of asphyxiation in their capsule, like the Russian Sputnik dog Laika, because they're all severely under trained for a space mission. Whoops!

The movie would be called *Crazy Space Death!*

In preparation for NASA Space Camp I study the NASA manual and memorize many space acronyms, so I can spout them freely and fit in during training with my space-enthusiast peers. Also, I devise my own spacesuit for "my mission": an orange jumpsuit, with "HUMANS #1" scrawled on the back, adorned with bits of Christmas tinsel to give it a futuristic "look of tomorrow." Like other NASA astronauts, I'm also wearing a diaper.

It's time for liftoff!

Inside a large NASA building, surrounded by walls lined with smiley pictures of past astronauts, I soon learn my fellow Space Camp-mates are spotty, pre-adolescent kids who have paunchy dads. I guess NASA is preparing for a time when children and paunchy adults are needed in space. These are my fellow astronauts, an elite squadron I'll recruit to be on my team when the alien invasion begins. I'm the only one dressed in space regalia. Yes, just a grown man alone, taking in NASA Space Camp.

"What are you wearing?!" asks the woman at the Space Camp check-in desk.

"It's a jumpsuit," I explain. "It gives me more space-mobility." Shifting from foot to foot, I demonstrate my space-mobility theory.

My Space Camp team leader, or commander, goes by the name of Roman; he's a happy man in a large "Space Camp" sweatshirt. Roman explains that he's a Space Camp leader for at least another six months; for some reason, he can't join the Police Department until then.

"Have you ever thought about joining the Intergalactic Police Force?" I suggest, thinking he'd make an excellent second lieutenant in my squadron. The question draws big Space Camp laughs. I elaborate further: "No, really, it might help with your EVA."

"My what?" Roman asks.

"EVA: extra-vehicular activity," I clarify with a smug laugh.

"Aah," is his reply. Apparently he hasn't memorized the NASA handbook. Maybe he wouldn't make a good second lieutenant after all.

"What are you wearing?" Roman asks after a moment of silence.

"It's a space-mobility suit," I explain.

Our purpose tonight is to master a few space simulators. The first is called the Five Degrees of Freedom simulator. It's an apparatus that floats on air and pivots on all axes, simulating what it would be like to fix a satellite station in the weightlessness of space.

"Who wants to try it first?" asks Roman.

"I will, sir!" I answer, giving my commander a respectful salute and butting in line in front of all the children and paunchy dads.

I'm strapped into something that looks like a high-tech, futuristic highchair. I feel like a big baby of tomorrow. I proceed to simulate raising a solar panel. It raises. Mission complete. So far, I'd have to say, space is kind of easy. I salute my fellow astronauts.

"I'm getting some LOS," I say.

"What?!" says Roman.

"Oh, *please!*" I remark indignantly. Doesn't he know that means Loss of Signal? Doesn't he understand my little space joke, from my sophisticated, intergalactic sense of space humor?

It's the next cadet's turn. He is 9 years old. He has trouble raising the solar panel. He is going ATO (Abort to Orbit). This is uncalled for. There's no room for the weak in my space squadron, and I'm the first to tell him so.

"Well, thank you very much! If this were a real mission, we'd all be dead!" I inform the 9-year-old. The cadet's mom, or mom-cadet, gives me a nasty look. But hey, if he can't take the pressure, he's not space material. One day she'll thank me for my stern approach to space preparation. Especially when we're blowing the antennas off of alien badasses!

We next go to the cockpit of the space shuttle. I immediately take position in the commander's chair. The screen has a view of the orbiting Earth. I put on the headset and start pushing all the buttons while making rocket noises. One of the paunchy dads makes the obvious joke:

"Houston, we have a problem!"

"Ha ha ha ha," everyone laughs.

"Shut up," I say under my breath. "Shut the hell up!"

The 9-year-old cadet wants to try out my commander's chair.

"GET LOST, KID!" I say.

He whimpers away. *(Commander's note: Court-martial the little bastard!)*

The headset is hooked to a mock Mission Control. I use this opportunity to be witty:

"Earth, surrender!"

"Luke, use the force!"

"Lock phasers on target."

The appreciation of my space humor is limited.

"Please don't push all the buttons," pipes in Roman.

The coolest thing at Space Camp is the Zero-G Wall. It simulates weightlessness in space. A specially designed swivel chair is attached to suspension ropes to create the anti-gravity effect, making it feel like the chair can float alongside the wall.

Our mission is to float to the top of the wall, maneuvering side to side while simulating exercises for constructing a space station. Space isn't all about floating around, you know; there's also responsibility! My thoughts turn to how great it would be to have one of these at home, to help with simulating "space sex."

Again butting in line to be the first to test Zero-G out, I bend my knees, jump, and soar to the top of the wall, like a normal spaceman floating around a space wall. This exercise will come in handy for hand-to-hand alien space combat. I refuse to come down from the wall, so my fellow astronauts must watch me with space envy.

Our last exercise is the Multi-Axis Trainer. It was built for the early Mercury space program and simulates not only a space capsule spinning out of control, but also what it's like to vomit in space. I'm strapped into a chair spinning on three axes. I'm spinning like a mother! Roman is finally getting his revenge on me, opening this baby up.

"ATO!" I scream for my safe word. *(Doesn't Roman know this means Abort to Orbit?!)*

I'm going to throw up space food. If this is a daily part of space travel, then space travel is certainly not for me!

"Abort mission! Abort mission!" I scream. The Multi-Axis Trainer comes to a halt. Screw the aliens. I'm dizzy as hell; I'll let someone else save the planet. I'm going to forfeit my potential alien anal-probe and remain here on Earth. We humans should just try to get along with the extraterrestrials, as best we can. I think the poem I wrote after my Space Camp sojourn best sums up my feelings:

Oh alien visitors,
Our little friends from beyond.
We welcome you in peace.
Or else, we'll disembowel you and put your head on a stick and parade it through the town square!

If You Must Go

Space Camp, U.S. Space & Rocket Center
One Tranquility Base
Huntsville, AL 35805
(800) 63-SPACE!

A Diseased Underbelly Salute To...

The Dumbest City In America: Fort Wayne, Indiana

Fort Wayne, Indiana has been named the stupidest town in America, by *Men's Health Magazine*, which based rankings on the number of bachelor's degrees per capita, the number of universities, inhabitants' SAT scores, state creativity scores as assessed by Catalytix and the Richard Florida Creativity Group, and the number of Nobel Prize winners for physics and medicine born within the towns' borders.

Here are a few cultural highlights of Fort Wayne Indiana – The Dumbest City in America:

- Fort Wayne is home to Piere's, the largest nightclub in the Midwest featuring nine bars, and nine huge dance floors. In 2006, Piere's was rated 4th in the entire world for ticket sales in 21+ venues. Piere's is your nightspot of choice if your idea of fun is being surrounded by hundreds of inebriated morons!

If You Must Go

5629 Saint Joe Rd.
Fort Wayne, IN 46825
(260) 486-1979

- Severe weather is not uncommon in Fort Wayne. Tornados occasionally occur in the area, particularly in the spring and summer. When this happens, residents of Fort Wayne are known to run outside in their underpants waving their arms in order to say "Hi," because they are dumber than a bag of mud.

- The major newspaper in the city is the independent *Fort Wayne Journal Gazette.* One striking feature of the paper is over 2/3 of the publication can be used as a coloring book because local residents have poo-for–brains.

- Insurance companies such as K&K Insurance, and Brotherhood Mutual Insurance Company, have their headquarters in the Fort Wayne. All their employees are paid in chocolate.

CONGRATULATIONS FORT WAYNE!
YOU ARE ONE DUMB CITY!

FLORIDA

Risque Business

STATE MOTTO In God We Trust!

NUMBER OF INMATES EXECUTED IN FLORIDA 64

WHO DROVE ACROSS FLORIDA WEARING A DIAPER A crazy astronaut lady.

TYPE OF VOTING MACHINE USED IN FLORIDA DURING THE 2000 PRESIDENTIAL ELECTION Diebold.

WILL PEOPLE IN FLORIDA TELL YOU WHAT THEY THINK OF FIDEL CASTRO? Yes.

FLORIDA FUN FACT Florida is a primary area for international drug trafficking and money laundering organizations, as well as a principal thoroughfare for cocaine and heroin transiting to the northeastern United States and Canada. Florida's over 8,000 miles of coastline provide virtually unlimited access and opportunities for drug trafficking.

It's get real sleazy once we cross the border into Florida. No longer do you see churches or hear Jesus radio. The first things I see are stands selling fireworks and billboards providing such information as, "Never Ever Shake a Baby!" *(Is baby-shaking a popular Floridian pastime?)*

"This Rest Area Patrolled by Armed Security," reads a posted sign, at this leg-stretching, bathroom-stop locale, set deep in the woods with the vibe of past atrocities including hooker/trucker blowjobs and abducted children heavy amongst the trees. This begs the question: what was this rest area like before they had armed security, and what made them finally put up the sign?

The entire State of Florida lacks any sort of class. Maybe it has to do with the tropical heat, Disney World, and faulty voting machines? Florida is all about big hair, tube tops, and long mullet ponytails sticking out the back of a clasped baseball hat; it's all business in front and party in the back! I-75 has a pure shadiness about it. This Interstate is where a large portion of our nation's drugs are trafficked. I heard stories about cunning drug dealers who will put the drugs in the trunk of their car, then call a tow truck, and simply have them tow it to their drug drop-off destination with no fear of being pulled over by the cops. And it's all here, on this Interstate!

Just like Hillbilly Junction in Missouri there's suddenly an emergence of billboards every few miles that highlight such things as *We Bare All, 24 Hours–Trucker's Discount And Showers,* then *Couples Welcome,* followed by *Pretty Women.* Though sleazy, it's a refreshing sight after spending days in Arkansas and Missouri amidst the sleaze of Jesusland. Yes, stretched 100 miles along the Interstate, 33 different billboards lure drivers to Café Risque which boast not only "We Bare It All," but also a delicious breakfast, lunch, and dinner.

Arriving in Central Florida, I take the Micanopy exit, where there's absolutely nothing but another place selling fireworks, a couple of gas stations and, of course, Café Risque.

MICANOPY FUN FACT:

Micanopy, by the way was the first distinct United States town in Florida, with settlement beginning after Spain ceded the Florida territory in 1821. When explorer and naturalist William Bartram visited in 1774, it was the site of a Seminole village called Cuscowilla. Now it's home to Café Risque where you can eat while seeing full nudity 24 hours a day! *(The combination of food and full nudity seems like it would be breaking various health codes... don't complain at what you might accidentally find in your burger; it comes with the turf!)*

I know I'm at the right place when I see 5 guys pushing a broken down van into the Café Risque parking lot *(there's ample trucker parking, but the prospect of free trucker showers creepifies me)*. Big-bellied truckers get out of their rigs, bolting for the front door wanting to live the fantasy they conjured in their mind after seeing 33 billboards reading *We Bare All,* not to mention the delicious breakfast, lunch, and dinner. *(The obstacles our steadfast truckers must face in moving the nation's essential goods in a timely fashion.)*

A singular white building blazoned with the club's logo stands alone in the darkness, while outside the air smells like bad feet. Assorted pictures of hot chicks with big hair, looking like they've stepped out of an '80s music video, grace the wall by the entrance *(who, I'm sure, <u>aren't</u> found inside)*. Yes, a secluded strip club, in the middle of nowhere right off the Interstate. It feels like a setting for the movie *Monster,* spawning a climate of hooker serial killers, where inside Aileen Wuornos might give you a lap dance.

A sign the entrance explains their justification for charging a cover, *"If You Ask a Woman at K-Mart If She'll Take Off All Her Clothes She Will Probably Slap You..."*

That's just a plain weird scenario to present potential customers, or a good insight into the type of patrons who regularly frequent Café Risque *(and what usually happens to them at K-Mart!)*.

On entering you are confronted with a paunchy, sleazy man with a mop of gray hair, working the door behind thick glass, reeking of mandatory back office blowjobs from strippers hoping to keep their jobs. He recites in a monotone, jaded manner, "We have no alcohol. The food is good. The girls are totally nude," stressing each point in the same mundane manner, asking for a $7 cover charge, stating there's a two-drink minimum. Also, he throws out that it's expected I *behave like a gentlemen (if I don't will I be tied to a tree in the swamp and left there?).*

Looking at the Café Risque menu, I ask the jaded man, "What's your most popular dish."

"The "Risque Special," he replies in a monotone manner. *(The "Risque Special" sounds like it involves a dead hooker stuffed into a car trunk. It's actually cheese-topped hash browns or home fries with eggs and toast.)*

Like all classy joints, not only do you have to be buzzed into Café Risque, but also buzzed out. Inside, it's half strip club, half adult sex shop, as strippers escort truckers to private rooms for lapdances *(I hope they utilized the free trucker showers first).*

What a shocker; the totally nude women dancing for truck drivers look just like strippers you'd expect to find at a strip-club-in-the-middle-of-nowhere-right-off-the Florida-Interstate. No surprises here, as cards on the table tell men the appropriate ways to act *(meaning the clientele need to be told how "gentlemen" behave).* I sit amongst a handful of truckers watching a stripper with stretch marks and visible surgical scars swinging like a crazed monkey on meth from a pole to a ZZ Top song. Trying to hold down my Risque Special, I pray her naked cottage cheese thighs comes nowhere near my cheese-topped hash browns *(again, possible health code violation).* The last time I had this sort of grim feeling about life, humanity and mankind, I was sitting at the Arrow Bar in Texarkana, Arkansas. All I can say about this sleazy trucker-den-of-nudity is: where are you now Jesus, where are you now?

"Could you possibly give me a lap dance while I eat a Reuben sandwich?" I ask the stripper with the surgical scars, devising a cunning plan to combine both full nudity, and the Café Risque fine dining.

"$30 for one song, $50 for two songs," she recites like a crack-fueled robot. Once again I look at the surgical scars and the truckers surrounding me. Buzz that door, oh jaded-gray-haired-man, I shall now be departing Café Risque! Adieu! Adieu!

If You Must Go

Cafe Risque
17035 SE County Road 234
Micanopy, FL,
(352) 466-3803

GIBSONTON, FLORIDA

Freaky Town

POPULATION 8,752

TOWN MOTTO Circus Carnie Capital of the World!

MY MOTTO FOR TOWN "Keeping Hush About the Lobster Boy Capital of America!'

GIBSONTON FUN FACT In its heyday Gibsonton was home to the likes of such sideshow folks as Pricilla the Monkey Girl, and the Anatomical Wonder, and Siamese twin sisters who ran a fruit stand.

WEIRD LOCAL SMELLS Un-bathed carnies and cotton candy.

EXTREMELY USELESS INFORMATION Gibsonton has the only post office in the country with a counter for midgets!

DID THE WORLD'S TALLEST MAN AND HIS WIFE – A LEGLESS 2.5-FOOT TALL WOMAN – OWN AN EATERY IN TOWN CALLED GIANT'S CAMP RESTAURANT? Yes!

MORE EXTREMELY USELESS INFORMATION The town offers unique circus zoning laws that allow residents to keep elephants and circus trailers on their front lawns.

WAYS TO GET YOUR ASS-KICKED Go to the Showtown Bar and ask about Grady Styles– The Lobster Boy.

CULTURAL HIGHLIGHT Lobster Boy Grady Styles

AN IDYLLIC LOCALE FOR Jo-Jo the Dog-Faced Boy, The Wild Men of Borneo, The Half-Boy, the Rubber-Skinned Man, and of course, Grady Styles—The Lobster Boy.

LEVEL OF CREEPINESS 1 if you're a carnie. 7 if you're not a carnie and really noisy about Lobster Boy Grady Styles.

Not only is Gibsonton the town where circus freaks go to retire, but the reason why I'm giddy as a schoolgirl to road trip here: it was the hometown of Grady Styles, a.k.a. The Lobster Boy.

A little back-story: Like his father, Grady Stiles was born with a genetic condition that caused his fingers and toes to twist like claws. He propelled himself around with his flipper-like legs *(he was known to be really quick too!)*. Though Lobster Boy was a sideshow sensation, he was also a bad drunk and one mean sonuvabitch! He was once convicted of shooting his daughter's boyfriend, but due to favorable testimony from two carnie neighbors *(a bearded lady and a fat man)* he was spared a lengthily prison term. Lobster Boy was such an a-hole that his wife and stepson *(a human blockhead)* paid a neighbor boy $1,500 to shoot him. On November 29, 1992, three bullets were put into Lobster Boy's lobster-head. Initially, police thought it was a robbery gone awry, but the loose-lipped neighbor bragged about being paid by Grady's wife to kill "Lobster Boy."

I must now walk in Lobster Boy's claw-like steps! Ten miles south of Tampa, I pull off I-75 at the Gibsonton exit. Venturing onward a few more miles to the city limits, Gibsonton at first appears to be a quiet Mecca for dilapidated mobile homes, with the occasional rusty carnival equipment sitting in people's driveways. I keep my eyes peeled for Frog Boy, Jackie the Half Girl, and the Dame Demure Madame Miniature. Encountering shirtless guys walking down the side of the road, I slow down to see if any could be Jo-Jo the Dog-Faced Boy *(they aren't)*.

Entering a convenience store, I approach the two men working by the register. *(Could they be the notorious sideshow oddity, Ronny & Donny – Siamese Twins Connected At The Convenience Store Counter?)*

"Do you know the bar where the circus carnies drink at?" I ask.

"Yeah, Showtown," says Ronny *(of Ronny & Donny – Siamese Twins Connected at the Convenience Store Counter)*.

After buying a Slim Jim, I'm given directions to a locale right down the road.

“Isn’t that where Grady Styles used to drink?” I question with delight, lighting up like a freak-seeking Christmas tree.

“I wouldn’t know about that,” abruptly snaps Ronny *(of Ronny & Donny—Siamese Twins Connected At The Convenience Store Counter)*, then immediately puts his attention to straightening the gum display.

Like a State Fair Midway, Showtown is a festive oasis in the tropical night. A huge, colorful, mural of circus performers graces the front of a building. Showtown looks like it might have bumper cars inside, and nothing but joy, joy, joy! How fun. Maybe there’s a house of mirrors, making it difficult to maneuver through in order to get a drink at the bar? I hope a car pulls up and dozens of tiny clowns continually get out. This is the place where Lobster Boy used to drink, whiskey and cokes clutched between his claws. As music *(not circus music)* spills out into the tropical night air from inside, it’s clear this place is going to be a pure delight!

In order to fit in I’ve duct taped a baby doll arm to my chest, so it can protrude out of the button of my shirt *(thus they’ll think I’m like legendary circus freak Laloo from India who had a small body growing out of his side)*. Walking towards the entrance, on closer inspection, eerily situated behind Showtown rests a large rundown trailer park *(I think that’s where Grady Styles was riddled with bullets?)*.

The heavily tattooed bouncer checks my ID *(Is he the sideshow strong man able to bend iron bars?)*. The whole place is plastered with carnival murals, attached to a restaurant *(do they serve cotton candy and corn dogs?)*. Passing a bulletin board with numerous Missing Person notices and a hand-scrawled notice offering carnie work in Indiana *(the only requirement, “No Drunk or Druggies”)*, the decor makes it look like this would be a delightful establishment. It’s actually one of the scariest bars I’ve ever been in. The clientele looks like hardened ex-cons with jail tattoos, many missing teeth, some not wearing shoes. These are the folks who set up the Tilt-A-Whirl and scam you out of your money trying to get you to knock over three milk bottles that are weighted down... carnies in the off-season with nothing to do but drink at the bar in front of their trailer park. *(Ironically, an arcade game in the corner gives people a chance to win a stuffed animal. Pointless. Why would carnie-folk need to win more stuffed animals?)*

Being their whole vocation involves sizing people up, I receive a cold welcome, constantly eyeballed, clearly designated as an unwanted outsider. *(The carnies look at me like I'm an undercover cop)* They don't want me here and they make it clear. *(Are they thinking, "Look at the freak!")*

Knowing they're aware of me, I take a seat in the corner, belly up to the bar, hoping my protruding baby-doll arm will warm people up like a kindred spirit. Ordering a beer, I wonder if the bartender, standing under a license plate that simply reads "Carnie," is the Incredible Bearded Lady with a fresh, clean shave?

"I should actually have two drinks," I say, gesturing to my faux appendage. *(Dead silence.)*

Three large, somber, crusty men walk in from the side entrance. They immediately give off a bad feeling *(like they've just came from a gangbang with the Amazing Torso Woman back at her trailer)*. Beneath the scariness there's a great sadness about all the people at the bar; outcasts who've banded together, finding each other, in order to escape their past and normal society. In the changing world where the flashy, high-tech rides at places like Magic Mountain have eclipsed old-school carnivals, these carnies are a dying breed.

Focusing on karaoke performed in front of a large mural of a ringmaster in the sky, a large man in shorts and yellow shirt hesitantly takes to the karaoke mike, singing Nancy Sinatra's "These Boots Are Made for Walking," in a really high, unintentional, girly voice.

Is this Joe and Josephine – The Amazing Half Man/Half Woman Hermaphrodite? When finished he/she sheepishly walks across the bar with his/her head down, emotionally drained from exposing himself in public, instantly leaving the bar.

While everyone pounds back the hard stuff, a normal-looking woman sips a can of Pepsi. Maybe she's a cousin of one of the carnies? Then she opens her mouth, revealing her teeth are all black. Yikes! It's the Amazing Black-Toothed Woman *(can she stop bullets with her teeth?).*

Like in Tod Browning's movie *Freaks,* I imagine everyone in the bar suddenly turning to me, chanting, "One of us! One of us!" Then I'm grabbed and transformed into The Platypus Boy.

A car outside pulls up into the drive-through liquor window. The driver boasts a normal-sized head and stumpy arms. Hurrah! It's a dwarf. Perhaps Tiny Tito – the World's Smallest Man who is married to Gargantuan Woman *(over 8 feet tall, from the jungles of the Andes),* on his way home to get liquored up.

I act like I'm intensely watching the TV over the bar, showing *Smokey and the Bandit,* hoping to strike up a Grady Styles conversation with the locals. A scene comes on with Burt Reynolds *(as The Bandit)* at a carnival.

"Hey, I was working the rollercoaster that day when they were filming," declares a gruff old man next to me. "That was in Atlanta." He turns to other people in the bar. "Hey I was working the rollercoaster that day!"

This is great; *Smokey and the Bandit* carnie insights.

"Was Burt Reynolds a nice man?" I ask, trying to get the conversation rolling.

"Really nice," *(to someone else)* "Hey I was working the rollercoaster that day!"

Ok, this is my *in* to find out true antidotes about Lobster Boy. After the excitement dies down, I ask, "Isn't this the bar where Grady Styles used to drink at?" hoping for great Lobster Boy antidotes. Perhaps I'll learn he was just a misunderstood man out of time? Maybe, if he called himself Lobster Man, he would've had more self-esteem and been less of a mean fucker! Perhaps Lobster Boy just wanted to be loved?! These are answers I want to know, and finally now is when I'll will find out!

After an uncomfortable silence the gruff old man looks me directly in the face, then at my drooping baby-doll arm.

"We don't talk about that around here!"

No further discussion.

If You Must Go

Showtown USA
10902 US Highway 41 S.
Gibsonton, FL, 33534
(813) 677-5443

Road Trip Lodging Quick Tip...

Consider The Refund Policy At Motels

If you stop at a questionable motel and there's a sign on the door that says "No Refund for Early Check-Out," you might want to think twice about staying there. It's a clear sign that the establishment might be a bit unsavory. The same holds true if the motel boasts Hourly Rates *(stressing you must pay for the entire hour)*. If they simply post a sign that says, "Don't Crap In The Bed!" highly reconsider because, as we all know, you just might want to crap in the bed, and why have THE MAN tell you what you can or can NOT do!

CONGRATULATIONS!
YOU NOW KNOW HOW TO CONSIDER
THE REFUND POLICY
AT MOTELS!

Where To Stay In Tampa?

Just when I thought I've ditched Jesus back in Arkansas, Sunday morning in the lobby of my motel RAMADA INN, I'm greeted by a loud preacher conducting and a clappity-clappity, "Hallelujah!" Jesus church service held in the meeting room adjacent to the checkout desk. While I get my motel bill and complimentary cup of coffee, I hear a scream of "In the name of Jesus! Testify!" followed by more shouts of Hallelujah! Again, you can never leave Branson. Going outside to snap some photos of the motel sign, at least the Ramada Inn doesn't get confrontational like the Cypress Tree Inn when you whip out a camera.

If You Must Go:

Ramada Inn
11714 Morris Bridge Road
Tampa, FL 33617
(813) 985-8525.

CELEBRATION, FLORIDA

Disneytown

POPULATION 3,244

TOWN MOTTO "A Place Where Memories of a Lifetime Are Made!"

MY TOWN MOTTO "Put A Gun In My Mouth Now!"

THE MEDIAN PRICE FOR HOME $835,100

FUN FACT It snows every year in the center of town the day after Thanksgiving. The snow is foam blown from a huge foam machine. The residents say that they love the fact that they get the snow without the winter chill and having to shovel. They also have a machine to simulate leaves falling. Well f**k me sideways!

EXTREMELY USELESS INFORMATION The band Chumbawamba penned a song called "Celebration, Florida," that satirizes the perceived excesses of American consumerism and nostalgia for a time they can't remember.

CULTURAL HIGHLIGHT Jordan Knight, from the '80s boy band New Kids on the Block, performed a concert at downtown Celebration in December 2006, exciting the citizens with both New Kids "classics," and songs from his current CD. Jordan currently bides his time appearing on *The Surreal Life* with other D-list celebrities.

AN IDYLLIC LOCALE FOR Stepford Wives, folks in a Valium-haze, those who fear minorities, lovers of "The Mouse."

LEVEL OF CREEPINESS 10. Be afraid; be very afraid!

Three cheers for the Disney-created city of Celebration, Florida! Unveiled in 1994, this $2.5 billion project – nestled on 4,900 acres a mere five miles south of Walt Disney World – may just be corporate branding's finest hour. These folks live in Disney Town! Celebration represents Walt Disney's dream of harnessing the power of his "imagineers" to fashion a futuristic city where crime, pollution and deviance are replaced by community, cleanliness and uniformity. This Disney fantasy sets the tone for the architect movement known as new urbanism – a sterile reality that, contrary to our bleary nostalgia, never really existed in the American landscape and can now only be captured through artificial means.

Read with me from Celebration's propaganda:

> "Celebration is a place where memories of a lifetime are made, it's more than a home; it's a community rich with old-fashioned appeal and an eye on the future. Homes are a blend of traditional southeastern exteriors with welcoming front porches and interiors that enhance today's lifestyles."

Think of the Magic Kingdom but without rides, where every day is filled with potluck dinners – or better yet, Main Street USA come to life on a suburban scale, where one might joyfully expect a jubilant fireworks display at dusk. *(Personally, I'm disappointed Disney didn't go with the direction of Tomorrowland, where every inhabitant would be entitled to their very own robot maid – not to mention jet-pack landing pad.)*

Read with me again:

> "Imagine how great it would have been...to live 50 years ago with all the neat gear you have today. Morning coffee on your front porch. An afternoon stroll to Market Street. Family evenings in the neighborhood park."

Ok, are you done vomiting? Great, wipe your chin, because it's been mentioned that beneath the small-town façade of such places as Celebration Florida lies a hidden mechanism of social control. Now read a comment made by a Celebration citizen and decide:

> "I live in a community with rules, by choice, because I like rules that ensure I won't have a neighbor who will drive me crazy with his lifestyle."
> *Sue Holland, writing about Celebration for MousePlanet.com*

Disney's Celebration citizens have many rules and conditions that dictate how their homes and yards must look in order to maintain the appearance of the "perfect suburb," specifying what people can and cannot do on their own damn property. You won't find Stinky McNasty, cars up on concrete blocks, or any other forms of personal expression in these neighborhoods – it would be clearly against the rules!

Celebration is connected directly to the Walt Disney World via World Drive, allowing residents direct access to the Magic Kingdom! Entering the community, and the realm of the surreal, I pass Celebration High School *(Home of the Storm!)*, looking Disney-movie picture-perfect; like the high school you'd find in such family classics as Flubber or The Computer Wore Tennis Shoes *(starring a young Kurt Russell)*.

WAYS TO GET KICKED OUT OF CELEBRATION, FLORIDA:

- Profanity!
- Being too "ethnic!"
- Drunkenness!
- Nudity!
- Driving a low-rider while playing loud hip-hop!
- Wearing a Mickey Mouse costume and Mayor's sash, telling residents, "I'm just checking up on the operation!"

The place feels as artificial as the back lot of Universal Studios. It's *The Truman Show* come to life. The houses are constructed in that turn-of-the-century Southern gothic style, drawing on the sensibilities of such turn-of-the-century places as Savannah, Georgia and Nantucket, Massachusetts, but yet look like they were built last week for a movie filming in the area.

There are no "weirdoes" here, no crime, no bad weather, probably no swearing, everyone has money, the homes all feel the same, people chat over picket fences, and your neighbors are cut from an identical cookie-cutter mold. Celebration feels like a new car with that new car smell even though this place has been here for over a decade; Celebration is so artificially sugar-sweet, it almost gives me a toothache!

You'd expect freckled-face Jimmy-the-paperboy to be riding his bike through the streets delivering the *Celebration Daily Gazette,* while backyard barbeques take place and hot apple pies cool on windowsills. Yet on this weekend afternoon, there're no kids to be found playing, and hardly any signs of life in the fabricated neighborhoods. *(The only minority I see is watering someone's lawn.)* It feels like you could turn and suddenly be at Space Mountain or encounter the Pirates of the Caribbean. (*Even Fake Iraq felt more real than this.)* Two picturesque old ladies on their front porch, with a Mickey Mouse wreath on the front door, are enjoying crumpets and tea served from an antique tea set. Is this a real scenario, or have they been hired by the Disney Corporation to do such for the benefit of people visiting Celebration? *(They could be animatronic old ladies).*

The expanse of identical neighborhoods leads to a big man-made Back to the Future-type town square *(where a potato sack race should be taking place),* and a 1920's art deco movie theater *(that looks like it was built last week).*

The fabricated small town charm feels forced, where citizens milling about look cast in their role. *(Dockers and blue shirts for men, Stepford Wife-composure for women.)* Celebration is as phony as the gondola ride at Vegas' Venetian Hotel, which tries to play itself off like the canals in Venice. You'd almost expect people to thrill at a mechanical shark spouting from the picturesque manmade pond. Perhaps once you move in, you learn the well-guarded secret, that Celebration is a Scientology-like cult, where all the residents are descents of a reptilian race from the planet Zenu?

The only thing slightly off about Celebration is a band of teenage girls in short-shorts conducting a Lolita car wash to booty shaking music, making me wonder what the hell would it be like to be a teenager in this pre-planned, artificial cultural wasteland community designed with conformity in mind? There would be nothing for the youth to do, nowhere to go *(except Disney World).* It would be like the '70s Matt Dillon movie *Over the Edge* where in the end, the alienated teenagers rebel by locking all the grownups in the Celebration High School *(Home of the Storm)* and setting it ablaze while wearing Little Mermaid outfits.

Passing the high-end corporate specialty shops, with names like Lollipop Cottage, Soft As a Grape, and Day Creams, Collectible Dolls & Bears, I encounter Celebration Market St. Café on Front Street, where Norman Rockwell families eat picturesque lunches on the outdoor patio.

"What are we doing?" questions one of three well-cast children at a table.

"We're going to pray," explains the archetypical dad. Simultaneously, they all fold their hands and bow their heads over their breakfast omelets. (*Are they praying to the almighty Mouse?)*

If You Must Go

Market Street Café
701 Front St.
Celebration, FL 34747
(407) 566-1144

I end up having lunch and strong alcoholic drinks inside the Celebration Town Tavern, served by the wry bartender who, like television's Sam Malone, always has a witty quip. Looking around at the packed restaurant, I ask, "Are these people tourists?"

"These are mostly locals." He adds, "It's busy because everyone is coming in from Church." *(Afterwards, I'm sure, it's onto the trains and off to the camps...to Disney World!)*

As the old guys next to me talk about how much their house is worth, more praying takes place amongst diners. Everything I learned about America, through my cross-country travels, tells me how fake this vision of America really is and how much this America doesn't exist; only under artificial, heavily monitored and secured means set to strict rules and regulations. Last night I was drinking with circus carnies and now here I am in Celebration sitting next to guys talking about their golf scores, wondering if they are really actors hired to create atmosphere.

"I'm thinking of buying a house in Celebration," I tell the bartender, who puts on a big, plastic smile.

"You'll love it here. It's really a great place."

I lean in closer, and whisper, "Hey! Do you know where I can buy any crack?"

If You Must Go

Celebration Town Tavern
721 Front Street
Celebration, FL 34747
(407) 566-2526

I wish I could bring everyone I've met on the road *(cockfighters, circus carnies, polygamists, guys who slit pigs' throats, Harrison KKK, Café Risque's manager)* – in other words, true Americans – here to the false America of Celebration.

NO
LOITERING